MW00622218

# The Partisan Republic

*The Partisan Republic* is the first book to unite a top down and bottom up account of constitutional change in the Founding era. The book focuses on the decline of the Founding generation's elitist vision of the Constitution and the rise of a more "democratic" vision premised on the exclusion of women and non-whites. It incorporates recent scholarship on topics ranging from judicial review to popular constitutionalism to place judicial initiatives like *Marbury v. Madison* in a broader, socio-legal context. The book recognizes the role of constitutional outsiders as agents in shaping the law, making figures such as the Whiskey Rebels, Judith Sargent Murray, and James Forten part of a cast of characters that has traditionally been limited to white, male elites such as James Madison, Alexander Hamilton, and John Marshall. Finally, it shows how the "democratic" political party came to supplant the Supreme Court as the nation's preeminent constitutional institution.

GERALD LEONARD is Professor of Law at Boston University School of Law and author of *The Invention of Party Politics: Federalism, Popular Sovereignty, and Constitutional Development in Jacksonian Illinois*.

SAUL CORNELL is the Paul and Diane Guenther Chair in American History at Fordham University and author of *The Other Founders: Antifederalism and the Dissenting Tradition in America, 1788–1828* and *A Well Regulated Militia: The Founding Fathers and the Origins of Gun Control in America*.

# New Histories of American Law

Series Editors

Michael Grossberg, *Indiana University*
Christopher L. Tomlins, *University of California, Berkeley*

New Histories of American Law is a series of bold, synthetic, and path-breaking interpretive books that will address the key topics in the field of American legal history, written by the leaders of the field, and designed for scholars and students throughout universities, colleges, and law schools.

## Other Books in the Series:

Mark Douglas McGarvie, *Law and Religion in American History*
Kunal M. Parker, *Making Foreigners: Immigration and Citizenship Law in America, 1600–2000*
Laura F. Edwards, *A Legal History of the Civil War and Reconstruction: A Nation of Rights*
Elizabeth Dale, *Criminal Justice in the United States, 1789–1939*
Jack P. Greene, *The Constitutional Origins of the American Revolution*
Barbara Young Welke, *Law and the Borders of Belonging in the Long Nineteenth Century United States*

# The Partisan Republic

*Democracy, Exclusion, and the Fall of the Founders'*
*Constitution, 1780s–1830s*

**GERALD LEONARD**
*Boston University*

**SAUL CORNELL**
*Fordham University*

CAMBRIDGE
UNIVERSITY PRESS

# CAMBRIDGE
## UNIVERSITY PRESS

University Printing House, Cambridge CB2 8BS, United Kingdom

One Liberty Plaza, 20th Floor, New York, NY 10006, USA

477 Williamstown Road, Port Melbourne, VIC 3207, Australia

314–321, 3rd Floor, Plot 3, Splendor Forum, Jasola District Centre, New Delhi – 110025, India

79 Anson Road, #06–04/06, Singapore 079906

Cambridge University Press is part of the University of Cambridge.

It furthers the University's mission by disseminating knowledge in the pursuit of education, learning, and research at the highest international levels of excellence.

www.cambridge.org
Information on this title: www.cambridge.org/9781107024168
DOI: 10.1017/9781139161930

© Gerald Leonard and Saul Cornell 2019

This publication is in copyright. Subject to statutory exception and to the provisions of relevant collective licensing agreements, no reproduction of any part may take place without the written permission of Cambridge University Press.

First published 2019

Printed and bound in Great Britain by Clays Ltd, Elcograf S.p.A.

A catalogue record for this publication is available from the British Library.

ISBN 978-1-107-02416-8 Hardback
ISBN 978-1-107-66389-3 Paperback

Cambridge University Press has no responsibility for the persistence or accuracy of URLs for external or third-party internet websites referred to in this publication and does not guarantee that any content on such websites is, or will remain, accurate or appropriate.

*Gerry Leonard dedicates this book to Abigail, Sarah, and Talia with love and admiration.*
*Saul Cornell dedicates this book to the memory of my mother Estelle Cornell, the memory of my wife's mother Ollie Selleck, and my wife Susan.*

# Contents

*Acknowledgments*                                                          *page* ix

  Introduction                                                                    1
1  The New Constitution                                                           8
2  The Federalist Constitution and the Limits of
   Constitutional Dissent                                                        42
3  The Democracy versus the Law: The Role of the Federal
   Judiciary, 1789–1815                                                          84
4  The Paradoxes of Jeffersonian Constitutionalism                             115
5  The White Democracy                                                         146
6  The Marshall Court, the Indian Nations, and the
   Democratic Ascendancy                                                       178
   Conclusion: The Constitutional Triumph and Failure
   of the Democratic Party                                                     210

*Bibliographical Essay*                                                        225
*Index*                                                                        239

# Acknowledgments

Gerry Leonard wishes to acknowledge gratefully the help of Khiara Bridges, Kris Collins, Tom Green, and Aaron Knapp, each of whom read sections of the manuscript and offered very helpful feedback. Portions of this book were presented at valuable workshops at the University of Connecticut School of Law and the Boston University School of Law.

Saul Cornell would like to thank Paul and Diane Guenther, whose generous funding of a chair in American Constitutional history at Fordham provided research support and leave time to work on this project. Faculty workshops at Boston University, the University of Connecticut, and Fordham School of Law provided lively venues to test many of the ideas in this book. Invaluable research support was provided by Stephen Leccese and Sophia Wise. Dan Kahan, Tracy Meares, and former Dean Robert Post welcomed me as a senior visiting research scholar at Yale Law School. Stephen Wilf and Richard Kay also provided congenial reception as a visiting scholar at the University of Connecticut School of Law.

Finally, we would like to thank the editors of this series, Michael Grossberg and Christopher Tomlins, for their patience and savvy editorial guidance.

# Acknowledgments

# Introduction

In the more than 200 years since the ratification of the U.S. Constitution, it has become conventional wisdom that the Supreme Court has the last word on the meaning of that document. At the same time, the American people widely take for granted that the Constitution is a charter of democracy, liberty, and equality. Those who wrote and adopted the Constitution, however, actually took a dim view of democracy, and their notions of liberty and equality embraced overt racial and gender discrimination. Moreover, few of them anticipated that their new Supreme Court would assume the role of final arbiter of the Constitution's meaning. They did believe that the courts were essential to the preservation of law and justice, as against the lawless whims of popular majorities. But they doubted that the courts could preserve or give meaning to the Constitution independent of other political institutions.

The most farsighted among the founding generation, particularly James Madison, expected the meaning of the Constitution to develop through a political process that included the Supreme Court but would typically be led by the political branches of the federal government, the state governments, and the electorate. At its core, this political process was to be republican, not democratic. Madison and the Framers designed the Constitution deliberately to limit the operational influence of the people – "the democracy" – and instead sought to empower a national, political elite to give force and energy to a new central government. They created new governmental structures that would modify and refine the raw democratic will of the people, inhibit democratic control of office-holders, and prevent the emergence of durable political parties, perhaps the most essential institutions of American democracy as it later developed but anathema to the republican founders.

The founding generation's republican vision – that is, the vision of the propertied white males who monopolized political power and promulgated the Constitution – can be reduced without too much distortion to a handful of fundamental ideas. The founders meant to create a republic, not a democracy. That is, the people would be recognized as formally sovereign, but real governing power would lie in the hands of the educated, the affluent, those of wide reputation – in short, a "virtuous" elite who might be expected to put justice, law, and the good of their country ahead of their own interests, forbearing the temptations of faction and party. The founders further meant to preserve a well-regulated liberty, not only by relying on the virtue of officeholders, but also by balancing enhanced power at the center against a substantial measure of reserved power for the states. Moreover, the preservation of liberty in a confederated republic depended on limiting full political participation and legal personhood to propertied white men. The majority of the population – women, black Americans, the indigenous nations, the poor – would take positions decisively subordinate to that of propertied white men in the new constitutional structure.

No part of this vision, however, went uncontested. Subsequent decades brought challenges to the Framers' vision, especially in the name of democracy and states' rights. Proponents of democracy never accepted the Framers' republican vision, before or after ratification. Rather, democrats gradually reimagined party organization as an essential feature of the now-democratic Constitution, notwithstanding the antiparty intentions of the Framers. Indeed, the triumphant radicals of the Jackson era deemed democratic party organization superior to courts and the elitist traditions of the law in determining constitutional meaning. Champions of states' rights also launched a persistent struggle over the meaning of federalism, the balance of power between the federal government and the states. Advocates of consolidated, national power and of radical state autonomy defined the ends of a continuum, along which battles raged constantly in the name of establishing the true route to liberty. Finally, proponents of the rights of women, black Americans, and the so-called Indian[1] nations challenged aspects of the Framers' plan but especially the

---

[1] Although "Indian" is an obviously problematic label for the diverse nations that inhabited the land that was to become the United States, it was the common label used by Euro-Americans in this period and remains a widely used label today, even among many of the

stark racism and chauvinism of the later democrats and states'-rights men. Periodically, they turned to the Constitution itself to advance their causes and principles, but the established authorities consistently found in that Constitution a charter of freedom for the white man alone.

Struggles along all of these dimensions played out over decades. Indeed, the story of what the Constitution became after ratification has no endpoint, although our narrative must: By the late 1830s, the republican vision of the founders had, in important ways, been turned on its head. The new Democratic Party had gained ascendancy by reading the Constitution as a fundamentally democratic, not republican, document, which belonged to the people rather than the courts. Joined with the party's notion of democracy was a commitment to strict construction of federal powers and fierce defense of states' rights. Yet this party of "the democracy" – so understood because its avowed purpose was to defend a populist constitutional order against a reinvented "aristocracy" of special interests – explicitly excluded all but white men from civic participation. If the white males of the founding generation had varied and fluid views of exactly how women, blacks, and Indians might fit into a republican hierarchy, the white male "democrats" of the 1830s starkly excluded all of these groups from their otherwise antihierarchical Constitution.

This book explains the Constitution's evolution from the putatively republican document of 1787 to a charter of democracy (of a sort) by the 1830s. It preserves courts and especially the Supreme Court as important shapers of that story, addressing the usual run of great cases in the constitutional history of the period. But it integrates judicial action into a much larger history of constitutional politics – in Congress, in presidential action, in the states, and in elections, political parties, newspapers, and the streets and fields. As the narrative seeks to demonstrate, this larger constitutional politics gave judicial action much of its meaning, as judicial action simultaneously informed that larger constitutional politics.

This book thus joins the important, traditional story of top-down constitutional development, centered on the Supreme Court, with a more modern, often bottom-up story. It draws on our own primary research and also synthesizes a generation of recent scholarship on the origins of judicial review, party formation, the plight of constitutional outsiders, and more. The result is a modern explanation of how diverse groups combined to supplant the founders' vision with a more "democratic"

descendants of those nations. So, while we often use "indigenous nations" or the like to describe these peoples, we also use "Indians."

understanding of the Constitution. This new democratic vision of constitutionalism, one bolstered by an expanded public sphere and an emerging
practice and theory of party politics, was premised on an exclusionary
understanding of citizenship that limited political access and legal personhood to white men. In short, this book suggests that a full understanding
of early American constitutional development requires a narrative that
places such figures as the Whiskey Rebels, the proto-feminist Judith
Sargent Murray, the African-American activist James Forten, and the
democratic party organizer Martin Van Buren in the same cast of characters as James Madison, Alexander Hamilton, and John Marshall.

The story's roots lie in the American Revolution and its challenge to
monarchy, aristocracy, and the legal omnipotence of Parliament. The
Revolution forced the American people to invent a government and
constitutional order that could preserve the people's sovereignty and
liberty without the familiar guideposts of hierarchical authority. Both
the facts on the ground and certain widely shared convictions dictated
that the new government would take the form of a confederation of states.
Only a confederation, it seemed, could protect the constituent republics
from aggression, foreign and domestic, while staying out of the internal
affairs of each member state. Each state would preserve its citizens'
liberties, as only modest-sized states could do, but would also be protected from the external threats that brought war, exaggerated military
authority, oppressive taxation, and consequent threats to liberty.

The Revolution seemed to vindicate the claim that confederation
would be an effective tool for the preservation of republican liberty. The
newly confederated United States won its war of independence without a
real national government but only an alliance among the states. The
Articles of Confederation thus persisted into the 1780s as the nation's
first constitution. But, as Chapter 1 of our story explains, its radically
decentralized structure came to seem a failure to many in the nation's
elite. These men bemoaned the excesses of democracy, the disregard for
law, and the anxious localism that crippled the nation in both foreign and
domestic affairs. The remedy was the new Constitution of 1787, which
was designed to deliver substantial power to the center, where it would be
wielded by an elite class putatively devoted to law rather than raw
democratic will. Yet, the framers of the Constitution also sought to retain
federalism and a limited sort of popular sovereignty. While trying to
maintain this delicate balance, the new Constitution made clear that
propertied white men were not yet prepared to grant civic equality to

women, black Americans, Indians, and the poor. These other Americans, constituting most of the population, would have distinctly subordinate roles, if any roles at all, in the constitutional hierarchy of the new federal republic. At the same time, the Founding and its immediate aftermath saw just enough agitation for the rights of each of these groups to suggest the possibility of a progressive expansion of rights under the Constitution over time.

The Constitution was ratified soon enough, but not without strong opposition from Anti-Federalists. There was little doubt that George Washington would be the nation's first president, but many Anti-Federalists stood ready to scrutinize the new administration's every step, even as they acquiesced in the new Constitution. Thus, Washington and his cabinet took the leading role in shaping the new government while facing criticism and skepticism at nearly every turn. As Chapter 2 explains, President Washington's ambitious Secretary of the Treasury, Alexander Hamilton, launched an energetic program for centralization of power in the national government. Although Hamilton believed that this Federalist program implemented the goals of the framers of the Constitution, opposition soon formed among elites and middling politicians, as well as democrats and populists. Representatives of marginalized groups also sought to carve out roles for themselves under the Constitution but with little success. Gradually the opposition to the Federalists coalesced under the Republican label and in 1800 delivered Jefferson to the presidency in the name of states' rights and popular sovereignty.

During the years of Federalist hegemony across the 1790s, the federal courts played an auxiliary role in legitimating the Federalist reading of the Constitution. After Thomas Jefferson's election in 1800, however, the cause of Federalist constitutionalism fell chiefly to the Supreme Court under Chief Justice John Marshall. Chapter 3 shows that Marshall's Court not only defended capacious federal power, but, as important, used the Court's opinions to promote a distinctively legalist understanding of the Constitution. That is, in the face of rising movements for states' rights and democratic control, the Court insisted that the judiciary was supreme over the other branches and even over the sovereign people in interpreting the Constitution. Moreover, according to Marshall, that document constitutionalized judge-made, common law principles of contract and property at the expense of the states' and the people's own understandings of the public good. At every step, Marshall's legalist campaign provoked resistance from the more-radical Republicans, who believed that the people – not the judges and not the common law – held the final and sovereign word on the meaning of the Constitution.

The Republicans, however, were never fully united. Although Jefferson's election in 1800 stood as important precedent for future efforts to organize a democratic party, the Republicans remained a loose movement comprising everything from radical democrats to "moderates" who were sometimes indistinguishable from Federalists. Chapter 4 shows how the Republicans in power after 1800 struggled to establish an alternative to Federalist constitutionalism. Under pressure from international crises, the Federalist judiciary, and a Federalist remnant in Congress and the states, the Jefferson Administration and subsequent Republican administrations actually expanded federal power in important respects. In so doing, they exacerbated the frustrations of the democrats and the firmest states'-rights men.

Chapter 5 begins the story of the democrats' breakthrough. After the War of 1812, the ascent of democratic culture did not mean the advent of universal equality but, instead, triumphant claims to the hegemony of the white man. The constitutionalism of the radical democrats came to dominate the Republican movement, gradually converting the movement into the Democratic Party and purging its more legalist and centralizing elements. As it did so, the democrats made clear that they read the Constitution not only as democratic but as white and, of course, male. The possibilities that many had seen in the Constitution for some measure of rights for black Americans, for women, and for the Indian nations virtually disappeared in the "democratic" reinvention of the Constitution.

Chapter 6 tells the story of Indian status under the Constitution, an important test case of the Marshall Court's resistance in the 1820s to the democratic, states'-rights reading of the Constitution. The climactic defeat of the Marshall Court occurred in 1832 when the Court tried to defend the residue of rights claimed by the Cherokee Nation against the aggressions of Georgia's people and government. In the teeth of a holding of the Supreme Court, President Andrew Jackson and the State of Georgia made clear that the Constitution and the laws would mean what the (white, male) people, not the Court, said they meant.

The story concludes with the creation and entrenchment of the Democratic Party by Martin Van Buren and other leaders of the democratic movement. This party would have been anathema to the framers of the Constitution and to nearly all of the ratifiers, both because of the simple fact that it was a permanently organized party and because it stood for a kind of radical democratic control and devolved federalism that seemed dangerously similar to the structure that had failed so miserably in the 1780s. For some of the founding generation, but certainly not for all, the horror of Van Buren's Democratic Party would also have included the starkness of its racism and its comprehensive exclusion of women, blacks, and Indians from any meaningful place in the constitutional order.

# The New Constitution

## INTRODUCTION

Freed from British imperial rule, post-Revolutionary Americans began to imagine what it would mean to build a genuinely "republican" government in place of monarchy and aristocracy. Americans prior to the Revolution had accepted that the British Constitution had achieved the perfect balance of Aristotle's three forms of government: monarchy, aristocracy, and democracy. In a few short years, however, they excised two of the fundamentals of British constitutional government, rejecting both monarchy and aristocracy and setting out to build a republic in which the people as a whole would be sovereign. But conventional wisdom held that the people could never govern themselves, that popular government reliably descended into factional struggle and the eventual emergence of tyranny. John Adams thus anxiously wrote that "public virtue is the only foundation of Republics. There must be a positive passion for the public good."[1] Without popular virtue, republicanism would fail.

In the decade following independence, Americans' faith in their ability to create a virtuous republic was tested. Economic dislocation, civic unrest, and a variety of external threats left the new United States in a precarious state. Their constitution, the Articles of Confederation, was little more than a treaty among independent states, adopted primarily to

---

[1] John Adams to Mercy Warren, April 16, 1776, in Philip B. Kurland and Ralph Lerner, eds., *The Founders' Constitution*, vol. 1, ch. 18, document 9 (2000; web edition): http://press-pubs.uchicago.edu/founders/documents/v1ch18s9.html.

win a war of independence. The Articles created a Congress with some power to coordinate the actions of the states but little power to coerce recalcitrant members of the confederacy. Thus, in domestic affairs, Congress had little capacity to address the postwar economic depression. Pro-debtor economic policies in many of the states only made things worse, at least in the eyes of the propertied classes. But, under the Articles, Congress had no way of forcing better policy on the states. Similarly, Congress had little leverage in foreign affairs, despite facing hostile Indian tribes, Spain's continuing control of much of the Southwest, and British refusal to relinquish western posts until the United States honored all the debts it owed British creditors. Without the protection of the powerful British Navy, American shipping even fell victim to pirates in North Africa.

Calls for reform were sounded from many quarters, with James Madison, Alexander Hamilton, and George Washington among the most important voices. In the summer of 1787, delegates from most of the states assembled in Philadelphia. The Constitutional Convention included some of the most important political figures in the nation and boasted many of the new republic's most gifted and innovative legal minds. Indeed, Thomas Jefferson, observing from his diplomatic post in Paris, described the gathering at the Constitutional Convention as "an assembly of demigods."[2] Yet many of the Framers' initiatives would prove controversial. Abandoning their charge to revise the Articles of Confederation, the delegates created an entirely new system of government that shared few features with the Articles.

The new Constitution proposed a powerful central government that diminished the roles of the people and the states. The Framers aimed to leave behind the mere alliance that was the Articles and substitute a genuinely national government. Structured correctly, the enhanced power at the center would equip the nation to act with unity and energy in foreign affairs. Equally important, it would control the tendencies toward democracy and faction in the states.

The Framers thus set themselves quite a challenge. They knew that a full consolidation of power at the center would not be acceptable. The states had to retain substantial authority, even as the Framers sought to

---

[2] Thomas Jefferson to John Adams, August 30, 1787, *Founders Online*, National Archives, last modified July 12, 2016, http://founders.archives.gov/documents/Jefferson/01-12-02-0075. (Original source: *The Papers of Thomas Jefferson*, vol. 12, *7 August 1787–31 March 1788*, ed. Julian P. Boyd [Princeton: Princeton University Press, 1955], 66–69.)

block policies that violated contract and property rights. Each state must believe that its essential interests would be adequately protected under the new Constitution. Most pointedly, the Constitution would never be ratified if it did not adequately protect slaveholders' interests in their human property. Similarly, the Framers knew that they must respect the sovereignty of the people, even as they sought to deliver operational power mainly to an educated, affluent elite. They further understood that even such an elite might fall prey to partisanship and factionalism if not hemmed in by structural checks and balances. The negotiation and drafting of the new Constitution thus required the Framers to achieve a delicate balance among multiple goals while keeping one eye on the larger public that would be asked to ratify the document.

And they succeeded, at least at first. By the middle of 1788, eleven states had ratified the Constitution, enough to launch the new government. But the contest was a difficult one, foreshadowing decades of constitutional contention, not the consensus that the Framers sought. If ratification of the Constitution seemed a triumph for the elitist republicanism of the Framers, it also drew in much more of the nation than just that elite. The lively debate gave voice even to the unpropertied (if not much to women, black Americans, or the indigenous) and demonstrated that the Framers' elitism would not go unchallenged. Rather, the Constitution would remain an object of debate, revision, and reinterpretation, even once ratified. Many of the votes for ratification depended on assurances that subsequent amendments would correct some of the deficiencies in the document. But even the addition of ten amendments in the early years of the new government did not eliminate profound tensions and conflicts in American society, derived from the American Revolution and manifested again in the ratification debate. Although no anti-Constitution party emerged after ratification, the next four decades would witness an almost ceaseless struggle over how to interpret and implement the Constitution.

## THE WEAKNESS OF THE ARTICLES OF CONFEDERATION

The Continental Congress created the Articles of Confederation in the midst of the Revolution. Although the creation of a sustainable wartime government for thirteen sovereign states was a remarkable achievement, the government was plagued by problems from the outset. The unicameral legislature gave each state an equal vote and lacked a permanent executive. There was no national system of courts to adjudicate matters between states or between the Confederation government and other legal actors, especially foreign debtors. In short, the Articles created a barely functional government, held together by gossamer threads.

The Treaty of Paris (1783) formally ended hostilities between Britain and the new United States of America. Peace did not, however, solve all of the new nation's many problems. Although America had won independence by force of arms, the young republic's strategic position after the conclusion of peace was precarious. On the frontier, British troops were still garrisoned in the Old Northwest, using these outposts to continue their lucrative trade with the Indians in fur and guns. Britain relied on the pretext that America had failed to pay prewar debts and compensate Loyalists for property confiscated during the war. Congress had little power to compel the states to live up to the nation's treaty obligations, even if that risked a dangerous alliance between the British and hostile Indian nations.

Relations with the Indian nations too remained tense. Neither the British nor the Americans showed much concern for Indian interests and rights in the peace negotiations, and the American government soon asserted its sovereignty over vast areas inhabited by indigenous nations. The Indian nations, for their part, had fought effectively with the British and were stunned that the United States presumed to treat them as if they had been defeated and were now a subject people. After several bloody encounters with Indian resistance, Congress faced up to its military weakness and retreated from its aggressive posture. Instead, it adopted a policy, often breached in later years, that Indian lands might be obtained only by good faith purchase.

Without a powerful navy to protect its commerce, American ships were easy prey for pirates, who were especially active in the Mediterranean, where the North African states of Morocco, Algiers, Tunis, and Tripoli, known as the Barbary States, sanctioned such practices. The Barbary pirates extorted money from merchant vessels in exchange for safe passage. Failure to pay resulted in the seizure of ships and imprisonment of sailors, who languished in prisons or were sold into slavery. In July 1785, when pirates captured two American ships, Algiers demanded nearly $60,000 in ransom to release the vessels and their crews. While the loss of trade as a result of piracy burdened the nation's fledgling economy, the sad fate of American captives became a source of national humiliation. Frustration built, but defending the nation's interests in the

Mediterranean would have to wait while America dealt with the more proximate threats posed by Indian nations, the British, and indeed the Spanish, who controlled territories on the southwest border.

Domestically, the failure to provide the Confederation government with even the basic power of taxation illustrated the problems with the Articles. Americans had resented British efforts to tax them prior to the Revolution, and their lingering sensitivity led them to severely restrict the Confederation Congress's power to fund its operations. Thus Congress was forced to rely on requisitions made to the states. Few states bothered to comply in a timely manner, and the new government of the United States was plagued by shortages of funds with which to pay for a war against the most powerful nation in Europe. Congress thus resorted to printing almost $250 million in paper currency, which was not backed by gold or silver and led to staggering inflation. By 1781, it took more than 150 Continental dollars to purchase what had cost one dollar in 1777.

Then the end of the war ushered in a host of new economic problems. Boycotts of British goods and the disruption of trade during wartime meant that consumers had been denied access to luxury items, including china, textiles, and wine. Demand for British goods surged after the war, and the new nation was flooded with imports. British merchants encouraged Americans to buy goods on credit. But few American goods went to Britain to offset the increase in imports. The trade deficit with Britain drained what little gold and silver reserves were available to the nation. American banks had to curtail loans. When merchants were forced to call in debts to satisfy their British suppliers, they in turn put pressure on consumers to pay off debts. This constriction of credit sent the economy into a tailspin. Agricultural prices plummeted, and wages fell. The result was the nation's first depression.

Within the states, the response to the economic crisis proved highly controversial. In many states, a new "middling" class of politicians rose to power and began to displace traditional governing elites, bringing with them debtor-friendly policies and a more democratic ideology. These men tended to favor policies to ease the burdens of farmers and artisans: "Stay laws" created generous grace periods for the recovery of debts and protected farmers from having their farms seized for nonpayment. "Tender laws" allowed farmers to pay debts with goods rather than hard currency. A turn to paper money eased the shortage of currency. But these policies also had the potential to hinder economic exchange by encouraging inflation and by indicating to creditors that they could not count on timely repayment at full value.

At issue in these debates was not just economic policy but also deep anxieties about the structure of power in the newly independent states. Before the American Revolution, men drawn from the upper ranks of society dominated the individual colonial legislatures. As one legislator noted, "It is right that men of *birth* and *fortune*, in every government that is free, should be invested with power, and enjoy higher honours than the people."[3] After the Revolution, however, democratic sentiment began slowly to assert itself. A writer calling himself "Democritus" captured the new mood when he urged citizens to vote only for men "of middling circumstances" and "common understanding," not members of a wealthy or educated elite. Such middling men were less likely to become corrupt and were better able to understand the needs of the vast majority of citizens. In nearly every state, a new type of politician emerged who embodied this more democratic version of republicanism: men such as New York's Abraham Yates, a shoemaker, and Pennsylvania's William Findley, a weaver.

Such tensions between the traditional authority of social elites and the insurgent claims of middling politicians touched on questions of legal authority as well as political power. Lawyers had taken a leading role in the Revolution and tended now to defend the conservative traditions of the common law as against the allegedly impulsive policymaking of democrats and middling men. The common law was a body of judge-made law drawn from a multitude of British court decisions, which venerated the obligations of contract and property rights, not the shifting policy preferences of the people. It was not surprising, then, that the democratic sentiment unleashed by the Revolution would encourage American farmers and artisans to prefer their own sense of economic justice, not that of British judges and the elite American lawyers who claimed to possess the keys to the obscure texts of the common law. Some of these democrats challenged the necessity of a learned judiciary altogether, arguing that little, if any, formal training in law was necessary to comprehend constitutional and legal texts. These radicals tended to favor legislatures, juries, the militia, and even the traditions of plebeian crowd action as the most genuine voices of the people and thus of the law. In the mid-1780s, the voice of the people frequently called for immediate economic relief, not stout defense of the common law's veneration of contract and property rights.

---

[3] *Virginia Gazette*, June 9, 1768; Samuel Adams to James Warren, November 4, 1775, *The Writings of Samuel Adams* 3: 235–237.

These simmering tensions came to a head in Massachusetts in 1786. The postwar economic downturn hit farmers there particularly hard. In contrast to some states, the Commonwealth's government refused to enact relief measures for private debts and also turned to tax increases to retire its public debt. The added burden on already strained farmers led to an increase in foreclosures. Frustration with the policy mounted, and in August of 1786 angry farmers, including a number of Revolutionary War veterans, marched on the town of Northampton to shut down the local courts and prevent the foreclosures. The armed crowd prevented the judges, dressed in long black robes and gray wigs, from entering the courthouse. The protesters here and across western Massachusetts, soon dubbed Shaysites after their leader Daniel Shays, believed they were protecting the "good of the commonwealth" and opposing the "tyrannical government in the Massachusetts State." But Governor James Bowdoin condemned the court closings as "fraught with the most fatal and pernicious consequences" that "must tend to subvert all law and government."[4] The governor dispatched the state militia, but a member of one crowd sympathetic to the Shaysites suggested putting the militia's next move to a vote: Supporters of opening the court stood to one side of the road, while those opposed crossed the highway. Nearly 800 of 1,000 members of the militia voted with their feet to join the rebels and keep the courts closed, challenging established authority and asserting a populist vision of law in which the rights of contract and property were tempered by notions of equity and justice.

Popular insistence on debt relief, sometimes spilling into mob action, had already alarmed many states' defenders of order and property, but the rebellion in conservative Massachusetts was the most alarming of all. Pro-government forces defeated Shays and his followers in a battle near the state arsenal in Springfield in early 1787, but the state government soon conciliated the rebels with measures of debt relief. If even Massachusetts, which had long held out for order and property, made concessions to rebels, then what was left of republican government? The one figure among the nation's Patriot elite who seemed relatively unfazed was Thomas Jefferson, who learned of the rebellion while posted in Paris. Jefferson believed that popular unrest in a republic was a tolerable inconvenience necessary to nurture liberty. Such events might actually be authentic expressions of the people's will and could be easily contained

---

[4] Governor James Bowdoin, Proclamation September 2, 1786.

by a conciliatory government exercising appropriate restraint. Brushing off the seriousness of the rebellion, he assured his friend James Madison "that a little rebellion now and then is a good thing, and as necessary in the political world as storms in the physical." Jefferson's views were not shared by George Washington, who typified most of the nation's elite in his distress at the events in Massachusetts. He feared that "if government shrinks, or is unable to enforce its laws," then "everything will be turned topsy turvey" and "anarchy & confusion must prevail."[5]

The economic, political, and diplomatic problems faced by the states and by the Confederation government inspired action among a small but talented group of politicians spread across the states. Many had long been advocating reform of the Articles of Confederation and creation of a stronger national government that could protect American interests abroad and control internal disturbances, such as Shays' Rebellion. For the nationalists the postwar era had proven the fragility of republicanism. Anarchy, not tyranny, had emerged as the true threat to American liberty. Delegates from Maryland and Virginia first gathered at George Washington's home in Mount Vernon in 1785 to discuss common economic concerns. A year later in Annapolis, Maryland, delegates from five states met to discuss the problems of the Confederation, particularly its financial woes. Finally, in 1787, delegates from 12 of the 13 states gathered in Philadelphia to reform the Articles of Confederation.

### A CONSTITUTION OF COMPROMISES

The 55 delegates who participated in the Philadelphia Convention in the summer of 1787 were an impressive cast of characters by any measure. Virginia's delegation included James Madison and George Mason, two of its most esteemed political figures, and also boasted George Washington, who was elected to preside over the meeting. Benjamin Franklin of Pennsylvania, then age 81, was the oldest delegate. Among New York's representatives was the brilliant, but sometimes brash, young lawyer Alexander Hamilton. Lawyers dominated the convention, and nearly all the delegates were wealthy men. To facilitate frank conversation among the delegates a strict rule of secrecy was imposed on the proceedings. The windows of the Pennsylvania State House were nailed shut and a guard

---

[5] George Washington to Henry Knox, February 3, 1787; *The Papers of Thomas Jefferson*, vol. 11, *1 January–6 August 1787*, ed. Julian P. Boyd (Princeton: Princeton University Press, 1955), 92–97.

posted at the door. This decision undoubtedly facilitated a more honest and wide-ranging debate among the delegates, but it also intensified rumors about their activities. One Pennsylvania newspaper warned of the "monster" being fashioned behind a "thick veil of secrecy."[6]

The delegates brought different agendas with them to Philadelphia. None were more ambitious than James Madison, who hoped to radically transform the trajectory of American constitutionalism. Like other delegates, he saw the politics in the states across the 1780s as reflections of too much democracy, in particular the rise of a new breed of politician, men of provincial and partisan views who had injected factionalism into politics. To cure this problem, nationalists believed that power must be substantially transferred to the political center. A new government capable of enforcing the law and collecting taxes had to be created. Further removed from local factions, national politics would draw from a larger pool of citizens and favor those with talent, education, and vision. A properly structured government would provide inducements to this elite to pursue the "permanent and aggregate interests of the community," rather than futilely pursuing personal or factional interests.[7] In short, Madison imagined a constitution that would simultaneously centralize powers in the national government and dampen the effect of localist partisanship.

Alexander Hamilton too brought a distinct constitutional vision to Philadelphia. Where Madison focused on neutralizing faction, particularly in the workings of state legislatures, Hamilton believed that the nation's primary problems lay in a central government that was too weak to guarantee America's survival as an independent nation. The Articles of Confederation had reflected popular perceptions that British-style government inevitably led to corruption and tyranny. The context of the Revolution had thus led Americans to hobble their new national government rather than grant it the tools necessary to build national power and prosperity. As early as 1781, Hamilton had observed: "As too much power leads to despotism, too little leads to anarchy, and both, eventually, to the ruin of the people. These are maxims well known, but never sufficiently attended to, in adjusting the frames of governments." By 1787, many of course agreed with Hamilton that the Articles had proven inadequate, but Hamilton was nearly alone in the Convention in actually

---

[6] "An Officer of the Late Continental Army," *Independent Gazetteer*, November 6, 1787.
[7] Jacob Cooke ed., Alexander Hamilton, John Jay, and James Madison, *The Federalist No. 10* (Middletown, Conn: Wesleyan University Press, 1961).

seeking to emulate important aspects of the British model, including a powerful executive charged with the building of an American empire.[8]

Madison and Hamilton each traveled to Philadelphia with great hopes for enhancing federal power, both to overcome provincial factionalism domestically and to establish a more truly independent and powerful United States in the community of nations. But no one man was able to direct the Convention. Over the course of the summer the delegates canvassed a bewildering range of issues, often digressing to discuss abstract issues in politics and law. Argument followed by compromise gave way to further argument, as earlier proposals were refashioned to accommodate the objections of different interests in the convention: small states battled larger states, slave states tangled with emancipating states, proponents of greater democracy debated defenders of elite governance.

Rather than follow their mandate to revise the Articles of Confederation, the Convention took up a bold proposal presented by the Virginia delegation. The Virginia Plan, drafted mainly by Madison, proposed a wholly new national government, supreme in those broad areas in which it was given authority. A federal structure would remain, and the states would retain substantial powers, but nothing like the autonomy they enjoyed under the Articles. The new federal government would comprise a single executive, a two-house legislature, and a separate judiciary. The lower house of Congress would be directly elected by the people, nodding to the principle of popular sovereignty, but the upper house would be elected by the lower house from a list provided by the state legislatures. Under the Articles of Confederation, small states such as Maryland had the same vote as large states such as Virginia. In place of this one-state one-vote principle, the Virginia plan offered each state representation in proportion to its population. The scope of authority of the new Congress was considerable: It would have power "to legislate in all cases to which the separate States are incompetent" or "in which the harmony of the United States may be interrupted by the exercise of individual [state] legislation." Although the plan did not explicitly address nettlesome issues such as the power to tax, such powers were clearly within the purview of this broad grant of authority. The authors of the Virginia Plan thus departed radically from the Articles,

---

[8] Alexander Hamilton, "The Continentalist No. 1," *The Political Writings of Alexander Hamilton: Volume 1, 1769–1789* (Cambridge: Cambridge University Press, 2017).

opting for a general grant of authority rather than a limited list of enumerated powers.[9]

Representatives from the small states opposed the Virginia Plan. Two weeks after it was introduced, William Patterson of New Jersey made a counterproposal, often dubbed the New Jersey Plan. Although it shared the Virginia Plan's determination to create a strong central government, it would have perpetuated the Articles' unicameral legislature, in which each state would have one vote. This arrangement would maintain the parity between small and large states. Although the New Jersey Plan was defeated, it had reminded the delegates that a federal structure was essential and a consolidated national government politically impossible. No consensus could be reached without accommodating the concerns of the small states, which feared a national government under the control of the larger states.

To address the conflict between large and small states, on June 29, Oliver Ellsworth of Connecticut reintroduced an earlier compromise that he and Roger Sherman (also of Connecticut) had devised. The plan provided for equal representation for large and small states in the upper house and a lower house in which representation would be apportioned on the basis of population. On July 16, the convention adopted what came to be known as the Great Compromise (or the Connecticut Compromise, a nod to its framers) overcoming what had been the major obstacle to a consensus plan of government.

Although the large and small states had battled each other on the question of representation, nearly all the delegates shared a suspicion of democracy. In the final scheme, even the popularly elected House would be chosen generally by white male property-holders (depending on each state's suffrage laws), in districts sufficiently large that only men of elite status and established reputations would be likely to gain office. These men would gather in the national capital at a sufficient distance from their constituents to foster independence of action and thus wise and effective governance. The upper house, the Senate, would not have titled aristocrats, but it too would be drawn from the "natural aristocracy." The two senators allotted to each state were not to be chosen directly by the people of the states, but by the state legislatures, who presumably would choose men of education, affluence, and accomplishment from among the

[9] *The Papers of James Madison, 27 May 1787–3 March 1788*, vol. 10, ed. Robert A. Rutland, Charles F. Hobson, William M. E. Rachal, and Frederika J. Teute (Chicago: University of Chicago Press, 1977), 12–18.

nation's commercial elite, planters, and lawyers. Granted a long, six-year term of service, the Senate was designed to be both smaller and more independent of the people than the House. Its structure would ensure that political decisions would be made in a calm and deliberate manner. In sum, the Framers designed the mechanisms for choosing the people's representatives to ensure that only members of the elite would rise to the most important positions in government.

Although the Great Compromise solved one of the most difficult problems the convention faced, it also focused attention on one of the nation's central contradictions: the persistence of slavery in a nation dedicated to liberty. Indeed, in James Madison's view, the greatest division in the convention was not the conflict between large states and small states, but the division between those that sought to protect slavery and those that did not. First, the compromise over the basis of representation had to determine whether to count enslaved persons in the apportionment of the new lower house. The southern states, seeking sufficient representation in the new legislature to protect slavery, were determined that their slaves be counted fully for this purpose. Opponents of slavery, by contrast, wished to see slaves taxed as property but did not wish to count them when calculating representation. The convention settled on a compromise in which slaves were counted as three-fifths of a person for purposes of both taxation and legislative apportionment. (The three-fifths ratio had been adopted by the Confederation Congress earlier, when it faced another issue pertaining to slavery.)

But representation was only one of the areas in which the persistence of slavery challenged the Framers' commitment to liberty. The question of the international slave trade prompted pointed but limited debate on the future of slavery. The convention's largest slaveholder, George Mason, argued that slavery undermined republican values and eventually turned even the most virtuous citizen into a vicious tyrant. He thus hoped for an immediate end to the "infernal traffic" that was the international slave trade (and an end to slavery altogether under state auspices). Representatives from Georgia and South Carolina viewed Mason's position cynically. Virginia had an excess of slaves and would profit enormously from an internal slave trade if the external trade with Africa were abolished. South Carolina's Charles Pinckney went further, justifying slavery by noting that all the great republics of the ancient world had accepted the necessity of slavery. His cousin, General Charles Cotesworth Pinckney, also from South Carolina, told delegates that his state would never accept the Constitution if the slave trade were banned. Roger Sherman of

Connecticut hinted at the in-between view of many in the convention when he assured those of antislavery sentiment that "the abolition of slavery seemed to be going on in the U.S. & that the good sense of the several States would probably by degrees compleat it." Connecticut's Oliver Ellsworth added that an increase in poor laborers (presumably white immigrants) would mean that, "Slavery in time will not be a speck in our country." The remarks of Sherman and Ellsworth reflected probably the dominant view in the convention: an abstract preference to be rid of slavery but an unwillingness to take affirmative steps or dictate to the states on the subject. Indeed, the Connecticut duo made clear that accommodation of such firmly pro-slavery states as Georgia and South Carolina was not simply prudent but the "sine qua non" of the Union. In the end, the delegates' widely shared antislavery sentiment was readily subordinated to their desire to achieve a Union that would firm up protections for property rights. So they adopted only a modest provision that permitted a federal ban on the international slave trade in twenty years' time.[10]

The Constitution's authorization of an eventual ban on the slave trade reflected the Founders' ambivalence, vindicating and limiting slaveholders' rights in the same provision. So too did the Fugitive Slave Clause, the other major slavery-related provision of the Constitution. This provision was less clearly a part of a conscious "bargain" among the states than was the slave trade clause. Rather, it was added late in the proceedings, largely without controversy or opposition and, like all other slavery-protective elements of the Constitution, without actually mentioning the word *slavery*. It thus reflected the Convention's unwillingness to frankly embrace slavery as a permanent institution under the Constitution. But it reflected much more strongly the Convention's conviction that the Union depended on constitutional recognition of property rights in persons. If South Carolina and Georgia had extracted a temporary protection for the international slave trade, no bargaining had been necessary to obtain a federal affirmation of slaveholders' property rights.

Hopeful anticipations of emancipation by delegates like Sherman and Ellsworth proved wildly optimistic in subsequent decades. Still, it is important to recognize the reasons why emancipation seemed a plausible prospect as of 1787. At this time, slavery remained legal in almost all states, but some had embarked on the road to abolition. At one end of the

---

[10] James Madison, *Notes of Debates in the Federal Convention of 1787* (New York: W. W. Norton, 1987), 503–509.

continuum lay parts of New England that had already abolished the institution. Massachusetts ended slavery by judicial decision in 1783, interpreting the provisions of its 1780 constitution in terms favorable to liberty and inimical to slavery. Rhode Island and Connecticut adopted gradual emancipation statutes in 1784. This was also the dominant path in the middle Atlantic. Pennsylvania enacted a gradual emancipation statute in 1780, while New York and New Jersey, with notably larger enslaved populations, would enact gradual abolition schemes in 1799 and in 1804, respectively. In the Chesapeake, a different model took hold. In the colonial era manumission often required a special act of the legislature. After the American Revolution slave owners were given the ability to free their slaves. Manumission laws in Virginia, Maryland, and Delaware led to a modest but steady increase in the number of slave emancipations. In the lower south, where the enslaved outnumbered free persons in many places, there were few illusions that slavery would end anytime soon. Still, for the most idealistic members of the Revolutionary generation, it was conceivable that a trend toward emancipation that extended all the way to Virginia – even one moving at a glacial pace – might eventually erode the viability of slavery even in the low country of the Carolinas and Georgia.

In sum, the Convention's deliberations reflected a founding ambivalence about slavery but also the de facto power of the slaveholding interests. Outside the lower south, many Americans sincerely hoped and believed that eventually the nation would find a path to emancipation, less often because of concern for the enslaved and more often because slaveholding was deemed corrosive to the personal character essential for republican government. Many shared a belief that history was on the side of eventual emancipation and that the anticipated end to the international slave trade indicated the nation's ultimate, emancipationist direction. On the other hand, the delegates had also chosen to require the return of the fugitive enslaved to their masters and implicitly to leave the question of slavery and emancipation to be decided by each state for itself. As of 1787, therefore, South Carolina, Georgia, and all who were committed to slavery had little reason to fear, despite the inchoate, emancipationist sentiments of many of the Framers. The interests of slaveholders were in no real danger under the new Constitution, which emphasized the protection of property rights, including the right to hold human property as slaves.

Less durably controversial than slavery, the shape of the new executive branch nevertheless proved a subject of debate in the Convention. The delegates generally agreed it required strength but also insulation from democratic will, as well as checks to prevent the accumulation of tyrannical power. They briefly considered George Mason's proposal for a three-man plural executive. Such an executive, Mason argued, could better represent the various regional interests of the nation. Instead, the convention settled on a unitary executive, but there was disagreement over the term of office. Some delegates favored a single term as long as seven years, while others argued that a shorter term with the possibility of reelection would provide a greater check on the president. Alexander Hamilton, perhaps the most ardent champion of executive power in the Convention, proposed a life term for the office of president, but this leaned too close to monarchy for most delegates. The convention ultimately settled on a four-year term with no limits on the number of terms a president might serve.

There was also considerable disagreement over how the president ought to be selected. James Wilson, in some ways the most democratic of the Framers, wanted the executive elected by the people, whereas Mason argued that the people lacked the necessary wisdom. Roger Sherman would have had the national legislature pick the executive, but this method raised concerns about separation of powers because it might have rendered the executive too much the puppet of Congress. The Convention ultimately settled on another elaborate filtering device to limit popular influence in selecting the president: an electoral college composed of electors selected by the state legislatures. This system not only created another deliberative body to elect the president; it also gave the state legislatures additional power, by making the president more directly a creature of the states, rather than making him directly responsible to the people.

The structure of the executive branch was laid out briefly in Article II of the Constitution, which declared that "the executive Power shall be vested in a President of the United States of America" and went on to list a number of specific responsibilities of the president. Although the president was endowed with considerable power, the convention did not create anything approaching a British-style monarch. Indeed, apart from a general commitment to the proposition that the executive branch would enforce the laws, there was little consensus or detail about how executive power would function in practice. Defining the scope of executive authority over treaty-making, the waging of war, and the removal of executive officers would prove to be exceedingly divisive in the early years of the new government.

The Convention's provisions for a new national judiciary not only corrected one of the glaring deficiencies of the Articles, but also responded to the rise of populist movements demanding radical reforms of law and society. Shays' Rebellion is the best known of these movements, but it was hardly the only one. One of the Framers' concerns about the politics of the states in the 1780s was that the people, acting through their legislatures or by direct action, had protected the interests of debtors at the expense of both creditors' rights and established procedures and principles of law. Although debtors shared in the rough consensus on the sanctity of property rights, populists believed that legal procedures designed to enforce contracts and debts had to be tempered by equity and justice. Indeed, during the war effort, even the most conservative members of the Founding generation recognized a need to take extraordinary measures such as confiscating Loyalist property, when popularly elected representative assemblies deemed such actions necessary. After the Revolution, however, antilawyer polemics and movements, court closings, and legislative relief for debtors seemed to call into question basic principles of contract and property.

To many Framers, such actions demonstrated the dangers of democracy and a growing threat to the rule of law. The Framers addressed these dangers in a number of ways. As we have already noted, the Constitution transferred substantial power to the political center of the new nation, created a series of structural mechanisms designed to restrain the popular will by checks on the legislative branch, and established a set of electoral processes designed to attenuate the influence of popular will on federal lawmakers. The Constitution further removed certain legal issues entirely from the control of the states, most importantly prohibiting any state law "impairing the obligation of contracts."[11] And, of course, Article III of the Constitution mandated the creation of a federal judiciary, consisting of at least one high court: "The judicial power of the United States, shall be vested in one Supreme Court, and in such inferior courts as the Congress may from time to time ordain and establish." This Court would be empowered to vindicate federal law, including the Contracts Clause, as the "supreme law of the land,"[12] and thus to control the states' propensity to violate principles of the common law. All of these provisions represented efforts to reinforce traditional legal concepts and procedures and insulate them from the democracy's untutored notions of "justice."

[11] See Article I, section 10 of the U.S. Constitution.
[12] See Article VI of the U.S. Constitution.

In Madison's view, two further provisions, which did not make it into the Constitution, would have been even more effective defenders of legal principles than the new Supreme Court. Madison favored both a congressional veto over state laws and a Council of Revision to review congressional statutes before they could go into effect. The veto would have empowered Congress to disallow any and all state legislation that it found unwise or unjust, but the proposal was motivated especially by the states' history of debt relief at the expense of contract and property rights. The Council of Revision, comprising the executive and members of the federal judiciary, would be tasked with assessing the constitutionality as well as the wisdom of federal legislation, thus defending law against the weaknesses of political will even within the national governing structure.

Neither of Madison's efforts to insulate law from the threat posed by democracy succeeded, but the Constitution did provide for constitutional review by the judiciary. Although the Constitution does not expressly mention the federal judiciary's power to conduct "judicial review," the existence of that power was clear, if occasionally controversial, from the outset. The "supremacy clause" of Article VI explicitly joins the federal Constitution with other federal laws and treaties as "the supreme law of the land," by which "the judges in every State shall be bound" in the normal course of adjudication, notwithstanding "anything in the Constitution or laws of any State to the contrary." This passage was not limited to *constitutional* review, but it did make clear both that the state courts must review state laws for constitutionality and that the Constitution was a sort of law that judges must recognize and apply in adjudications. If the Constitution was cognizable law in state cases, then logically it must have been so in federal cases as well. And it was clearly supreme over legislation wherever it applied.

Debate in the Convention, moreover, was punctuated by delegates' endorsements of judicial review. Elbridge Gerry, for example, explained his opposition to a national council of revision in part by noting that the judges would "have a sufficient check agst. encroachments on their own department by their exposition of the laws, which involved a power of deciding on their constitutionality." There is little doubt that among members of the nation's judicial elite, there was broad agreement that the power of judicial review was a simple matter of lawyerly logic, following directly from judicial oaths to apply the law.

For those not familiar with lawyerly culture, the great North Carolina lawyer and future Supreme Court Justice James Iredell spelled out the logic of judicial review under the North Carolina Constitution a year before the drafting of the federal one. In a newspaper essay, he explained that the "duty of [the judicial] power . . . is to decide according to the laws of the State." And, "[i]t will not be denied, I suppose, that the constitution is a law of the State," just the same as "an act of Assembly, with this difference only, that it is the fundamental law, and unalterable by the legislature, which derives all its powers from it." The power of judicial review, as we now call it, was inherent in the judicial office, he argued, once one understood the nature of judicial duty under a written constitution embodying popular sovereignty: "The judges, therefore, must take care at their peril, that every act of Assembly they presume to enforce is warranted by the constitution, since if it is not, they act without lawful authority. This is not a usurped or a discretionary power, but one inevitably resulting from the constitution of their office, they being judges for the benefit of the whole people, not mere servants of the Assembly."[13]

The creation of a federal judiciary was one of the most important departures from the weak government created by the Articles of Confederation. For decades to come, the federal courts would deploy the Contracts Clause and the power of judicial review to effectively constitutionalize the common law and thereby tame the democracy.[14] Yet, compared to the delegates' extensive elaboration of the structure and duties of the other branches of the federal government, the Constitution provided only the barest outlines of the judiciary. It mandated the creation of a Supreme Court and allowed for the creation of lower federal courts, but it did not specify the scope and structure of the federal judiciary any further than that. Rather, it charged Congress with filling out this vital part of the constitutional design. It authorized a number of categories of federal jurisdiction, but, again, left Congress to determine how much of this jurisdiction would actually be assigned to the federal courts and how it would be distributed.

The Judiciary Act of 1789, consequently, created the federal court system that the Constitution had barely hinted at. Beyond creating the Supreme Court, Congress erected a modest system of thirteen district courts and three circuit courts. Presiding over the circuit courts were two circuit-riding justices of the Supreme Court along with the local district judge. One might have imagined that these courts would mainly adjudicate cases governed by federal law, especially because the

---

[13] "To the Public," *Life and Correspondence of James Iredell*, vol. 2, 148, ed. Griffith J. McRee (New York: D. Appleton & Co. 1858).
[14] See especially *Fletcher v. Peck* (1810), to be discussed at length in Chapter 3.

Constitution seemed to mandate such general federal jurisdiction, announcing that the "judicial power shall extend to all cases, in law and equity, arising under this Constitution, the laws of the United States, and treaties made, or which shall be made, under their authority." But, in fact the Judiciary Act granted the courts a more limited jurisdiction. The most important provisions assigned the circuit courts appellate authority over the district courts and, more important, original jurisdiction in "diversity" cases, cases between citizens of different states – but not the general, federal question jurisdiction evidently contemplated by the Constitution. Rather, the Act left most federal cases to the state courts. The bread and butter of the federal courts would not be matters of federal law but diversity cases, involving litigants from different states and generally turning on state law. In these cases, it was imagined, one or another party might reasonably fear some bias on the part of a state court and so gained the right to insist on a federal forum, which was presumed to be relatively neutral. The task of preserving uniformity in the mass of state court interpretations of federal law fell mainly to the Supreme Court, which was given the power to review state court judgments by writ of error when necessary to defend federal law.

All of this amounted to a limited reach for the federal courts in comparison to the jurisdiction actually authorized by Article III. But few doubted that Congress could limit the jurisdiction of the federal courts as it liked. At least for the moment, the most nationalist-minded members of Congress were content to limit their ambitions when it came to the courts, mollifying those like Pennsylvania Senator William Maclay, who feared that the federal courts would "swallow all the State Constitutions by degree."[15]

In sum, the Constitution sought to reinvigorate law as a check on the democratic excesses of the post-Revolutionary period. Both the design of the federal Congress and the creation of a federal judiciary aimed at restoration and enforcement of the property and contract rights that so much state policy had endangered. Although the Constitution achieved this goal in important measure, it did not generate the comprehensive subordination of the states to the federal courts feared by men like Senator Maclay.

Two delegates from New York, Robert Yates and John Lansing, left the Convention before the document was completed and therefore did not

<hr />

[15] Maeva Marcus, ed., *The Documentary History of the Supreme Court of the United States, 1789–1800*, vol. 4 (New York: Columbia University Press, 1992), 473.

sign it. Three other delegates – Edmund Randolph, George Mason, and Elbridge Gerry – refused to sign their names to the Constitution because of their reservations about its defects. Most delegates, however, would have agreed with Benjamin Franklin's assessment of the work of the Convention. It was doubtful, he wrote, "whether any other convention we can obtain may be able to make a better Constitution ... [I]t ... astonishes me ... to find this system approaching as near to perfection as it does."[16]

Whether all the compromises of the Convention produced a Constitution "near to perfection" is open to debate, but there is no doubt that the framers produced an impressive and innovative design. It was a radical departure from the Articles of Confederation, centralizing power in a governing elite, deliberately insulated and removed from the people. The new government had power to constrain the states' ability to erode property rights and the rule of law. The powerful national legislature created by the Constitution was given authority to enact all laws "necessary and proper" to carry out responsibilities delegated by the Constitution. It had two houses, a House of Representatives resting on relatively large districts and a Senate elected by the state legislatures. Each state had equal representation in the Senate, while representation in the House of Representatives was based on population, with each enslaved person counting as three-fifths of a person. Amendments to the Constitution would be difficult, requiring the approval of three-quarters of the states, though not the unanimous consent required under the Articles. Where executive power under the Articles of Confederation had been weak, the new president could veto legislation, negotiate treaties, and issue pardons. The ill-defined structure and powers of the federal courts left many wondering if the judiciary would be the weakest of the three branches, but the Contracts Clause and judicial review made the courts a force to be reckoned with. The new federal Constitution also broke with well-established precedents from the state constitutions, neither declaring the rights and liberties retained by the people, nor announcing the basic republican principles upon which government rested. In contrast to many states, which directly elected their governors, the Framers chose indirect election of the president through the Electoral College, affirming again that they had designed a republic, not a democracy. The national government also gained control of the power to tax and streamlined the process

[16] James Madison, *Notes of Debates in the Federal Convention of 1787* (New York: W. W. Norton, 1987), 653.

by which it could wage war and conduct foreign policy without obstruction by the states.

No delegate, including the supposed Father of the Constitution, James Madison, could claim to have obtained all that they desired. Madison was not feigning modesty when he dismissed the idea that his hand had given form to the document: "This was not, like the fabled Goddess of Wisdom, the offspring of a single brain. It ought to be regarded as the work of many heads and many hands."[17] Most of the delegates sincerely believed that the Constitution provided the only workable, if imperfect, plan for republican government available to America in 1787. Only a handful of delegates had concluded that the frame of government was so radically defective that they could not in good conscience sign their names to it.

### RATIFICATION: THE PEOPLE DEBATE
### THEIR CONSTITUTION

On September 18, 1787, a broadside version of the final text of the Constitution was printed for public distribution, and by the first week of October the Constitution had been reprinted in at least fifty-five different newspapers across the nation. Ratification inaugurated one of the most boisterous public debates in American political and legal history. Citizens paraded, raised their glasses to toast or attack the proposed government and even rioted to express their sentiments. Opponents of the Constitution in Carlisle, Pennsylvania, burned an effigy of James Wilson, one of their delegates to the Philadelphia Convention and an ardent champion of the new plan of government. Supporters of the Constitution were not shy about taking to the streets to express themselves and occasionally to intimidate their opponents, including smashing their opponents' printing presses. These types of disturbances were the exception, however, not the rule. The debate over ratification was heated, but Americans usually confined their passions to the printed page or passionate words in taverns, coffee shops, town squares, and the steps of local courthouses. Newspapers teemed with argument, both praising and denouncing the Constitution. In those regions of the nation where newspapers were hard to come by, advocates and opponents distributed broadsides and pamphlets to local residents.

---

[17] James Madison to William Cogswell, March 10, 1834, "James Madison to William Cogswell, 10 March 1834," *Founders Online*, National Archives, last modified June 13, 2018, http://founders.archives.gov/documents/Madison/99-02-02-2952.

A writer in a Providence paper optimistically proclaimed that America "exhibits to the World a most unusual spectacle," a new Constitution crafted by "the wisest and Best Men," who were "uninfluenced by Party Faction."[18] In New York, Hamilton, Madison, and John Jay adopted the pen name Publius in coauthoring the now-famous newspaper essays known as *The Federalist*. In the first of these, Hamilton too pointed to the exceptional nature of America's situation: "it seems to have been reserved to the people of this country, by their conduct and example, to decide the important question, whether societies of men are really capable or not of establishing good government from reflection and choice." Arrayed against this unprecedented opportunity, he warned, were "Ambition, avarice, personal animosity, party opposition."[19] General Henry Knox, one of George Washington's most trusted confidants, captured the fears of many supporters of the Constitution, commenting that "the germ of opposition originated in the convention itself. The gentlemen who refused signing it will most probably conceive themselves obliged to state their reasons publickly." The highly public dissents of the nonsigners, texts that circulated widely both in manuscript and later in print, did provide ample fuel for those critical of the new document. Thus, Knox predicted correctly that "the presses will groan with melancholy forebodings, and a party of some strength will be created."[20]

The supporters of the Constitution described themselves as Federalists, thus saddling their opponents with the name Anti-Federalists. The latter complained that they were the true supporters of federalism and attacked pro-Constitutional forces as "consolidationists," men who wished to destroy the states and create a single, consolidated national government. But the labels of Federalist and Anti-Federalist stuck and at least indicated accurately that the struggle was mainly about the operative meaning of federalism.

For the talented Federalist wordsmith Joel Barlow, a man whose career included writing poetry, playing politics, and serving as a diplomat, American federalism was one of the greatest achievements in the science of government. In his view it was "the only resource that nature has offered us at least in the present state of political science for avoiding at once the two dangerous extremes of having the republic too great for any

---

[18] *United States Chronicle*, September 27, 1787.     [19] *The Federalist No. 1*.
[20] To George Washington from Henry Knox, October 3, 1787," *Founders Online*, National Archives, last modified June 29, 2017, http://founders.archives.gov/documents/Washington/04-05-02-0327.

equitable administration within, or too small for security without."[21] Probably, both sides of the ratification debate would have agreed with that abstract statement. But, in this formative period of American constitutional development, federalism proved to mean very different things to different actors in different contexts.

An inchoate version of federalism had evolved under the dual structures of imperial government created by Britain's system of colonial rule. Colonists recognized the authority of the metropolitan government in London in certain areas of imperial life, but also affirmed the legal authority of their local legislatures in matters of internal governance. Still, everyone held firm to the principle that sovereignty itself could never be divided. Sir William Blackstone, one of the most influential British jurists of the eighteenth century, authoritatively declared that in every nation there must be one "supreme, irresistible, absolute, uncontrolled authority ... in which the rights of sovereignty reside." The notion that one might divide sovereignty, making different governments supreme over different regions or for different purposes within a single state, was denounced as a "solecism" at best or at worst a "monster."[22] Prior to the imperial crisis, most Americans would have accepted this notion as irrefutable. All loyal subjects of Great Britain in the years before the American Revolution, anywhere in its far-flung empire, acknowledged one "sovereign and uncontrollable authority in making, confirming, enlarging, restraining, abrogating, repealing, reviving, and expounding of laws."[23]

The drafting of the first state constitutions fit within the received model of sovereignty. Many states included express provisions stating the terms of the social compact and making explicit both the powers granted to government and those retained by the people. The Articles of Confederation was unambiguous in stating that the states remained sovereign. "Each state retains its sovereignty, freedom, and independence, and every Power, Jurisdiction and right, which is not by this confederation expressly delegated to the United States, in Congress assembled." The states were permanently allied, but each remained sovereign. Their "perpetual

[21] Joel Barlow, "To His Fellow Citizens, of the United States" in Charles S. Hyneman and Donald S. Lutz, eds., *American Political Writing during the Founding Era, 1760–1805*, 2 vols. (Indianapolis Liberty Fund, 1983), 1105.

[22] Iredell, "To the Inhabitants of Great Britain" (1774), in Griffith J. McRee, *Life and Correspondence of James Iredell* (New York: Appleton, 1857–1858), I: 205–220.

[23] William Blackstone, *Commentaries*, vol. 1 at 49. Parliament according to this theory was omnipotent and could "do every thing that is not naturally impossible." Ibid.

union" created "a firm league of friendship with each other,"[24] not a new, sovereign government.

But Americans were soon compelled to repudiate this theory of sovereignty. Supporters of the Constitution, most notably James Wilson and James Madison, admitted that the proposed government was a radical departure from traditional, federal theory. In Madison's words, the novel system was "partly national; partly federal." If sovereignty under traditional British constitutional theory was indivisible, then America's Constitution had in effect "split the atom of sovereignty."[25] But many Americans, particularly those who became Anti-Federalists, continued to accept the traditional Blackstonian view that sovereignty was indivisible. New York's Anti-Federalist governor George Clinton denounced the new government in familiar terms, describing it as "the political absurdity of imperium in imperio" (a state within a state), a system that was "destructive to every idea of good government."[26]

Anti-Federalists united in opposition to the Constitution's disruption of traditional ideas of federalism and sovereignty, but they divided on matters of governance and political economy. Anti-Federalism drew together a diverse coalition. Backcountry farmers opposed the Constitution, particularly those disconnected from major commercial markets. Many state politicians were strongly Anti-Federalist, especially the newly empowered men of moderate wealth and humble origins who dominated politics in states such as Pennsylvania and New York. Finally, in parts of the South, wealthy planters became Anti-Federalists out of fear that a distant and powerful government would not represent their interests. The genius of Anti-Federalism lay precisely in the fact that its localism allowed individuals and groups who might share little else to rally around the same constitutional position. Rich planter aristocrats who feared that a distant government would trample on their liberties could unite with middling democrats who feared the power of a distant government dominated by "well born" members of the "natural aristocracy."

---

[24] *The Founders' Constitution*, vol. 1, Chapter 1, Document 7, available at http://press-pubs.uchicago.edu/founders/documents/v1ch1s7.html.

[25] This metaphor was coined by Justice Kennedy in his concurrence and has achieved some popularity among modern legal scholars writing about this issue: "The Framers split the atom of sovereignty. It was the genius of their idea that our citizens would have two political capacities, one state and one federal, each." *U.S. Term Limits, Inc. v. Thornton* (93–1456), 514 U.S. 779 (1995).

[26] Herbert J. Storing, *The Complete Anti-Federalist*, vol. 6 (Chicago: University of Chicago Press, 1986), 180.

Amos Singletary, a member of the Massachusetts ratification convention from the heart of Shaysite Worcester county, captured the fears of
many Anti-Federalists in this impassioned speech: "These lawyers and
men of learning, and moneyed men that talk so finely, and gloss over
matters so smoothly, to make us poor illiterate people swallow down the
pill, expect to get in Congress themselves." Exploiting their economic and
cultural advantages, the rich and well born "expect to be managers of this
Constitution, and get all the power and all the money into their own
hands." Singletary's class indictment of the Constitution shared little with
the views of his own state's leading Anti-Federalist, the merchant Elbridge
Gerry, who had been the most vocal critic of democracy within the
Philadelphia convention. Gerry attributed America's problems to an
"excess of democracy." Partisan politics in his home state of Massachusetts and Shays' Rebellion taught him the danger posed by "designing
men," the populist demagogues who exploited the "the levilling spirit"
unleashed by the American Revolution in some quarters. Although Singletary and Gerry stood at opposite poles regarding democracy, they
shared a state-centered vision of federalism. For different reasons, they
each feared that the transfer of power to a distant government would not
be good for the future of republicanism.[27]

Indeed, the different factions of Anti-Federalism could both point to
the conventional wisdom that republicanism could survive only in a small
state, a view championed by political philosophers from antiquity down
to the eighteenth-century eminence Montesquieu. Gerry might have
agreed with the Federalist claim that factionalism and the spirit of party
threatened America's bold new experiment in republican government. But
he also believed that the Federalists' proposed cure was worse than the
disease. Gerry believed that a distant government of a huge nation could
never have adequate knowledge of the people, would therefore lose the
people's confidence, and would inevitably turn to force to enforce its
dictates. In keeping with this fear, Gerry became one of the most outspoken critics of the Constitution's military provisions, including its
contemplation of a powerful standing army and its weakening of state
control of the militia.

For Federalists, however, the transfer of power so feared by Singletary
and Gerry was vital to the survival of the nation. The Framers thus made
one of their major innovations in claiming that their design would render

---

[27] Quoted in Saul Cornell, *The Other Founders: Anti-Federalism and the Dissenting Tradition in America, 1788–1828* (Chapel Hill: University of North Carolina Press, 1999).

republicanism practicable over a large territory. In *The Federalist*, this novel theory was laid out with considerable elegance. Provocatively, Madison argued that only a large and diverse republic could contain the threat posed by faction. In such a large republic, encompassing so many regions and interests, politics would function like a kaleidoscope: Constantly shifting political patterns would prevent durable coalitions from forming. Factions would inevitably coalesce from time to time, but no one group would perpetually dominate the others. A large republic would also create a better filtering mechanism because electoral districts would have to be large, thus weeding out candidates of excessively local and partisan views. As Madison wrote, "In the extent and proper structure of the Union, therefore, we behold a republican remedy for the diseases most incident to republican government."

Federalists possessed a number of clear political advantages over their opponents. Supporters of the Constitution organized themselves around a well-defined goal: ratification. By contrast, Anti-Federalists could not provide a clear and consistent alternative. Some opponents favored another convention to draft a new Constitution. Others favored amending the Constitution to correct its most serious flaws. A few clung to the idea of returning to the Philadelphia Convention's original task, revising the Articles of Confederation. Federalists were also more effective at getting their message into print. Newspapers were generally located in larger commercial centers and hence were more likely to lean Federalist. In fact, many newspaper editors refused even to print Anti-Federalist materials.

Early and decisive Federalist successes in Delaware, New Jersey, Pennsylvania, Georgia, and Connecticut established a momentum that Federalists capitalized on to achieve their goal of unconditional ratification. If states with powerful, well-organized Anti-Federalist coalitions, such as Virginia, had held ratification conventions earlier, the dynamics of ratification might have been different. The Constitution might have been defeated or those seeking more significant alterations might have forced substantial changes. New Hampshire's vote to ratify on June 21, 1788, gave Federalists the nine states needed to ratify the Constitution. Despite divisive debates in both the Virginia and New York ratification conventions, and the continuing presence of strong Anti-Federalist movements in North Carolina and Rhode Island, eventually all of the states accepted the Constitution as the supreme law of the land.

Commenting on the debate over the Constitution, Thomas Jefferson confessed that he found fault in both the Federalist and Anti-Federalist positions. As was true generally for the Founding generation, Jefferson loathed the idea of party and perhaps appreciated the irony that a Constitution designed to neutralize party had been adopted only by the victory of one party over another. Indeed, shortly after the adoption of the Constitution he wrote, "If I could not go to heaven but with a party, I would not go there at all."[28] But the barely organized Anti-Federalists did not continue as a movement past ratification. Accepting the framework established by the Constitution, they disappeared as a movement, yet many of them simultaneously looked for ways to interpret the new Constitution in line with their state-centered version of federalism. Elite Anti-Federalists feared anarchy as much as Federalists did, turning peacefully to courts, legislatures, and newspapers to defend state sovereignty. Some of the more populist, localist voices among Anti-Federalism would return to the streets, occasionally arraying themselves in military fashion, to protest grievances under the new Constitution. None looked to create a party or movement to overturn the Constitution itself. With time, however, parties of a sort would emerge in a new form to renew the constitutional conflict between states' rights and consolidation.

## AMENDMENTS AND THE CREATION
## OF A LOYAL OPPOSITION

The divisions between Federalists and Anti-Federalists cast a shadow over the first congressional elections. In Virginia, for example, erstwhile Federalists were eager to have James Madison run for Congress. Madison agreed but, sharing the strong antiparty ethos of his friend Thomas Jefferson, he balked at actively campaigning for a seat, a kind of self-promotion inconsistent with traditional ideas of republican virtue. Electioneering, in his view, was not only unpleasant and undignified, but tread too close to party politics for him. Faced with the prospect of a delegation dominated by former Anti-Federalists, eager to weaken the powers of the new central government, he finally relented and took his case directly to the people.

Amendments to the Constitution were the primary issue in the campaign. His opponents charged that Madison opposed the Amendment process. Madison explained that he had opposed amendments before ratification, but now, with the Constitution securely in place, he would

---

[28] Thomas Jefferson to Francis Hopkinson, March 13, 1789; *The Papers of Thomas Jefferson*, vol. 14, *8 October 1788–26 March 1789*, ed. Julian P. Boyd (Princeton, NJ: Princeton University Press, 1958), 649–651.

"espouse such amendments as will, in the most satisfactory manner, guard essential rights, and will render certain vexatious abuses of power impossible." The one thing Madison adamantly opposed was any effort to weaken the powers of the central government and restore power to the states.[29]

Madison won the election to Congress and quickly emerged as one of the most effective and articulate members of the new body. Ironically, among the chores that fell to him was, in his words, "the nauseous project of amendments."[30] Urged on by Jefferson, Madison recognized the political necessity of the project, concluding that, if properly framed, amendments might go a long way to assuage lingering Anti-Federalist suspicions of the new federal government.

Madison pared down the dozens of amendments proposed by the state ratification conventions to seventeen. The Senate then whittled these down to twelve provisions and sent them to the states to ratify. The states did not adopt the first two proposed amendments, one of which dealt with legislative apportionment and the other with congressional salaries (although the latter was indeed ratified 200 years later). The remaining ten amendments were quickly approved and eventually came to be known as the Bill of Rights.

These amendments assuaged the concerns of most moderate Anti-Federalists even if they did not satisfy the most ardent opponents of federal power. The debate reveals the way that rights were enmeshed in questions of federalism. For example, the First Amendment, now the putative source of individual rights of speech and religion as against any governmental entity, originally limited only federal action. It did so partly to protect individual rights against federal abuses but, just as important, to preserve the prerogatives of the states in *limiting* those individual rights. Thus, many a state at the time impinged on religious freedom by perpetuating a religious establishment. The First Amendment did not limit the states' right to do so. Rather, in the name of federalism, it denied the federal government authority to legislate regarding religious establishments at all. Similarly, the amendment's ban on any federal law "abridging the freedom of speech" conspicuously left the states free to restrict

[29] *The Papers of James Madison, 7 March 1788–1 March 1789*, vol. 11, ed. Robert A. Rutland and Charles F. Hobson (Charlottesville: University of Virginia Press, 1977), 428–429.

[30] James Madison to Richard Peters, August 19, 1789 in *The Founders' Constitution*, vol. 1, Chapter 14, Document 53, http://press-pubs.uchicago.edu/founders/documents/v1ch14s53.html (Chicago: The University of Chicago Press).

speech through the common law of seditious libel, as they traditionally had, or to withdraw such restrictions. Any doubts about the states' continuing authority to regulate most rights were calmed by the Tenth Amendment's guarantee that "[t]he powers not delegated to the United States by the Constitution, nor prohibited by it to the states, are reserved to the states respectively, or to the people."

The Bill of Rights, therefore, certainly protected some individual rights, but, as the case of the Second Amendment further illustrates, this function had a complex relationship with its equally important purpose of protecting the prerogatives of the states. Although it is hard for modern Americans to imagine, most of the early state constitutions did not explicitly protect the right to bear arms. Nor did the right of individual self-defense emerge as a significant issue during ratification; there was little reason to fear that the new federal government posed any real threat to this venerable right enshrined in the common law. Federalists and Anti-Federalists agreed that matters of criminal law largely remained with the states, and there was little evidence that any of the states had threatened the right of self-defense the way they had supposedly undermined the "obligations of contract." The Anti-Federalist Brutus had made this point expressly when he wrote, "[I]t ought to be left to the state governments to provide for the protection and defence of the citizen against the hand of private violence, and the wrongs done or attempted by individuals to each other ..."[31] Federalist Tench Coxe echoed this understanding, writing that "[t]he states will regulate and administer the criminal law, *exclusively of Congress.*" The police power of the states would not be diminished under the new Constitution and the individual states would continue to legislate on such matters as "unlicensed public houses, nuisances, and many other things of the like nature."[32]

The concerns that led to the Second Amendment grew mainly from the problem of federalism, not individual rights. The militia was a local and state institution, but the Constitution gave Congress new powers to call out the militia and to "provide for organizing, arming, and disciplining, the Militia, and for governing such Part of them as may be employed in the Service of the United States, reserving to the States respectively, the Appointment of the Officers, and the Authority of training the Militia

[31] Brutus, Essays of Brutus VII, 2 The Complete Anti-Federalist 358, 400–405

[32] Tench Coxe, *A Freeman,* Pa. Gazette, January 23, 1788, *Friends of the Constitution: Writings of the "Other" Federalists,* 82, ed. Colleen A. Sheehan and Gary L. McDowell (Indianapolis: Liberty Funds, 1998).

according to the discipline prescribed by Congress."[33] Anti-Federalists thus feared that federal authorities might rob the states of the ability to command the militia in times of need, including, some argued, when necessary to resist a tyrannical federal government, repress agrarian insurrections, or put down slave rebellions.

Congress endorsed the Second Amendment's "right of the people to keep and bear arms" less to protect an individual right to a broad range of legitimate uses – though some such right was widely assumed – and more to protect the "well regulated militia" of the states. It chose to do so by affirming an individual's right to bear arms insofar as that was necessary to preserve the effectiveness of the militia. In this sense the original debate over the Second Amendment fits neither the rhetoric of modern gun rights nor that of modern gun control, neither of which prioritizes the sort of militia contemplated by the Second Amendment.

For a number of former Anti-Federalists, the Second Amendment was inadequate, not because it failed to protect an individual gun right firmly enough, but because it failed to protect the states. It neither guaranteed the structural support necessary for the preservation of a militia nor limited Congress's new power to regulate the militia. Centinel, a prominent Pennsylvania Anti-Federalist author, attacked an early draft of the Second Amendment for merely stating a republican truism: a well-regulated militia was the best protection for liberty in a free republic. The problem, Centinel wrote, was that the Amendment did not actually "provide for, the establishment of such a one. The absolute command vested by other sections in Congress over the militia, are not the least abridged by the amendment."[34] Thus the Amendment was perhaps worse than useless because it could lull the unthinking into a false sense of security.

After ratification of the amendment, the distinguished jurist St. George Tucker took a contrary view. In a lecture to his students at William and Mary, Tucker suggested that the Second Amendment could serve a vital role in supporting federalism, preserving to the states a tool with which to check federal tyranny. It was for precisely this reason that "the first Congress appears to have been sensible by proposing an Amendment to the Constitution, which has since been ratified and has become a part of it, viz. 'That a well regulated militia being necessary to the Security of a

---

[33] Article I, § 8.
[34] "Centinel, Revived, No. XXIX," *Independent Gazetteer* (Philadelphia), September 9, 1789.

free State, the right of the people to keep & bear Arms shall not be infringed.'" He further argued that, "If a State chooses to incur the expence of putting arms into the Hands of its own Citizens for their defense, it would require no small ingenuity to prove that they have no right to do it, or that it could by any means contravene the Authority of the federal Govt." Tucker noted that the Tenth Amendment buttressed the Second Amendment's federalism-reinforcing function: "[W]e may add that this power of arming the militia, is not one of those prohibited to the States by the Constitution, and, consequently, is reserved to them" under the Tenth Amendment. To affirm that the states had a power of armed resistance as an ultimate check on potential federal tyranny might be hard for modern Americans to fathom, given the outcome of the Civil War, in which the North deemed armed resistance by the Southern states treason and eventually crushed it. But in 1791, that right of resistance seemed to Tucker an essential feature of federalism: "[T]o contend that such a power would be dangerous ... would be subversive of every principle of Freedom in our Government." The question of how militias would function to preserve federalism turned out to be far more complex than anyone imagined at the Founding.[35]

Although modern Americans are apt to read Congress's early amendments primarily as protectors of individual liberty, it is important to recall that Madison viewed the amendments as having two intertwined functions: asserting individual rights and limiting federal power relative to the states. For most former Anti-Federalists, the first eight amendments were far less important than the tenth, which made explicit the states' and the people's retention of powers that had not been delegated to the federal government. Even more than Madison, former Anti-Federalists believed that protection of rights was best achieved by keeping power dispersed to the localities, where it could be watched by politicians closely tethered to their constituents. Thus, when Congress debated the wording of the Tenth Amendment, some argued that it should restrict the new government's powers to those "expressly delegated," the language used in the Articles of Confederation. But this last-ditch effort to further limit federal power was resoundingly defeated.

For some Anti-Federalists, the failure to limit federal powers to those "expressly delegated" rendered the Bill of Rights worse than useless. Even though many of the amendments helped preserve the states' authority – both

---

[35] Saul Cornell, "St. George Tucker's Lecture Notes, the Second Amendment, and Originalist Methodology: A Critical Comment," 103 *Nw. U. L. Rev. Colloquy* 406 (2009).

to preserve and to regulate individual rights – many Anti-Federalists were dissatisfied. Without structural changes in the nature of federalism, Anti-Federalists feared that any protections for liberty embodied in the Bill of Rights would be circumvented by the federal courts and Congress. Moreover, the inclusion of such a text might lull the people into a false sense of security. Today, Americans speak with reverence of the Bill of Rights and its protection of individual freedoms, but the Anti-Federalists' original goal was mainly to use amendments to sharply limit federal power and preserve state autonomy. Although they accepted defeat on the final form of some of the amendments, the battle over the scope of state and federal power would continue unabated.

## CONCLUSION

The drafting and ratification of the new American Constitution made a profound difference to American constitutional history. Indeed, it may have prevented the disintegration of the American confederacy altogether. And it channeled American constitutional conflicts into a new set of institutions. It did not, however, settle or eliminate those conflicts. The pre-1787 tensions between advocates of democratic reform (in one version or another) and an elitist republicanism persisted after 1787. So too the tensions between defenders of state autonomy and advocates of enhanced federal authority persisted despite the apparent triumph of the Federalists.

The weaknesses of the Articles of Confederation, both in domestic and foreign affairs, made constitutional reform increasingly likely as the 1780s wore on. The Articles had been drawn for the purpose of winning one particular war, so it was no surprise that they would at least need substantial revision to serve as the constitution of the nation going forward from the Revolution. There was, however, no consensus on the nature of the necessary revision. Not everyone agreed that the states' efforts to relieve farmers' debt burdens, for example, produced a grave injustice that required federal power to insist on unbending rights of contract. Nor did all agree that the nation's troubles in foreign affairs required, for example, a standing army or other features of a powerful, British-style nation–state. More generally, agreement on the need for constitutional reform did not indicate agreement on the balance between democracy and republicanism or that between federal and state authority.

The Convention itself skewed decidedly in the direction of enhanced federal power and elite management of the people's government. For the delegates, the 1780s had been plagued by too much democracy and too much localism, which predictably led to government controlled by party and faction rather than by virtuous republican statesman. The delegates thus largely agreed on a set of institutions that would insulate federal representatives from the whims of the people and the dangers of faction. Large electoral districts, long senatorial terms, indirect election of the president, an independent system of federal courts, and other features were designed to ensure a powerful federal government under elite management. This elite would see the wisdom of energetic action in foreign affairs and restoration of the principles of the common law as the foundation of economic policy. Fundamental rights of contract and property would be protected both by the affluent members of Congress and by the insulated federal courts.

There were, of course, conflicts in the Convention. Large and small states battled over the question of representation in the national government, but the Great Compromise settled matters by giving the large states an advantage in the House, the small states a large measure of protection in the Senate. At least as important, the mostly nascent tensions among the states regarding slavery resulted in a compromise on the international slave trade but a clear consensus on protecting the property rights of slaveholders, not the natural rights of the enslaved to liberty and equality. Both the Fugitive Slave Clause and the Three-Fifths Clause gave slaveholders firm assurances that the new republican government would present no challenge to slaveholding.

The process of ratification and the subsequent addition of amendments (later to be known as the Bill of Rights) gave the nation its new Constitution in roughly the form it would hold until the Civil War. But that same process revealed that the old conflicts would not go away. Struggles over democracy and federalism would continue now within and around a brand new set of institutions, but they would indeed continue. The Framers' hope that these institutions would generate a centralized, elitist structure of power was well understood by all but rejected by many. The ratification debates made clear that there was no easy or stable conclusion available to the question of how the federal republic would operate and who would control it.

The adoption of the Constitution solved many of the problems posed by the Articles of Confederation, but did so in a manner that created an entirely new set of issues for Americans. The distribution of power between the states and the new powerful central government created by the Constitution meant that defining and policing the boundaries of federalism would become a central problem in American law. The tensions evidenced in the Philadelphia Convention and in the spirited ratification debate were not resolved in 1788. Americans continued to be deeply divided across a wide range of legal issues. The Framers of the Constitution and its leading champions hoped that the new system of government would diminish both the partisanship and the localism in American politics. Although the Constitution changed the terms of legal debate and recast the structural elements defining these battles, it did little to diminish the intensity of these divisions. In the coming decade, virtually every contentious issue in American politics would become constitutionalized at some moment, forcing Americans to define with greater precision their constitutional ideologies and legal agendas.

## 2

# The Federalist Constitution and the Limits
# of Constitutional Dissent

In 1789, South Carolina politician and historian David Ramsay offered this cautious assessment of America's future under the recently adopted federal Constitution: "Time and experience only can fully discover the effects of this new distribution of the powers of government." Nonetheless, he was optimistic that the new system was "well calculated to unite liberty with safety, and to lay the foundation of national greatness, while it abridges none of the rights of the States, or of the people."[1] Many Americans agreed with Ramsay's assessment of America's future under the Constitution. One measure of this optimism was the grand federal processions staged in many of the nation's cities and larger towns. Pennsylvania Federalist Francis Hopkinson organized one of the most elaborate of these celebrations, with as many as 5,000 marchers representing Philadelphia's many trades, professions, and religious denominations.[2] Printers, for example, marched alongside a printing press mounted on a horse-drawn cart that churned out an ode that praised the Constitution. A banner with the name "Publius," the author of *The Federalist*, flew proudly above the press, and the printers sported caps with "Liberty of Press" written in large letters. Similar but less-elaborate parades were

[1] David Ramsay, *The History of the American Revolution*, Foreword by Lester H. Cohen (Indianapolis: Liberty Fund, 1990), vol. 2. http://oll.libertyfund.org/titles/547#lf0015-02_mnt489.

[2] Francis Hopkinson, "The Raising: A New Song for Federal Mechanics," in *The Miscellaneous Essays and Occasional Writings*, 3 vols. (Philadelphia: Printed by T. Dobson, at the stone-house, no. 41, Second Street, 1792), 2: 320.

staged in other cities. In all of these celebrations, the rituals were designed to symbolize harmony and promote consensus.

These processions could not, however, obliterate lingering divisions. Given the rancor of much of the ratification process and the close votes in many key states, the fact that no organized Anti-Federalist movement survived ratification is remarkable. In fact, once the new government was launched, headed by the universally admired George Washington, virtually no one thought of challenging the Constitution itself. Rather, opposition to the Framers' agenda for completing the project of constitutional reform was momentarily suspended, submerged beneath a renewed spirit of nationalism. This brief hiatus did not last long as the longstanding tensions in American politics and law reemerged. Rather than turn their ire against the new Constitution, opposition would coalesce around the Federalist implementation of the Constitution.

With the crucial support of President Washington, Secretary of the Treasury Alexander Hamilton sought to implement an ambitious program of centralized state building. His comprehensive plan for a British-inspired fiscal-military state quickly provoked opposition, however, including the unanticipated opposition of one of his closest former allies, James Madison. Opponents of Hamilton's agenda did not immediately coalesce into an organized force. Some, like Madison, still adhered to an elitist vision of constitutional reform and were reluctant to go beyond newspaper essays and legislative resolutions in opposing the government's alleged distortion of the Constitution. Others took views that revived localist and democratic elements of the Anti-Federalist critique of the Constitution. Some began to embrace elements of proto-party organization in the form of the new Democratic-Republican Societies. Finally, plebeians resurrected the methods of Shays and others, turning to crowd action and even armed rebellion, to resist the policies of Hamilton. Contrary to the goals of the Philadelphia Convention, constitutional debate had not become refined and deliberative, but continued to rage beyond the control of the elite ensconced in the new, national government.

As the 1790s progressed, nonelite white men increasingly tested their constitutional voices in public. But it remained clear that these stirrings of democracy were intended to reach *only* white men. It is true that some free blacks were able to vote from the earliest days of Union and that a limited number of women in New Jersey also had the vote for a time. As unpropertied white men chipped away at exclusions of class, however, whiteness and masculinity became ever firmer requirements for constitutional participation, despite proto-feminist ferment and persistent flashes of resistance by black Americans, both free and enslaved.

Amid these early struggles to establish the locus of power under the new Constitution, the French Revolution injected major new issues into American public life. The Revolution simultaneously disrupted the international order, creating major foreign policy challenges for the new nation, and reinvigorated the democratic movement in the United States. In consequence, it also sparked a conservative reaction. These effects came together in the politico-constitutional struggles over the Federalist administration's pro-British policies, such as the Jay Treaty of 1794, and its efforts to cripple the opposition through the Alien and Sedition Acts of 1798.

The French Revolution's intensification of partisanship in the United States shaped the presidential election of 1800 in important ways, putting a fine point on the central constitutional questions of the 1790s. Would the United States continue down Hamilton's path to a centralized, fiscal-military state capable of competing with the British Empire and other international powers? Or would it turn down the road of limited government and states' rights, a model most fully articulated in Thomas Jefferson's vision of the United States as a decentralized confederation of yeoman republics? Jefferson deemed his election the Revolution of 1800, a vindication of states' rights and a rejection of the Federalist program. For many of the younger Jeffersonians, however, that election seemed a decisive turn to a constitutional future far more democratic – but always white and male – and far more sympathetic to party organization than Jefferson or other members of the Founding generation could ever endorse.

## A CONSTITUTION FOR A FISCAL AND MILITARY STATE: HAMILTON'S BOLD AGENDA

Although few Federalists would have been so naïve as to believe that ratification had solved every legal question and political challenge, the adoption of the Constitution was a signal achievement. It jettisoned the radical decentralization of power associated with the Articles of Confederation, and it substituted a structure that divided power between the states and the new national government. Yet, even among the ardent Federalist supporters of the Constitution, tensions were evident from the start. Some, particularly James Madison, believed it vital to conciliate those who had opposed the Constitution in order to cement support for the new government. Other Federalists, led by Alexander Hamilton, cared less for conciliation and more for using the Constitution to launch an ambitious project of state building.

Beginning with the First Congress, Hamilton and his group of pro-British Federalists embarked on a bold program to endow the central government with powers beyond anything that Madison and other moderate Federalists had envisioned in Philadelphia. Hamilton sought to emulate Britain's fiscal-military state by creating a national bank, a consolidated national debt funded by new taxes, and an effective military establishment. He not only wished to place the new national government on a solid financial basis but also to bind the wealthy to the new nation by aligning their economic interests with those of the new government. He further recognized that a powerful nation state would require the ability to project military force when necessary. In pursuing this agenda, he would lay the foundations for an ascendant national government that could establish the United States as a force in the community of nations.

Although his opponents attacked him as a crypto-monarchist, Hamilton's vision was not antirepublican. "As to my own political Creed," he wrote to the Virginian Edward Carrington in 1792, "I give it to you with the utmost sincerity. I am *affectionately* attached to the Republican theory. I desire *above all things* to see the *equality* of political rights exclusive of all *hereditary* distinction firmly established." There was, however, a profound gulf separating Hamilton's statist vision of republicanism and the more decentralized vision of his opponents. The clarity of Hamilton's agenda would help crystalize opposition to that program and lay the foundation for the rise of a party politics centered on conflicting interpretations of the Constitution.[3]

The first aim of Hamilton's program was to restore confidence in the American economy. To explain his vision, Hamilton authored a series of economic reports. His "Report on Public Credit" addressed the war debt of the states and the federal government. The debt from the Revolution consisted of many different types of paper currency, securities, and other types of financial instruments. Although many viewed the debt as a

---

[3] Hamilton to Carrington, May 26, 1792, 11 *The Papers of Alexander Hamilton, February 1792–June 1792*, ed. Harold C. Syrett (New York: Columbia University Press, 1966), 426–445.

serious threat to America's future, Hamilton believed that if properly managed and adequately funded a permanent national debt could become an engine of economic growth. Taking his cues from recent British history, Hamilton saw an opportunity to bring American finances into the modern era, embracing debt as an essential tool of state economic policy.

In addition, Hamilton saw that consolidating the debts of the individual states into the federal debt could strengthen the fledgling government. Creditors who held state-issued financial instruments would exchange them for a new type of federal security that promised to pay interest until the bearer redeemed the original value of the note. Hamilton's "Second Report on Public Credit" focused on financing this scheme with income from various taxes, including a new tax on whiskey. The plan was controversial from the outset. The value of state- and Confederation-issued paper had declined steadily by the 1790s as the hard-pressed states and the weak national government simply printed more currency to pay their debts. After the adoption of the Constitution, a few financial speculators had purchased large amounts of this devalued paper, hoping that the new government would redeem it at face value and net them a huge profit. Believing it was vital for the new nation to maintain excellent credit with investors – and hoping further to tie the interests of the wealthy to the success of the federal government – Hamilton insisted that the government had an obligation to honor the debt at face value.

Others within Washington's cabinet were less sympathetic to Hamilton's arguments. Opponents feared that Hamilton's funding scheme would not only give a windfall to speculators but would also create a powerful financial interest that would become a potential source of corruption. Hamilton's opponents, led by his former ally Madison, favored paying the full value of the debt to the original holders but giving speculators only a fraction of the original value. Speculators would reap some profits but not a windfall. Hamilton argued that such discrimination among creditors would violate the sanctity of contracts and undermine the credit of the new government, two of the evils the Constitution had been framed to prevent.

Outside of Washington's inner circle, opposition to Hamilton's agenda began to unite remnants of the former Anti-Federalist opposition with moderate Federalists such as Madison. Anti-Federalists had feared precisely the creation of a powerful fiscal-military state modeled on Great Britain, which now seemed slowly materializing. In their view, Federalists under Hamilton's spell were bent on a deliberate process of consolidation that would render the states mere ciphers and endanger the liberties of the people. Virginian Henry Lee wrote to Madison, declaring that "[Patrick] Henry already is considered as a prophet, his predictions are daily verifying."[4] Henry had been probably the greatest Anti-Federalist orator during ratification, but Madison now seemed to move toward such former opponents.

As this opposition to government policy gradually coalesced, it revived the founding generation's anxiety about party and faction. The very first number of *The Federalist*, the collection of pro-ratification essays authored by Madison, Hamilton, and John Jay, had emphasized this concern. Writing as "Publius," a pen name designed to invoke Roman republican ideals, the authors warned that "nothing could be more ill-judged than that intolerant spirit which has, at all times, characterized political parties."[5] Thus the growing opposition to Hamilton's program adopted the descriptor "republicans" not as a party label but because they genuinely believed themselves defenders of America's republican form of government, now under siege by champions of British monarchism.

The rise of a concerted opposition, led by Jefferson and Madison, troubled Hamilton, both because of its character as a faction, as it seemed to him, and because of Madison's seeming reversal on questions of federal power: "Mr. Madison cooperating with Mr. Jefferson is at the head of a faction decidedly hostile to me and my administration, and actuated by views in my judgment subversive of the principles of good government and dangerous to the union, peace and happiness of the Country." Hamilton had expected that Madison would be an ally who shared his view "that the real danger in our system was the subversion of the national authority by the preponderancy of the state governments." He now believed Madison's opposition to the funding of the debt arose from an erroneous belief that Federalists were engaged in "a dreadful combination against state government and republicanism; which according to them, are convertible terms." Quite apart from their misguided critique of his economic agenda, Hamilton honestly feared that "once rendered odious," it would be difficult for the national government to regain the powers needed to deal with domestic and foreign threats. Attacking specific policy was one thing, but the factional assault on the Federalist vision of the Constitution threatened to destabilize the entire political and

---

[4] Henry Lee to James Madison, April 3, 1790, and Fisher Ames to George Richards Minot, May 14, 1789, in Lance Banning, *Liberty and Order: The First American Party System* (Indianapolis, IN: Liberty Fund, 2004), 66, 110.

[5] *Federalist No 1*.

legal edifice created in Philadelphia. Hamilton remained convinced that
the greatest danger facing America in the future would not be a government too powerful, but one too anemic to control the "spirit of faction
and anarchy."[6]

Hamilton revealed another key part of his program in his "Report on a
National Bank." He recommended that Congress create a Bank of the
United States to hold government funds, bolster confidence in government
securities, make loans, and provide the nation with a stable currency. The
government would own part of the stock in the new Bank, but would
allow private investors to buy the majority. At the time of his proposal,
there were only three private banks in the United States. So, from a
Hamiltonian perspective, the services of a national bank were critical.
Moreover, like the federal assumption of state debts, a national bank
would further align the interests of the wealthy with the government.

The Bank debate divided Americans on issues of political economy. It
also spawned an important early debate on the meaning of the Constitution and the appropriate methods for interpreting it. Federalists, most
notably Hamilton, believed that the power to charter a bank was readily
inferable from the powers delegated to Congress by the new Constitution,
such as the power to regulate interstate and international commerce. In
his view, "a power of erecting a corporation may as well be implied as any
other thing, it may as well be employed as an instrument or mean of
carrying into execution any of the specified powers."[7] Here, the English
model of state building again influenced Hamilton's views of the Constitution. British experience demonstrated that a bank could facilitate economic growth and help stabilize the economy. Such highly desirable goals
weighed in favor of finding that the Constitution implied the necessary
powers.

Madison and Jefferson recognized, of course, that Congress had the
power to regulate commerce and even that a better banking system might
serve the nation well. But, they argued, the Constitution granted only
limited powers. Preservation of the fundamental, federal structure of the
government forbade reading an unstated power to charter banks into an
explicit grant of authority over commerce. Secretary of State Jefferson

---

[6] Alexander Hamilton to Edward Carrington May 26, 1792 in Harold C. Syrett et al. eds.,
*The Papers of Alexander Hamilton*, vol. 11 (New York: Columbia University Press,
1961–1979), 442.
[7] Alexander Hamilton, "Opinion on the Constitutionality of the Bank" February 15, 1791,
in Banning, *Liberty and Order*, 80–86.

noted that "to erect a bank, and to regulate commerce, are very different acts."[8] In Congress, meanwhile, Madison emphasized the "essential characteristic of the government, as composed of limited and enumerated powers." From that characteristic, he derived a rule of constitutional interpretation that "condemn[ed] the exercise of any power, particularly a great and important power, which is not evidently and necessarily involved in an express power."[9]

Hamilton won the debate over the Bank, defeating his disorganized opposition. The Bank received a Congressional charter in 1791. He also succeeded in implementing his plan for assumption of the state debts. The final part of Hamilton's plan, however, was unsuccessful. Hamilton's "Report on Manufactures" called for a comprehensive program to encourage domestic industry by providing incentives for industrial development and tariffs to help American industry compete against cheaper, imported foreign goods. But Congress refused to follow Hamilton's recommendation to raise these tariffs sharply, and his grandiose scheme to encourage industrial development generated little interest in Congress.

The opposition mostly failed in its challenge to Hamilton's program, but in doing so, it began to discover itself as an opposition, not just in Congress but also in the public sphere generally. Members of the elite and populists alike produced key texts that gave the opposition its shape. Only time would allow the diverse opposition to come together as a movement to defend a state-centered republicanism.

Apart from Madison's own speeches on the Bank and the debt, a key example of early opposition writing among the elite was the work of John Taylor of Caroline, a wealthy Virginian and an ally of Jefferson and Madison. Taylor was a lawyer, legislator, planter, and intellectual, whose criticism of Hamilton's economic program drew directly from the English radical Whig ideology that had informed the Revolution itself. That ideology was rooted in aristocratic defense of liberty against the encroachments of power, as exemplified by the corruption and party-building of the eighteenth-century English Court. Taylor applied radical Whig language to Hamilton's neo-British financial system, but importantly added a distinctively American concern with federalism and

---

[8] "Opinion on the Constitutionality of the Bill for Establishing a National Bank, 15 February 1791," *Founders Online*, National Archives, last modified June 29, 2017, http://founders.archives.gov/documents/Jefferson/01-19-02-0051.
[9] Madison's Speech on the Bank Bill, February 2, 1991: http://oll.libertyfund.org/pages/1791-madison-speech-on-the-bank-bill.

republicanism: "The funding system was intended to effect, what the bank was contrived to accelerate. 1. Accumulation of great wealth in a few hands. 2. A political moneyed engine. 3. A suppression of the republican state assemblies, by depriving them of political importance, resulting from the imposition and dispensation of taxes."[10] The ultimate goal, according to Taylor, was to reduce the state assemblies to nonentities in a consolidated system of government. State legislatures, the only truly representative bodies in the new federal system, would be rendered impotent by the machinations and manipulations of the corrupt, paper banking interest.

Populist writers shared Taylor's hostility to centralized power but tended to frame the fundamental issues more in class terms. As newspapers were passed from hand to hand in taverns and coffee houses, populist writers showed that they were not confined by legalistic modes of constitutional interpretation, such as those employed by Jefferson, Madison, and Taylor. Nor were they inclined to defer to educated and wealthy members of the natural aristocracy. In language sometimes reminiscent of the antilegalism that framed Shays' Rebellion, popular essayists insisted that the people could interpret the Constitution for themselves and must always be wary of the manipulations of "the few."

This view was reflected in the work of William Manning, a Massachusetts tavern keeper, who compared the Constitution to "a Fiddle, with but few Strings." He charged that the Framers of the Constitution had deliberately written the text in such general terms as would allow them to use artful legal constructions to "play any tune upon it they pleased." Manning argued that "in making laws in a free Government" the people ought to be wary of efforts to obscure constitutional texts in legalistic terms and urged that such texts be crafted plainly "to be understood and not too numerous." Summarizing his views of government and law, Manning wrote: "In short a free Government is one in which all the laws are made judged and executed according to the will and interest of the majority of the people and not by the craft, cunning, and arts of the few."[11]

As such language makes clear, Manning was less interested in the ideas of radical English Whigs or common law precepts, than in protecting "the

---

[10] John Taylor, *An Enquiry into the Principles and Tendency of Certain Public Measures*, (Philadelphia: Thomas Dobson, 1794), 85–87.

[11] Michael Merrill and Sean Wilentz, eds., *The Key of Liberty: The Life and Democratic Writings of William Manning* (Cambridge, MA: Harvard University Press, 1993), 148, 180.

many" from relentless exploitation by "the few." "The few have great advantage over the Many in forming and constructing Constitutions and laws," Manning wrote, and "are highly interested in having them numerous intricate and inexplicit as possible." Creating constitutional texts in vague language gave an advantage to elites who would then give "them such explanations as suits their interests." The proof of such danger was provided by Hamilton's arguments in favor of the Bank, applying a theory of broad construction to vague constitutional language in the interests of the moneyed few.[12]

Manning believed that Hamilton's policies favored the interests of wealthy financial speculators. Not only had the Secretary of the Treasury's policies provided a windfall for speculators, but also new taxes enacted to pay off the speculators bore down hardest on the common people. If not checked, Hamilton's plan would "eventually prove the Destruction of our Dear bought Liberties & of all the State Governments." The Federal Constitution had facilitated this process by shifting power away from the states to a central government more remote and insulated from the popular will.

Although there was much that separated the worlds of William Manning and John Taylor, they shared crucial commitments. For both, a defense of state and local authority was essential to the preservation of liberty and republicanism. More immediately, both believed that Hamilton's economic program and constitutional vision favored the relentless ambitions of a corrupt few, at the expense of the popular sovereignty won in the Revolution. The two men parted company when it came to envisioning the nature of local government. Taylor was a member of Virginia's natural aristocracy who feared excessive democracy. The tavern keeper William Manning was an unabashed populist democrat.

### PARTISANSHIP AND THE POLITICS OF THE EMERGING PUBLIC SPHERE

In their *Federalist* essays and elsewhere, Madison and Hamilton had agreed that a major goal of adopting a new Constitution was to hinder the sort of factional politics that had distorted the policies of the states in the 1780s. Now faced with the rise of Hamilton's Federalist agenda, a de facto program of constitutional revision in its own right, Madison refined

---

[12] Merrill and Wilentz, *The Key of Liberty*, 146.

his thinking about factions and politics in relation to the Constitution. In a 1792 essay in the *National Gazette,* "A Candid State of Parties," he conceded that America had become divided into a "Republican party" and an "antirepublican party" (the Federalists). By modern standards, the parties Madison described were hardly parties at all. Neither Federalists nor their Republican opponents operated on a national scale or tried to enforce party discipline among their members. These proto-parties were not committed to a wide-ranging policy agenda, but rather had a single purpose each, according to Madison: to save republicanism or, as he accused the Federalists, to restore monarchy or aristocracy. Moreover, Madison's "party," such as it was, could never be content with a mere majority, as in a modern two-party system. Rather, the very legitimacy of the Republican Party rested on its claim to encompass the people as a whole, "the mass of people in every part of the union, in every state, and of every occupation."[13] Of course, Federalists disputed this picture, but they agreed that there was an emergent party struggle that would decide the fate of the Constitution.

To fight effectively, each side realized it was vital to manage public opinion by some means, and that means was increasingly print culture, particularly newspapers. "Public opinion sets bounds to every government," Madison noted, "and is the real sovereign in every free one." A free government, therefore, called for "a circulation of newspapers through the entire body of the people."[14] It is hardly surprising, then, that the number of newspapers doubled in the period between 1788 and 1800. Although an earlier generation of printers had represented themselves as repositories of republican virtue, it had become increasingly clear that they could not act as neutral facilitators of public deliberation. They had to take sides on matters that would determine the fate of the Constitution and the republic. The rise of partisan politics and the expansion of the press were symbiotic developments, generating that essential institution of the early republic, the partisan newspaper.

While eastern port cities still supported the most papers, many interior market towns also boasted papers by the end of the 1790s. Many of these papers aligned themselves with one or the other of the main political movements in the country. Some papers even established themselves as national platforms. John Fenno's *Gazette of the United States* proudly

---

[13] James Madison, "A Candid State of Parties," *National Gazette,* September 26, 1792. https://founders.archives.gov/documents/Madison/01-14-02-0334.

[14] James Madison, "Public Opinion," *National Gazette,* December 19, 1791.

asserted its goal was "to endear the General Government to the people," articulating the Federalist point of view. To combat Fenno's influence, Jefferson and Madison persuaded the poet Philip Freneau to found the *National Gazette,* which rallied opposition to Hamilton and the Federalists.

Although newspapers were central to the expanding public sphere of the new republic, Madison and other Republicans did not see print as the only sphere of public deliberation. Madison believed that the federal system itself could contribute to the expansion of a public sphere of rational debate. In essays published in the *National Gazette* in 1791–1792, he endorsed "[w]hatever facilitates a general intercourse of sentiments" and listed "good roads, domestic commerce, a free press, and particularly a *circulation of newspapers through the entire body of the people,* and *Representatives going from, and returning among them*" as "favorable to liberty."[15] In his essay "Consolidation," Madison argued that the state legislatures, closer to the people and distributed across the extended republic, were vital instruments to both influence and ascertain the public mind. At their best, they could be deliberative assemblies that could gather, refine, and focus public opinion. By contrast, efforts to consolidate power at the center robbed the legislatures of this ability and fostered a tyrannical government out of touch with its people.[16]

These arguments foreshadowed Madison's later effort to use the Virginia state legislature to mobilize opposition to the Alien and Sedition Acts. They also marked an important shift of emphasis from the Madison of 1787, who sought to shift power to the center. Now, Madison believed the greatest threat to liberty came from Hamiltonian consolidation, not the states' tendencies to provincialism and factionalism. Hamilton believed Madison had abandoned his earlier commitments, but Madison claimed that the political pendulum had simply swung too far in the opposite direction. Notwithstanding his former disdain for the state legislatures, he now expressed optimism that these bodies would work in concert with an invigorated public sphere of print to educate citizens and produce "one paramount Empire of reason, benevolence and brotherly affection."[17]

At roughly the same time that Madison was publishing these thoughts, William Manning too emphasized the importance of public opinion in

[15] James Madison, "Public Opinion," *National Gazette*, December 19, 1791.
[16] James Madison, "Consolidation," *National Gazette*, December 3, 1791.    [17] Ibid.

his populist constitutionalism. Like Madison, Manning reacted to Hamilton's economic program, particularly the "Disputes in the public papers about funding & the Manner of paying the Continental & State Debts." But Manning's populism contrasted sharply with Madison's elitist perspective, albeit one now weighted toward increasing state power. Madison continued to believe that the interest of "the many" was best discerned by a virtuous elite, composed of those possessing wealth and education, who could translate the needs of all into a coherent pubic good. But Manning did not see the interests of "the many" and "the few" harmonizing as Madison did. Rather, he believed that the few comprised too many of "those that live without Labour," who were "ever opposed to the principles & operation of a free Government." Where Madison thought the few could be induced to serve the interests of all, Manning believed that the few would always seek to dominate the many. The remedy was to create new institutions that could gather and advance those popular interests.[18]

For Manning, democratic principles required that legislators "all feel as acting in the presents of their Constituents & act as servants & not masters." The goal was not to refine the popular will, but to faithfully mirror it, which required new institutions to accurately identify that will. One of the keys to liberty, then, was the expansion of the press and the creation of a network of laboring societies. Manning took a cue from the nation's most elite organization, the Society of the Cincinnati, a fraternal organization composed of American and French Revolutionary war officers. Working people needed to create similar organizations so that their voices might be heard more effectively.[19]

Although Manning's vision of a laboring society never materialized, the notion of creating political societies to gather, improve, and disseminate republican ideas helped to drive the creation of Democratic–Republican societies across America. These societies' avowed purpose was "to cultivate a just knowledge of rational liberty – to inquire into the public conduct of men in every department of government, and to exercise those constitutional rights which as freemen they possess."[20] Between 1793 and 1794, forty-six of these organizations emerged across the nation. In addition to publishing their sentiments about political

---

[18] "Manning, *The Key of Liberty*, 128.     [19] Ibid., 162.
[20] "W.T.," *National Gazette*, July 4, 1792; "Democratic Society of Philadelphia, 9 October 1794," in Banning, *Liberty and Order*, 186.

issues, the societies staged celebrations, gave festive dinners, and sponsored public orations.

In the view of Republicans, the Constitution on its own was not enough to protect the people. Rather, the people had to protect the Constitution by strengthening the public sphere of political discourse and ensuring that the elected branches did the people's will. As one proponent of the Societies observed: "the security of the people against any unwarrantable stretch of power is not confined to the check which a constitution affords or the periodical return of elections." Popular vigilance was also required and could best be cultivated by a network of Democratic–Republican societies. Although the Constitution made no mention of such institutions, Republicans believed them both necessary and a constitutionally protected form of association implicit in the freedom of assembly.[21]

Federalists saw the societies in a different light. Denouncing them as factions aimed at fomenting discord and dissent, some even linked them to French revolutionary Jacobin clubs, and others saw them tainted with the "sour leaven of antifederalism."[22] No Federalist was more scornful of the Democratic–Republican societies than Fisher Ames. In his view, the Societies undermined government by "perverting the truth and spreading jealousy and intrigue throughout the land."[23]

Federalist opposition was not aimed just at the particular activities of individual societies. Rather, Federalists objected to the very idea that that a private organization could set itself up as an intermediary between the people and their government. President Washington himself condemned any "self created, *permanent* body" of this sort. Like other Federalists, the president did not dispute the right of "the people to meet occasionally, to petition for, or remonstrate against, any Act of the Legislature," but he condemned any body that would "declare that *this act* is unconstitutional, and *that act* is pregnant of mischief; & that all who vote contrary to their dogmas are actuated by selfish motives, or under foreign influence." While Committees of Correspondence and other temporary, extra-legal organizations had been necessary during the American Revolution,

---

[21] "Correspondent," *General Advertiser*, May 16, 1794.

[22] Fisher Ames, "Debate Over the Propriety of Replies to the President's Speech," in W. B. Allen ed., *Works of Fisher Ames*, 2 vols. (Indianapolis, IN: Liberty Fund, 1983), II: 1053–1081. "Bifrons Janus," [Fisher Ames,] untitled essay, "Against Jacobins," ibid., 974–984. Fisher Ames to Christopher Gore, December 17, 1794, ibid., 1087.

[23] Fisher Ames, "Debate over the Propriety of Replies to the President's Speech," in W. B. Allen ed., *Works of Fisher Ames*, 1053–1081.

Federalists argued that the Constitution now supplied all of the necessary institutions of republican government. They rejected the claim that the "Constitution countenances, much less acknowledges, that any set of men, few or many, shall *set themselves* up as umpires between the people and the government the people themselves have established." Indeed, for many Federalists, the notion of permanent, political organizations outside the government seemed to mock a Constitution that had been designed specifically to neutralize partisan combinations. Federalists continued to believe that, although the people might elect their leaders, they must defer to them once elected.[24]

When Federalists sought a Congressional censure of the societies, Republicans challenged such action as an unlawful assertion of federal power. For Republicans it was far worse for Congress to assume unwarranted authority than it was for the people to create the societies. According to William Giles of Virginia, "We are neither authorized by the Constitution, nor paid by the citizens of the United States, for assuming the office of censorship." Indeed, if "such a clause had been inserted in the Constitution, it would never have gone through. The people would have never suffered it."[25]

Still, Federalist condemnations of the societies only echoed values that many Republican leaders had themselves espoused in both public writings and private correspondence. In *Federalist 10,* Madison had decried the problem of excessive popular influence and factionalism. The new federal system created by the Constitution would check such tendencies, filtering and refining popular opinion rather than deferring to it. Even Jefferson approached democracy with a good deal of caution. Jefferson resolutely affirmed the ideal of popular sovereignty, but his vision of representation shared Madison's elitist assumptions. Both men were egalitarian in the sense that they believed the "talents" necessary to leadership were "sown as liberally among the poor as the rich."[26] Still, it was a meritocratic elite, the natural aristocracy, who should be trusted to govern in the normal course, not the people themselves. Popular participation was limited to voting, militia duty, and jury service. This vision made no place for direct action by an assertive people, nor did it consider representatives as mere

---

[24] "E. F., Desultory Remarks on Democratic Clubs," *Gazette U.S.*, July 21, 1794.
[25] *Annals of Congress* 3rd Congress, 2nd session, (November 1794), 917–918.
[26] Thomas Jefferson, *Notes on the State of Virginia*, ed. William Peden (Chapel Hill: University of North Carolina Press, 1955), 148.

agents of the popular will, two essential attributes of William Manning's constitutional vision.

It is easy to forget that Madison and Jefferson shared an opposition to party politics, a veneration for law as a constraint on democratic excess, and faith in a virtuous governing elite. All of these beliefs placed them closer to the elitist vision of Hamilton and other Federalists than it did to populists such as William Manning. Only gradually over the course of the 1790s did Madison and Jefferson come to accept a greater role for popular institutions outside the government. Only the radicalism of Hamilton's statist agenda moved both to make alliances with other opponents of Hamilton's agenda and consequently to accept a more fully democratic notion of politics.

### THE WHISKEY REBELLION AND THE CHALLENGE OF POPULIST CONSTITUTIONALISM

Whatever differences Federalists and Republicans may have had over the Democratic–Republican Societies, they were soon overshadowed by an even more radical assertion of populist democracy. Pennsylvania's Whiskey Rebellion of 1794 challenged an excise tax that was an important part of the Federalist program. This violent uprising tested the limits of lawful protest as well as the ability of the federal government to maintain order in the face of violent resistance.

The cause of the Whiskey Rebellion lay in the taxes enacted to fund Hamilton's economic program. Tax protests eventually turned violent in parts of western Pennsylvania and Kentucky. The most violent and sustained popular protest since Independence, the Whiskey Rebellion highlighted the fragility of the new federal system. Federalists blamed the uprising on the Democratic–Republican societies and other critics of the government. In Washington's view, for example, the insurrection was "the first *ripe fruit* of the Democratic Societies. I did not, I must confess, expect it would come to maturity so soon, though I never had a doubt, that such conduct would produce some such issue."[27] Republican leaders sympathized with the protesters' economic grievances, but few prominent

---

[27] George Washington to Burges Ball (September 25, 1794) *The Papers of George Washington*, Presidential Series, vol. 16, *1 May–30 September 1794*, ed. David R. Hoth and Carol S. Ebel (Charlottesville: University of Virginia Press, 2011), 722–724.

figures went so far as to endorse armed rebellion as a constitutional mechanism. Republican leaders did insist, however, that the federal government had no power to act against the rebels unless called upon by state authorities.

For the Whiskey Rebels themselves, Revolutionary ideas of popular constitutionalism, including mob action, remained very much alive. These radical localists doubted even the state-centered theory of federalism that motivated democratic-minded Republicans like Pennsylvania Congressman William Findley. Populists believed that the people under the new Federal Constitution were hardly better off than under British rule. In contrast to members of the Republican elite, including its most democratic elements, these radicals rejected the authority of both state and federal governments to impinge on the autonomy of local communities. Plebeian radicals also continued to embrace the symbols and tactics of the Revolutionary tradition, erecting liberty poles and applying coats of tar and feathers to those who violated community norms or facilitated federal power. Nor did radicals limit their opposition to symbolic protests; they mustered themselves as local militia units and resisted efforts to collect federal taxes. The rebels clung to an understanding of the local militia as the people's tool for checking external power, even as the radical potential of the militia was challenged by the Constitution's placement of each state's "well regulated" militia under federal control.

Republican critics of Federalist policy were placed in a difficult position by the populist resistance. Congressman William Findley of western Pennsylvania, for example, was one of the era's great champions of democracy and acknowledged that the protests sprang from legitimate sources of complaint. Yet even he stopped short of endorsing the rebels' radically localist vision and believed that their turn to violence exceeded the limits of constitutional protest. He did, however, defend strict limits on federal power, insisting with other Republicans that the Tenth Amendment's reservation of powers to the states required the federal government to stand back until the state requested help.

Hamilton and other Federalists, however, believed that the rebellion was a direct challenge to federal authority and had to be met with a swift and forceful federal response. Washington sought advice from other members of his cabinet who were more cautious. Former Attorney General Edmund Randolph, a Virginian who had become Washington's Secretary of State, noted that dissatisfaction with the excise tax extended beyond Pennsylvania and suggested that the state militias might not cooperate: "if the militia of other States are to be called forth, it is not a decided thing that many of them may not refuse."[28] Washington took a serious gamble in overriding both Randolph's fears and statements by the Governor of Pennsylvania that assistance was not needed. Fortunately for the Federalists, the militias of neighboring states did respond to Washington's call, and the rebellion crumbled, a major victory for Hamilton's project of establishing the authority of the national government.

For Republicans, the Washington administration's decision to use force confirmed the consolidating designs of Hamilton and his allies. Still, few Republican leaders were willing to grant constitutional legitimacy to extralegal violence or accept that local militias might exercise a constitutional checking function on their own, a prospect that seemed closer to mobocracy than republicanism. Mainstream Republican constitutional theorists accepted that public meetings and the press might be used to rally opposition but they avoided endorsing violence.

The whiskey excise tax also prompted nonviolent protest politics out of doors. In particular, liberty poles, which had been symbols of protest during the American Revolution, were revived by the whiskey protesters. Typically, the poles were used to post placards or hoist banners with a variety of slogans or symbols. Some were innocuous, affirming "Liberty and Equality." Others were more pugnacious, declaring defiance to government measures through slogans like "Liberty or Death" or "Liberty and no excise, and no asylum for cowards or traitors." Ordinary citizens across Pennsylvania raised poles, claiming their rights to free speech, but not everyone agreed that this form of protest counted as protected speech. The Federalist Judge of the County Courts of western Pennsylvania, Alexander Addison, made clear in a grand jury charge that erecting a liberty pole was both a nuisance under the common law and, in the context of the rebellion, seditious. Even among Republicans sympathetic to the rebels, such as William Findley, there was little support for pole-raising under such circumstances. Although he argued that liberty poles were not inherently seditious, he conceded the "bad effect, which the erecting of liberty poles had in encouraging the insurgents in western Pennsylvania."[29]

[28] Edmund Randolph to George Washington, 5 August 1794, The Papers of George Washington, Presidential Series, *1 May–30 September 1794*, ed. David R. Hoth and Carol S. Ebel (Charlottesville: University of Virginia Press, 2011), 523–530.

[29] *Independent Gazetteer*, September 17, 1794 at 2; *The Baltimore Daily Intelligencer*, September 10, 1794 at 3; Edmund Randolph to George Washington, 5 August 1794, The Papers of George Washington, Presidential Series, *1 May–30 September 1794*, vol. 16, ed. David R. Hoth and Carol S. Ebel (Charlottesville: University of Virginia Press, 2011), 523–530.

Still, while state prosecutions for raising liberty poles enjoyed some success, federal prosecutions for the same crime were largely unsuccessful in Pennsylvania. Federalist prosecutor William Rawle initiated twenty-six misdemeanor charges for speech-related infractions, the majority of which involved pole raisings, but juries sometimes produced "unexpected acquittals" while grand juries sometimes declined to indict "contrary to what appeared a grounded expectation."[30] In the case of federal prosecutions, Pennsylvanians used the jury, as well as a reluctance to testify against their fellow citizens, to interpose between the government and protesters.

Thus in the end the Whiskey Rebellion produced a victory for Hamiltonian policy, but also a reminder that popular constitutionalism could serve as a check on government power in certain circumstances. The controversy generated by liberty poles during the Whiskey Rebellion revealed that the scope of freedom of expression, the boundaries of the public sphere, and the mechanisms of popular sovereignty were sharply contested in the early 1790s. In fact, despite broad hostility to Federalist constitutionalism by 1794, the resistance remained deeply divided in its own constitutional visions.

The most significant casualty of the Whiskey Rebellion was the Democratic–Republican societies, which Federalists blamed for instigating the insurrection. The notion that extraconstitutional political organizations might act to correct constitutional defects clashed with the Founding era's antiparty ethos, notwithstanding the societies' insistence on their right to assemble and to influence politics in a peaceful manner. Federalists and Republicans each claimed to be true to the Revolution's affirmation of the ideal of popular sovereignty. Yet, the question of how the sovereign people's will would be collected and given effect remained deeply contentious. As of 1794, for most Americans, openly embracing a party organization was little different than supporting the radicalism of the Whiskey Rebels.

CONSTITUTIONAL OUTSIDERS: ENSLAVED AMERICANS

Rural white men were not the only Americans prepared to claim the full, radical promise of the American Revolution. The most glaring contradiction between the Revolution's promise of liberty and American reality

---

[30] William Rawle to Alexander Addison, August 15, 1795 in *Pennsylvania Archives, Second Series*, (19 vols., 1874–1893), 450.

remained slavery, as famously observed by the English literary figure Dr. Samuel Johnson in 1775: "How is it that we hear the loudest yelps for liberty among the drivers of negroes?"[31] The enslaved were aware of this contradiction and pressed the case for abolition even before the Declaration of Independence had publicly declared liberty an "unalienable right" of "all men."

The most common course of action for an enslaved person determined to gain liberty was simply to run away, effectively freeing themselves, an action that did not normally occasion a declaration of rights. Others petitioned legislatures for their freedom and expressly invoked the ideas of the Revolution. In 1773, 1774, and 1777, enslaved persons petitioned the government of Massachusetts for their freedom using language that echoed Patriot rhetoric: "We have in common with all other men a naturel right to our freedoms without Being depriv'd of them by our fellow men." Such petitions failed, but in 1781 the enslaved Mum Bett successfully sued for her freedom. A jury in western Massachusetts cited the state's Declaration of Rights, which stated that "All men are born free and equal, and have certain natural, essential, and unalienable rights; among which may be reckoned the right of enjoying and defending their lives and liberties." Just two years later, in the case of Quock Walker, Chief Justice William Cushing of the state's highest court invoked the same language from the Massachusetts Constitution and declared that it effectively abolished slavery in the state.

Slaveholding survived in virtually every other state, but some began to enact gradual emancipation statutes. Pennsylvania, for example, adopted such a plan in 1780, requiring all slaveholders to register their property by November of that year. Any master who failed to meet the deadline would lose claim to his or her slaves immediately. The impact of the law was dramatic. By the time of the first federal census in 1790, almost two-thirds of the state's enslaved persons had been emancipated.

Gradual emancipation did not mean that freed people in Pennsylvania had achieved equality under the law. Nor did the law eliminate all the threats to the newly freed. In 1781 the legislature considered a revision that would have granted slaveholders who missed the registration deadline a two-year grace period, a change that would have allowed them to

---

[31] Samuel Johnson, *Taxation No Tyranny* (London: T. Cadell, 1775), 89.

re-enslave some free Pennsylvanians. Members of the free African-American community petitioned the legislature in a manner that made clear both their commitment to liberty and their continuing subordination in a society built on racial hierarchy: "We are fully sensible, that an address from persons of our rank is wholly unprecedented, and we are fearful of giving offence in the attempt." But the petition boldly pointed to the Revolution itself and the "common rights of mankind" in urging the legislature to leave the emancipated secure in their freedom.[32] The petition effort succeeded, and the Assembly held firm on the registration deadline.

Still, the vast majority of black Americans remained enslaved, and even free blacks remained civically subordinated. Activists formed antislavery societies in New York, Delaware, Rhode Island, Pennsylvania, Maryland, and even Virginia. But these societies were gradualist, forswearing the immediate abolition of slavery out of deference to the property interests of slaveholders. Consequently, pockets of significant change like the Pennsylvania emancipations made only a dent in the national commitment to slavery.

An alternative route to freedom was insurrection, a threat that loomed large in the white political imagination but that seldom achieved success in the United States. Jefferson had articulated white fear in the early 1780s when he predicted that "a total emancipation" was all but inevitable but hoped that it could occur "with the consent of the masters, rather than by their extirpation."[33] The successful 1791 rebellion of the enslaved in Saint-Domingue (modern Haiti) helped to cement the fear of insurrection as a major concern of American slavery policy right up to the Civil War. The Washington administration gradually accepted the need to establish relations with the new government of Saint-Domingue, and some Federalists even urged Washington to renew the lucrative trade with the former French colony. Republicans opposed such relations, however, mostly because of the party's commitment to protecting slavery. Republicans feared that enslaved Americans might emulate their oppressed brethren in the Caribbean. Although fears of slave insurrection were most keen in the South, Northern Republicans also voiced concerns. Congressman

---

[32] Letter of Cato and Petition by "The Negroes who Obtained Freedom by the Late Act," in *Postscript to the Freeman's Journal*, September 21, 1781.
[33] Thomas Jefferson, *Notes on Virginia*, Query 18.

Albert Gallatin of Pennsylvania warned that supporters of the rebels might "spread their views among the Negro people [in America] and excite dangerous insurrections among them."[34]

America faced its own rebellion less than a decade after the uprising in Saint-Domingue. Gabriel Prosser, a skilled Richmond artisan, planned to seize the Virginia state arsenal and distribute weapons to all who would join him to overthrow the system of slavery. His owner allowed the enslaved blacksmith to hire himself out, which enabled him to make contact with others among the enslaved as well as among free blacks. Gabriel not only knew about the uprising in Saint-Domingue and the French Revolution but was also keenly aware of the ideas of the American Revolution. The conspirators planned to march under a banner with the words "death or liberty" emblazoned on it, converting Patrick Henry's revolutionary credo into a rallying cry for an uprising against slavery. Moreover, he expected "poor white people" and other "democrats" to rally to his cause and planned to spare all those whites deemed "Friendly to liberty," notably "Quakers, Methodists, and Frenchmen."[35] All others were to be slaughtered.

Word of the plot leaked, however, and Virginia's militia was called into action. Virginians then discovered that this venerated institution and primary defense against slave insurrection was poorly prepared to serve its primary function. Arms and ammunition were in short supply in many counties, which meant that Gabriel's plan was not as far-fetched as it might seem. Had the rebels seized the Richmond arsenal, the outcome of the rebellion might well have turned out badly for white Virginia. Indeed, the plot was only discovered because a torrential rainstorm delayed the rebellion, creating time for some wavering conspirators to reveal its dimensions to the authorities. A special court tried the conspirators without the benefit of a jury. Ultimately twenty-six of those put on trial were convicted and sentenced to death. The remaining convicted rebels were deported.

Gabriel's Rebellion demonstrated the racial limits of the nation's republican ideals. By using the language of American constitutionalism – particularly the rights discourse of the revolutionary heritage – to rally

---

[34] "Speech of Albert Gallatin," *Annals of Congress*, vol. 9, 5th Cong., 3rd sess., 2752 (January 22, 1799).
[35] Testimony of Ben Woolfolk, *Governor's Office, Letters Received, James Monroe, Record Group 3, Library of Virginia*, available at www.lva.virginia.gov/exhibits/deathliberty/gabriel/gabtrial17.htm.

support for their insurrection, Gabriel and his followers reminded the nation of the savage contradiction in American constitutional thought. The official response to this frightening but abortive rebellion was far more severe than the punishments meted out to the white men of the Whiskey Rebellion and Fries's Rebellion (another Pennsylvania protest against another Federalist tax), the two most violent protests in the previous decade. Perhaps the explanation was in part that Gabriel's rebels had slaughter on their minds, however justified, but at least as important – and thoroughly entwined with that explanation – was the slaveholding elites' decision to meet its internal contradictions with redoubled violence.

### CONSTITUTIONAL OUTSIDERS: WOMEN

If post-Revolutionary principles of equality and liberty generally did not reach black Americans, neither did they reach American women. The experiences of black men and white women were hardly the same, to say nothing of the compound challenges facing black women. But white men, regardless of social class, deployed race, gender, or both to effectively silence all others and render them constitutional outsiders.

Republican theory ascribed the capacity for virtue – an essential ingredient of constitutional durability – to independent, property-owning male citizens. Patriarchal ideals were woven into the fabric of republicanism. Still, a few far-sighted thinkers pushed the principle of equality to its logical conclusion, adumbrating a critique of the gendered law of the Founding era. For a fleeting decade or two, this critique suggested the prospect of a meaningful space for women in public life. The possibility of such change was reflected in a growing body of American magazines and book culture, in the growth of female education beyond the merely domestic arts, in the extension of the suffrage itself to a limited number of women in a single state, and in embryonic arguments against coverture, the English legal doctrine that subsumed a married woman's legal personhood entirely within that of her husband. However, this sense of possibility existed mostly among an elite stratum of women and remained on the fringes of American public life in the years of Federalist dominance across the 1790s. In the larger scheme of things, the bubbling of proto-feminist argument did not oblige even the Federalists to give serious thought to opening public life to women. What few opportunities emerged during the generation after the Revolution soon gave way to a Republican ascendancy that firmly remasculinized public life, just as it solidified the supremacy of the white democracy.

Few of the proto-feminists of the 1790s actually campaigned for female voting, but their arguments for female intellectual equality, female education, and female attention to public affairs all carried the germ of an argument for full equality in public life. Such arguments faced a stout line of masculine resistance, but there was nevertheless meaningful change in the world of education. The Federalist author Judith Sargent Murray, among others, argued that women should at least receive educations suited to their intellectual capacities, even as these arguments often disavowed any claim to the vote, jury service, office-holding, or the like. Her view was complemented by that of the eminent Philadelphia physician Benjamin Rush, who offered a robust statement of the need to educate women for their role as mothers of future citizens of the republic. But this role remained in the private sphere, raising boys and men of virtue for active roles in public life. Women attended James Wilson's law lectures at the University of Pennsylvania, but those in attendance would have heard the distinguished jurist reinforce Rush's point, reminding women that their primary function in a republic was moral, not political. Although women did not act directly in a political capacity, he noted, they "had a most intimate connexion with the effects of a good system of law and government."[36] The Philadelphia Young Ladies Academy was typical of the new institutions for educating women. In addition to music, dance, and needlework, these new schools instructed girls in rhetoric, oratory, and history, topics once exclusively taught to boys. Occasionally, such education led to serious questioning of society's gendered power structures. Priscilla Mason's 1793 salutatory oration exposed how men had "seized the scepter and the sword" but had "denied women the advantage of a liberal education" and "doom'd the sex to servile or frivolous employments, on purpose to degrade their minds, that they themselves might hold unrivall'd, the power and pre-eminence they had usurped."[37]

The most radical champion of gender equality was the English writer Mary Wollstonecraft. She argued that women equaled men in virtually every quality relevant to establishing political equality, most importantly in their capacity for reason. Women's subordinate status resulted only from society's denying them access to education and other opportunities.

[36] James Wilson, *Law Lectures*, 1: 88.
[37] "The Salutatory Oration, Delivered by Miss Mason," in *The Rise and Progress of the Young-Ladies' Academy of Philadelphia* (Philadelphia: Stewart & Cochran, 1794), 92.

She thus championed female education and even the right of a woman to earn a living for herself. Indeed, women deserved the right of suffrage and full representation in government.

By the end of the 1790s there were more copies of Wollstonecraft's feminist tract *A Vindication of the Rights of Woman* in American libraries than there were copies of Thomas Paine's *Rights of Man*. An enthusiastic early review drew a favorable comparison between her work and Paine's, noting that, "while thousands are shedding their blood in asserting the Rights of Man, a female has lately wielded her Pen, and we think with great success, in vindicating the Rights of Woman." Negative responses to Wollstonecraft also appeared, particularly once stories about her nontraditional attitudes toward sex and the family filtered back to America. The president of Harvard, John Thornton Kirkland, imagined the framers of the Constitution falling under Wollstonecraft's sway and the unfortunate results that would have followed, asking of women in America: "Are they not as free, as lovely, as respectable, and happy, in their present situation of society, as they would be" if they assumed the employments and responsibilities of men? Kirkland presumed to answer for American women, asserting that the sexual division of labor liberated women from the "drudgery and danger" of full political and legal equality. By the time Thomas Fessenden published his poem "The Ladies Monitor" in 1818, he could comfortably mock her ideas: "Dame Nature tells us Mary's rights are wrongs" and that her vision of "female freedom is a Siren-Song."[38] Wollstonecraft's radical critique of gendered inequality did not disappear but required decades before a sustained campaign for women's rights would pursue her goals. In the meantime, mainstream thinkers often used her name as shorthand for the host of evils they feared would flow from women's rights, including Jacobinism, free love, and socialism.

Although the authors of the Declaration and the Framers of the Constitution never felt the need even to consider the place of women in the republican constitutional structure, elite women sometimes tried to convince their powerful husbands and brothers to do them justice. In 1776, for example, Abigail Adams reminded her husband "to remember the ladies" when drafting a new "Code of Laws," one that would free them from being their husbands' "vassals," subject to whatever "cruelty and indignity" they might inflict. Drawing on the universalist principles of the Revolution, she warned that women would "foment a Rebellion, and will

---

[38] Thomas Fessenden, "The Ladies Monitor: A Poem" (Vermont, 1818), 59.

not hold ourselves bound by any Laws in which we have no voice, or Representation." John Adams's response reflected a deeper anxiety: "We have been told that our Struggle has loosened the bands of Government every where," Adams wrote, "That Children and Apprentices were disobedient – that schools and Colledges were grown turbulent – that Indians slighted their Guardians and Negroes grew insolent to their Masters." Comparing wives to the consummate outsiders, American Indians, Adams concluded by mocking his wife: "But your Letter was the first Intimation that another Tribe more numerous and powerfull than all the rest were grown discontented."[39] John's dismissive response offered no logical argument or legal principle to refute Abigail's point, but dispatched his wife with condescension. He confessed that he "cannot but laugh" at her suggestion and that everyone knew that husbands "are the subjects. We have only the Name of Masters."

Hannah Corbin, Richard Henry Lee's sister, likewise held her Patriot brother accountable to the radical ideas of the Revolution, demanding to know why widows with property were not allowed to vote. Republican theory's emphasis on property as the foundation for representation and political stability supported Corbin's point, as Lee understood: "The doctrine of representation is a large subject, and it is certain that it ought to be extended as far as wisdom and policy can allow; nor do I see that either of these forbid widows having property from voting." Yet, Lee made no suggestion that married women should control property or vote, nor that he would lift a finger to advance the cause even of widows' voting. Simple disregard of women's self-evidently logical claims proved effective in this generation, thanks to the sheer weight of custom.

The boldest experiment in applying the radical ideas of the Revolution to women's rights came in New Jersey's 1776 Constitution, which omitted the typical gender exclusions found in every other state's suffrage provisions. The state preserved a property requirement for voting, and there is not much evidence about voting practices in the years immediately following adoption of the state constitution. But by 1787 women were appearing on poll lists, and in 1790 the legislature expressly granted the franchise to single, propertied women in seven counties in the southern part of the state. This limited female suffrage was expanded to the entire state in 1797. No other state followed New Jersey's example, but in this

---

[39] John Adams to Abigail Adams, April 14, 1776. *The Adams Papers*, Adams Family Correspondence, vol. 1, *December 1761–May 1776*, ed. Lyman H. Butterfield (Cambridge, MA: Harvard University Press, 1963), pp. 381–383.

one state, by the time of the contentious election of 1800, Federalists and Republicans were vying for the votes of propertied single women.

New Jersey's brief experiment with female suffrage, however, did not much alter the gendered quality of republican language or practice. Just months before the election of 1800, the (Newark) *Centinel of Freedom* printed a list of "Ladies' Toasts" from a ladies-only Fourth of July celebration, paralleling the traditional male events. The female correspondent who submitted the toasts noted that the group would "acknowledge no other lords or masters but their husbands" and therefore felt free – although evidently with their husbands' permission – to engage in this unprecedented meeting. The toasts included one to "a free and chaste press for to instruct and delight [the] United States," and another to "sentiments without coquetry." Chastity, of course, was a core ideal of middle-class womanhood. Coquetry, by contrast, represented a peculiarly female form of dissembling and corruption, the antithesis of female republican virtue. These toasts echoed themes in early American novels such as Hannah Foster's *The Coquette* and in widely popular morality tales of sentiment, seduction, and sorrow. Other toasts too reinforced gender roles, such as the toast to "Our fathers, husbands, and brothers, who fought for the rights of man and thereby secured those of the women." What exactly those rights of women were, the toasts did not indicate, other than the right to "reward" men who were true to their public duties. Nevertheless, one of the concluding toasts was offered to "The rights of women – may they never be curtailed."[40]

Within two years of the publication of these toasts, the idea of female suffrage was generating vigorous criticism. One observer conceded that the legislature had "acted from a principle of justice, deeming it right that every free person who pays a tax should have a vote," but argued that this worthy republican experiment had been undermined by the usual villain, partisanship: "When party spirit began to rear its hideous head, the female vote became its passive tools, and the ill consequences of their admission have increased yearly." Citing the republican fear of political corruption, Republicans led an effort to strip both women and blacks of the right to vote, which succeeded in 1807. No evidence corroborates the idea that party spirit and corruption were somehow worse when women and blacks held the suffrage. More likely, Jeffersonian animus to female and black voting resulted from the Federalist inclinations of

---

[40] "The Ladies' Toasts," *The Centinel of Freedom* (Newark, NJ), July 29, 1800.

propertied women and free blacks as well as the raw, white masculinist prejudice of the time.

Like the world of politics, the world of law resisted the feminism that surfaced in cultural criticism, novels, and poetry, such as this bit of newspaper verse objecting to married women's legal subordination:

> That I hate all the doctrines by wedlock prescribed
> Its law of obedience could never suit me
> My spirit's too lofty, my thoughts too free.[41]

The courts were not won over by such poetic appeals, a fact made abundantly clear in the Massachusetts case, *Martin v. Commonwealth* (1805). *Martin* addressed a claim by the son of a Loyalist father. The younger Martin sought to reclaim his mother's land, which had been forfeited during the Revolution. He relied on the common law notion that a married woman's legal identity was practically merged into that of her husband. Thus her abandonment of her country to join the British was not her decision at all but that of her husband. James Sullivan, the state's Attorney General, rejoined that the mother had chosen freely to follow her husband out of Massachusetts to adhere to the British, rightly depriving her (and her son) of her land. She could not escape her responsibility to her country by pointing to the higher authority of her husband. Rather, Sullivan insisted, she bore the privileges and responsibilities of a constitutional actor in her own right.[42]

Sullivan's argument counted as remarkably progressive for its time, treating a married woman as a person of independent will and responsibility, but the argument proved unpersuasive. Rather than accept that a woman had legal agency, the court deemed Martin's mother a *feme covert*, legally a mere appendage of her husband. Her withdrawal from the state had been her husband's doing, not her own. Any attempt on her part to resist that withdrawal – to choose patriotism over her husband's treason – would have been unthinkable. In the face of the principle of equality that justified the Revolution, the law considered the subordination of women so fundamental as to excuse even what otherwise would be treason. The outcome in *Martin* was not surprising. Most legal commentators accepted the traditional doctrine of coverture. Thus Connecticut jurist, Zephaniah Swift, author of one of the earliest legal treatises

---

[41] *Centinel of Freedom* (Newark, NJ) October 21, 1800.
[42] *Martin v. Commonwealth*, 1 Mass 347 (1805).

written in the new republic, affirmed that "the husband and wife" were "one person" and hence had "one will."[43]

The one notable voice of dissent on this point was another Connecticut jurist and legal scholar, Tapping Reeve, a prominent Federalist, proprietor of the nation's only law school, and a judge on Connecticut's highest court. He insisted that "the law does not view the husband and wife as one person." Although Reeve's views were unorthodox, his professional status lent them weight. The state legislature included a number of graduates of Reeve's law school, and in 1809 they helped enact a landmark piece of legislation expanding married women's property rights. The legislation declared that "married women shall have the power of disposing of their estates by last will and testament." Connecticut preceded New York and other states by three decades in undertaking significant reform in this area. So the significance of Reeve's accomplishment was notable, although the pace of change in women's rights remained glacial.[44]

Prevailing legal and constitutional ideas among the white male elite allowed no public role for women under the Constitution. Excluding women from full political participation required no lengthy justification. Republican ideas defined the outer limits of women's sphere of action in the world of politics and law in terms of women's responsibility to imbue children with republican values and restrain the excesses of an increasingly aggressive partisan culture.

Indeed, the Federalist 1790s would remain the high water mark of feminist possibility for decades to come. The Jeffersonian and Jacksonian ascendancies brought only retrenchment. Eventually, the Federalists' Whig descendants in the 1830s exhibited a modest openness to the participation of women in public affairs as the moral consciences of their families and communities. Thus women petitioned Congress, attended campaign events, and joined reform societies in the name of Indians' rights, antislavery, temperance, and other reforms that were more generally identified with the Whigs than the Democrats. But the dominant Democrats maintained a firm hostility to any sullying of the female character through involvement in the partisan battles of public life. So, while individual women of means occasionally carved out space for

---

[43] Zephaniah Swift, *A System of the Laws of the State of Connecticut* (1795); T. Reeve, *The Law of Baron and Femme; of Parent and Child; of Guardian and Ward; of Master and Servant; and of the Powers of Courts of Chancery* (New Haven, CT: Oliver Steele, 1816).

[44] "An Act in Addition to 'An Act Relating to the Age, Ability and Capacity of Persons,'" ch. VII, 1809 *Connecticut Public Acts* 15 (May Sess. 1809).

public accomplishment and even power – perhaps in the form of literary success or skilled facilitation of a husband's political career – nothing resembling a campaign for women's constitutional rights gained any traction in this era of white, masculinist democracy.

## THE FRENCH REVOLUTION IN AMERICA AND THE INTENSIFICATION OF PARTISANSHIP

Political and constitutional struggle in the 1790s was profoundly influenced by the tumult following the French Revolution of 1789. At first there was broad support in the United States for the French Revolution's toppling of the monarchy. Even the arch-Federalist *Gazette of the United States* described the Revolution as "one of the most glorious objects that can arrest the attention of mankind." Republican James Madison added that events in France were "so glorious to this country, because it has grown as it were out of the American Revolution." The impact of the French Revolution in America touched everything from fashion to forms of address. Pro-French Republicans in Philadelphia and other cities began addressing each other as "citizen," after the fashion of revolutionary France. Many Republican women followed suit, some using the term *citizen* and others *citizeness* or *citess* among themselves.

The increasingly radical turn of the Revolution, especially the rise of the Terror, including the execution of the King, Queen, and other enemies of the Revolution, led Federalists to turn against France and its Republican apologists in America. As Hamilton observed in 1794, "The excesses which have constantly multiplied, with greater and greater aggravations have successively though slowly detached reflecting men from their partiality for an object which has appeared less and less to merit their regard."[45]

As revolutionary France's foreign policy also became increasingly aggressive, particularly toward Great Britain, the Washington administration attempted to maintain its neutrality. The British navy dominated the Atlantic trade routes and sought to isolate and weaken France, particularly its lucrative trade with its Atlantic colonies. Of course America had signed a Treaty with France in 1778, whose terms seemed to require that the nation adopt a pro-French policy, something that many

---

[45] *The Papers of Alexander Hamilton*, vol. 26, *1 May 1802–23 October 1804, Additional Documents 1774–1799, Addenda and Errata*, ed. Harold C. Syrett (New York: Columbia University Press, 1979), 738–741.

Republicans, most notably Jefferson, urged with considerable force. America was caught between two major European powers, each aiming to strangle the trade of the other. Washington dispatched Supreme Court Justice John Jay as a special envoy to negotiate with Great Britain. Negotiating with little leverage, Jay's Treaty failed to exact any major concession on the right of American ships to enjoy neutral trade with Europe. Federalists nevertheless lauded Jay for making the best of a bad situation, while Republicans denounced him for acting in bad faith and allowing British interests to trump American. The hostility to the Jay treaty was so intense that effigies of the Supreme Court Justice were set on fire and, in Philadelphia, even placed in pillory and marched to a guillotine.

Republican suspicions of Federalist diplomacy also spawned a lively debate over constitutional limits on the conduct of foreign affairs. The Republican-dominated House sought copies of Jay's negotiating instructions, threatening to withhold funding to implement the treaty. Federalists insisted that the Constitution gave the treaty-making power to the president and the Senate alone, not the House, but a Republican writer, assuming the name "Franklin," reminded readers that the people must have the final constitutional word: "'We the People' made the Constitution and the Officers under it." Naturally it followed that the people "will have some influence on the laws which are made to bind us."[46] For Franklin, Federalists had turned republican theory upside down, acting as if representatives were independent of the people, when they ought to be their faithful servants. Republican resistance failed in this instance but represented an important step in the growth of a self-conscious, democratic-leaning opposition to Federalist constitutionalism.

Washington's decision not to seek a third term meant the 1796 election would be colored by the deepening partisan divisions that had grown since the adoption of the Constitution. In his Farewell Address, drafted by Alexander Hamilton, Washington warned Americans "in the most solemn manner against the baneful effects of the spirit of party." Moreover, it was vital for America to avoid permanent alliances that would involve the nation in European politics and war, themselves intensifiers of partisan divisions at home. Although Washington hoped his address would contribute to the lessening of partisan fervor, its publication, one

---

[46] "Franklin," *The Independent Gazetteer* (Philadelphia) March 11, 1795.

Federalist observed, acted like a "signal, like dropping a hat, for the party races to start."[47]

Although the nation was deeply divided and clear political factions had emerged in Congress and in most state legislatures, the dominant anti-party ethos continued to inhibit the development of modern techniques of party organization. The Constitution had not anticipated the rise of parties, nor presidential tickets with designated candidates for president and vice president running together. Rather, the individual with the most votes was to be president, and the runner-up was to be vice-president. The system was designed to ensure that the executive contained the two men best qualified to lead the nation, not the nominees of parties. Yet, by 1796, it was clear that the next president would be chosen in a contest of parties, with Adams and Jefferson the consensus choices to lead the Federalists and Republicans.

Still, there were no modern party devices – like nominating conventions – and strong antiparty convictions prevented the candidates from taking active roles in the campaign. The task of getting each candidate's message out fell to their subordinates and the press, and these surrogates acted within their own local contexts and with an eye to local and regional issues. As a consequence, more than a third of presidential electors broke ranks and cast their votes for nine alternative candidates, reflecting local concerns, state interests, loyalties, and grudges as much as the national debate between Federalists and Republicans. The campaign, then, continued the traditional politics of local interests and personal loyalties, while simultaneously planting the seeds of durable party conflict. The press adopted intense partisan rhetoric that sharpened the ideological differences between the candidates, most notably on matters of foreign affairs and federalism. Adams was cast as a monarchist and Jefferson as a libertine and atheist, a debauched devotee of revolutionary France's worst vices. In the end Adams edged out Jefferson by a mere three electoral votes, and hopes for a politics above party progressively dimmed.

Adams inherited a diplomatic mess, as relations with France grew increasingly hostile. Adams's preference for diplomacy over military force angered Federalists aligned with Hamilton, who hoped to use the opportunity to both strengthen America's military and isolate the pro-French

---

[47] "Farewell Address, 19 September 1796," *Founders Online*, National Archives, last modified June 29, 2017, http://founders.archives.gov/documents/Washington/99-01-02-00963.

Republicans. When diplomatic overtures failed, the Hamiltonians got their wish. The undeclared, naval "Quasi-War" of 1798–1800 gave the Federalists the opportunity to expand the military, funded by a new property tax on land, slaves, and buildings.

At the same time, the Federalists clamped down on the opposition at home, enacting the Alien and Sedition Acts to protect America from the foreign and domestic subversion that they associated with Francophile Republicans. The three Alien Acts made it more difficult to become a citizen and gave the government far-reaching powers to deport resident aliens. The Sedition Act made it a crime to "combine or conspire together with the intent to oppose any measure or measures of the government of the United States." The Act criminalized any attempt to "write, print, utter, or publish" statements "false, scandalous, or malicious" against "the government of the United States, or either house of Congress of the United States, or the President." Conspicuously absent were penalties for attacking the Vice President, who was then the Republican Thomas Jefferson. The Federalist press was free to hurl whatever invectives it chose at Jefferson, while prosecutions under the Act would be directed exclusively at Republicans.

No part of the Federalist agenda did more to inflame political passions than did the passage of the Alien and Sedition Acts. Federalists defended the Acts as necessary to prevent foreign agents, radical refugees, and their domestic allies from undermining American republicanism. They pointed out that the Sedition Act actually was a restrained measure: Unlike the common law offense of seditious libel, it allowed truth as a defense, thus nurturing a free press but not a licentious one. For most Republicans, however, the chief problem with the Act was not its restraint on the press, as such, but its appropriation of such a power to the distant national government in disregard of the carefully drawn constraints of the federal system. Republicans generally accepted that state governments could continue the common law's rules of seditious libel to prevent licentious use of the press. But the Constitution had explicitly barred the federal government from making such laws and displacing the policies of the states.

Republicans in Congress attacked the Sedition Act on grounds that linked federalism and the First Amendment. Virginia's John Nicholas "looked in vain amongst the enumerated powers given to the Congress in the Constitution, for an authority to pass a law like the present" but did find in the First Amendment "an express prohibition against passing it." Albert Gallatin of Pennsylvania reminded his audience that during ratification a decade earlier Americans had worried that the new federal government might run amok in precisely this fashion: The Sedition Bill "justified the suspicions of those who, at the time of the adoption of the Constitution, had apprehended that [the Necessary and Proper Clause] might be distorted" for just such a purpose. "It was in order to remove these fears, that the [First] amendment was proposed and adopted."[48] According to the Federalists, however, the power to prosecute sedition was an essential power wielded by all governments. The individual states had exercised such powers, and it would be folly to deprive the federal government of the same essential powers.

When Republican resistance proved futile in both the Congress and the courts, Republicans were forced to think of new ways to protect individual liberty, restore the federal government to its proper sphere, and defend state sovereignty. Although federalism was a cardinal tenet of dissenting constitutionalism and had been invoked in nearly every major constitutional debate in the decade after ratification, relatively little attention had been devoted to exploring how federalism's checking function would actually operate in practice. Would the judiciary exercise the final check when a corrupt faction gained control of the federal government and threatened the liberties of the people? Would the individual state legislatures rally to the defense of liberty? In an extreme situation could special conventions of the people of the states act? Or, if necessary, might the people act through their state militias, using armed resistance as the final barrier between a tyrannical federal government and the people?

Republican elites predictably favored a mode of resistance somewhat removed from the people, preferring the refined and filtered voice of the people as articulated by state legislatures to the unfiltered voice of the people themselves. Jefferson and Madison again took the lead, penning resolutions to be adopted by the legislatures of Kentucky and Virginia. Each text drew on the anticonsolidationist rhetoric that had defined dissenting constitutional discourse since ratification. In each case, the authors asserted that protection of each individual's liberty depended on preserving the balance of the larger federal structure. States' rights and individual rights continued to be linked in oppositional constitutional discourse.

The two documents also elaborated a theory of the Union as a compact among sovereign states rather than a government created by the American

---

[48] *The Debates and Proceedings in the Congress of the United States*, July 10, 1798 (Washington, DC: Gales and Seaton, 1851), 8:2139, 2159.

people as a whole. The Kentucky Resolutions affirmed that the states had agreed to create a "general government" of limited powers, and, "as in all other cases," involving a "compact among parties having no common judge, *each party has an equal right to judge for itself, as well of infractions as of the mode and measure of redress.*" Jefferson's original draft of the Kentucky Resolution drew the further inference that a state, as a party to the compact, might nullify acts of Congress on its own judgment of unconstitutionality, although this language was omitted from the final version. Even without asserting the right to nullify federal laws, the Kentucky Legislature appeared to claim an independent right to determine their constitutionality.[49]

Madison's more temperate Virginia Resolutions did not assert an individual state right, but noted that in extraordinary cases, when the Constitution's safeguards had broken down, the states "have a right, and are duty bound to interpose for arresting the progress" of federal encroachment on state authority. By invoking the right of the states, not of an individual state, and employing the vague concept of interposition, Madison avoided the confrontational language of nullification. But the Virginia Resolutions shared with the Kentucky Resolutions an emphasis on the Union as a compact among the states.

In New England, Federalist-controlled legislatures were unsparing in their criticism of both documents. Rhode Island's legislature used the occasion to claim that the Constitution assigned the power of constitutional review exclusively to the federal courts: "In the opinion of this legislature, the second section of the third article of the Constitution of the United States, in these words, to wit, – 'The judicial power shall extend to all cases arising under the laws of the United States,' – vests in the Federal Courts, exclusively, and in the Supreme Court of the United States, ultimately, the authority of deciding on the constitutionality of any act or law of the Congress of the United States."[50] Massachusetts was even more forceful, praising the Alien and Sedition Acts as "expedient and necessary" and denouncing the state resolutions as inimical to the Constitution. The Resolutions got a more sympathetic response in some parts of the South, but even in these instances, the preferred solution was not "interposition" by special state conventions, but the much more

---

[49] "The Alien and Sedition Laws, and Virginia and Kentucky Resolutions" (Young & Minns: Boston, 1798), 2.
[50] "The State of Rhode Island and Providence Plantations to Virginia, February 1799" in Banning, *Liberty and Order*, 237.

restrained recommendation that each state's congressional delegation be instructed to seek repeal of the Sedition Act.

The disappointing reaction of the states to Madison's and Jefferson's innovative mode of resistance only led Jefferson to double down. In the subsequent Kentucky Resolutions of 1799 the term "nullification" was reintroduced. Asserting that the individual states could judge issues of constitutionality, the resolutions also affirmed that in extreme circumstances nullification was the rightful remedy. The threat of nullification was tempered by the promise that Kentucky would in this instance "bow to the laws of the Union" while continuing "to oppose, in a constitutional manner, every attempt ... to violate that compact." Nevertheless, Jefferson flirted with the notion of secession as the ultimate response to the tyranny of the Alien and Sedition Acts. Although Madison counseled him out of this radical position, Jefferson had done enough to provide constitutional cover to the South Carolina nullifiers and secessionists of subsequent generations.

What united the Virginia and Kentucky approaches was the belief that individual state legislatures might take the lead in collecting and organizing opposition. That belief followed from the assurances of the Federalists themselves in 1788 that the states would rally against any potential threat from the federal government. More than ten years later, responding to other states' skepticism of interposition, Madison reaffirmed this gloss on federalism: "The appeal was emphatically made" in 1788 "to the intermediate existence of the state governments between the people and the government." The individual states, Madison observed, "would descry the first symptoms of usurpation" and "sound the alarm to the public." In defending the rights of states, Madison even suggested that the states' authority was superior to that of the federal judiciary, but he quickly assured his audience that the states would resort to this authority in response to only the most "deliberate, palpable, and dangerous" violations of the Constitution.[51]

Conspicuously absent from Madison's arguments, to the modern eye, is any reference to political parties as the natural institutions of resistance, because, of course, real party organization remained anathema to Madison and most others. In the end, the Virginia and Kentucky Resolutions were failures in their own terms. They inspired no effective support among their intended audience, the other state legislatures. Moreover,

---

[51] James Madison, "Report on the Virginia Resolutions," reprinted in *The Founders' Constitution*, vol. 1, ch. 8, document 42.

they failed at both a theoretical and practical level to establish the state legislatures – the parties to the "compact" – as the ultimate authorities on the federal government's constitutional limits. The door was now open to the middling politicians, who were less squeamish about party organization. These men had experience managing elections and mobilizing the press in a way that allowed them to see both the possibility and the necessity of new institutions to harness the growing opposition to Federalist constitutionalism. It was these men who would soon set the stage for a party-driven constitutional order.

### THE ALMOST REVOLUTION OF 1800

As the election of 1800 approached, the Resolutions played a critical role in inspiring a movement of constitutional resistance among the people as a whole. If resistance to the Federalist program in Congress, the courts, and even the state legislatures had failed – indeed, if the peaceful protests of the Democratic–Republican Societies and even open rebellion had failed in their immediate objectives – they nonetheless energized the opposition movement. Neither the Republican elite nor their more plebeian allies had transcended the antiparty ethic of the Founding period, but there existed, especially in northeastern states like New York and Pennsylvania, an emergent core of party-oriented politicians who knew how to organize and how to make use of the nation's expanding print culture. Now, they would turn Jefferson's candidacy for the presidency in 1800 into a victory for an unprecedented type of party organization, suggesting to future democrats that party was the institution by which states' rights and popular notions of constitutional meaning might be most effectively defended.

In 1800, Federalist and Republican congressional caucuses met to choose their presidential candidates, settling predictably on President John Adams and Vice President Thomas Jefferson. In one sense, the caucuses were forerunners of party nominating conventions, but the participants remained attached to an antiparty ethos. Many caucus participants continued to describe their actions in terms of a traditional code of honor among gentlemen, pledging themselves to support the selected candidates. Electors might be shamed or cajoled into upholding these pledges, but the culture of honor among gentlemen played at least as strong a role in securing this outcome as did party loyalties.

If the nation's political elite continued to inhabit a world informed by traditional gentry values and antipartyism, much of the electorate lived in an increasingly democratized world. Indeed, the Federalist minister Samuel Miller lamented that "in the last twelve or fifteen years," the nation had "exhibited a spectacle never before displayed among men, even yet without parallel on the earth. It is the spectacle, not of the learned and the wealthy only, but of the great body of the people; even a large portion of that class of the community which is destined to daily labour, having free and constant access to public prints, receiving regular information of every occurrence." The unfortunate result, Miller complained, was that ordinary people were now "attending to the course of political affairs." The impact of print on politics was most dramatic in the many places where new partisan newspapers began publishing. For example, Federalists had dominated the elections of 1796 in Lancaster, Pennsylvania. By 1799 Lancaster had two Republican newspapers, one publishing in English and the other in German. Perhaps as a result, voter turnout more than doubled between 1798 and 1800. Republicans actually won the town of Lancaster and cut the Federalist margin in the county as a whole by a factor of three.[52]

Partisan animosities were both cause and effect of the expanding partisan press. Inflammatory political rhetoric was the norm in the campaign of 1800, not the exception, each side denouncing the other in apocalyptic terms. Republicans attacked Adams as a monarchist and a tyrant and prayed for deliverance from "Tories" and "Aristocrats." Federalists cast Jefferson as an atheist and a Jacobin, intoxicated by the radical theories of the French Revolution that had left France bathed in blood. One Connecticut Federalist minister declared, "I do not believe that the Most High will permit a howling atheist to sit at the head of this nation."[53]

Complicating the election was a growing division within the ranks of Federalists. Supporters of Alexander Hamilton believed Adams too lukewarm in his support for Federalist policies, most importantly fiscal and military policy. Adams had also demonstrated his weakness as an

---

[52] Samuel Miller, *A Brief Retrospect of the Eighteenth Century*, 2 vols. (New York: T. and J. Swords, 1803), 2:253. Data for the elections is available from the Lampi Collection of Early American Election Data, American Antiquarian Society (2007). The example of Lancaster, Pennsylvania, is illustrative of the changes in political culture, see Jeffrey L. Pasley, "1800 as a Revolution in Political Culture: Newspapers, Celebrations, Voting and Democratiziation in the Early Republic" in James Horn et al. *The Revolution of 1800: Democracy, Race and the New Republic* (Charlottesville: University of Virginia Press, 2002), 144–149.

[53] *Diary of Thomas Robbins, D. D., 1796–1854*, vol. 1 (Boston: Beacon Press, 1886), 114.

executive when he pardoned the Pennsylvania rebel leader John Fries, who had taken up arms to protest the new taxes enacted to pay for military expansion during the Quasi-War. The rift between Hamilton and Adams spilled into the popular press, with Hamilton personally publishing his doubts about "Mr. ADAMS'S temper" and "the correctness of his maxims of Administration."

Taking advantage of Federalist disunity, Republicans in certain key states worked to establish mechanisms of Republican Party unity. Less encumbered by revolutionary republicanism's antiparty ethos, these new politicians learned an important lesson from the chaotic years of resistance across the 1790s. Protecting the integrity of the Constitution required supplementing the Constitution with popular organizations that might deploy public opinion to prevent abuses of power. Of course, the Republicans' experience with political organization was mixed. Opponents of the Federalists had experimented with new institutions such as the Democratic–Republican societies, but America had not been ready for this innovation. By the end of the decade matters had changed. Techniques of political organization had been repeatedly tried and refined, especially in the local politics of states like New York and Pennsylvania, and these would prove central to the triumph of Jefferson and states' rights in 1800.

Indeed, in lieu of a full accounting of the election of 1800, one might boil the story down to the Federalists' internal divisions, on one side, and, on the other, the organizational skill of New York City's Republicans, especially Aaron Burr. Far from the world of Madisonian theory and Jeffersonian principles, the reality was that the election turned in significant part on who controlled New York's electoral votes, which would be cast by the New York State legislature. And the composition of the legislature would turn on who controlled the municipal elections in New York City in the spring of 1800. The man who effectively seized control of those elections was the Republican operative Aaron Burr, a sophisticated political organizer and power-seeker, largely free of any antiparty ethos or any constitutional philosophy at all. When he managed the turnout in New York City to provide arguably the most important building block in Jefferson's electoral edifice, he not only equipped Jefferson to claim a mandate, but he also provided the precedent that would legitimate party organization a generation later. (Importantly, as things turned out, he also claimed the Republican nomination for the Vice-Presidency as his reward.) Working on that New York campaign as an eighteen-year-old enthusiast of both states'-rights constitutionalism and the magic of party organization was Martin Van Buren. In later years, Van Buren, the nation's eighth president, would rarely mention Burr's name, but would endlessly invoke Jefferson and the Revolution of 1800 to legitimate his injection of party organization into the increasingly "democratic" constitutional system.

Although the Republican victory at the polls in 1800 did not bring down the judgment of heaven, it did trigger a constitutional crisis that few among the Framers of the Constitution could have predicted. The actual vote in the Electoral College had produced a tie between Jefferson and Burr, the two Republican candidates. The Constitution did not direct presidential electors to cast separate ballots for president and vice president, so a tie meant that the sitting House would decide.[54] The new Republican-dominated House would not be seated until March 1801, so the fate of the presidency rested with the lame-duck Federalists, creating an explosive political situation. Rumors of deals and conspiracies circulated widely. The Republican governors of Pennsylvania and Virginia both mobilized their militias, sending a message that they would not sit by if scheming politicians in Congress cast aside the will of the people.

Many Federalists' fears of a Jefferson presidency rendered Burr the preferred alternative, but Alexander Hamilton, who had been Burr's rival in New York politics for more than a decade, explained to his fellow Federalists why Jefferson was the lesser evil: "Mr. Jefferson, though too revolutionary in his notions, is yet a lover of liberty and will be desirous of something like orderly Government. – Mr. Burr loves nothing but himself ... and will be content with nothing short of permanent power in his own hands."[55] At the same time that Hamilton lobbied against Burr, Jefferson provided private assurances to select Federalists that he would not undermine all of the hard-won Federalist policies of the previous decade. Despite the dire predictions of so many Federalists, then, Jefferson was elected, and the Republic survived.

The tense election of 1800 ultimately produced a peaceful transfer of power from Federalists to Republicans, a notable achievement amid the fraught political atmosphere of the 1790s. Aware of the intensity of partisanship, Jefferson adopted a conciliatory rhetoric on assuming the

---

[54] To avert future deadlock in presidential elections, the Twelfth Amendment, adopted in 1804, required that electors cast separate ballots for president and vice president.

[55] Alexander Hamilton to Harrison Gray Otis, December 23, 1800 in David B. Davis and Steven Mintz, eds., *The Boisterous Sea of Liberty* (New York: Oxford University Press, 1998), 282.

presidency. In his Inaugural Address he reminded Americans that, "We are All Federalists, We are all Republicans." But the rhetoric would not prevent the rapid resumption of conflict once he assumed office.

### CONCLUSION

If one were to believe many of the Federalists of the 1790s, one would think the Republican opposition a movement for mob rule. Whereas, if one were to believe many of the Republicans, the Federalists would appear to be a counterrevolutionary, monarchist conspiracy. Not everyone embraced such extreme views, but the rapid emergence of sharp conflict on the operational meaning of the Constitution made clear that ratification had failed to resolve the struggle between centralizers like Hamilton and defenders of states' rights like Jefferson. The first decade under the Constitution was marked, on the one hand, by Hamilton's aggressive effort to treat that document as authorization for the federal government to assume every power that might advance national military and economic greatness. But it was marked, on the other hand, by constant defenses of state autonomy and constrained federal power as the necessary conditions for individual liberty. Moreover, as Hamilton sought to create a kind of artificial aristocracy, closely tied to the federal government by holding its debt and benefitting from its economic policies, assertive democracy began to bubble up from below in numerous forms: armed, antitax rebellions, the Democratic–Republican Societies, election of "middling" politicians, and more. Each assertion of democratic rights could be counted on to bring contempt from Federalist defenders of an older and still vital politics of deference.

Although the conflicts were real and had a tendency to go to extremes, they also had their limits. For one thing, they were conflicts almost entirely among white men. These white men widely shared the view that, whatever one thought of republicanism or democracy, women and black Americans must remain excluded from public life. There were exceptions, of course. Even some white men accepted arguments for a measure of gender and racial equality. A limited number of women had the vote for a while in New Jersey, and free black Americans who could meet property requirements and other qualifications had a formal right to vote in a number of states. But these exceptions added up to a negligible quantity of voters who were other than white and male. And the exclusions were even starker when it came to office-holding or other participation in public life.

The raging conflicts of the 1790s led some of these white men to consider a resort to arms in the electoral crisis of 1800. Yet, in the end, Republicans pulled back, and the Federalists accepted the electoral outcome. The struggle to remake the Constitution on one model or another – that of a compact among the states or a consolidated government of the nation as a whole, that of elite control or of democratic transformation – would continue within the institutional frame of the still-infant Constitution.

# 3

## The Democracy versus the Law: The Role of the Federal Judiciary, 1789–1815

### INTRODUCTION

The story of constitutional development in the years immediately after ratification was mainly a story of politics, not courts. The Washington and Adams administrations had worked to centralize power in a national government and empower a national elite that would keep the democracy at bay. The nascent Republicans, for their part, had tried any number of mechanisms to resist the Federalists' ambitions. The elites of the movement turned to formal political initiatives like the Virginia and Kentucky Resolutions. But middling republicans and unapologetic democrats – albeit overwhelmingly white and male – often employed more-populist methods of resistance, from the Democratic–Republican Societies to New York–style party-building and even actions out-of-doors, including in the extreme case the Whiskey Rebellion.

The Republicans generally turned to politics rather than courts for a number of reasons. Federalist political control of the executive and legislative branches meant they also controlled the judiciary. Thus, political resistance provided the only means available to Republicans. Moreover, many in the Republican coalition continued to favor a populist, antilegalist ideology that opposed the vesting of significant power in judges and courts at the expense of popular will. And behind these context-specific reasons for turning to political resistance lay the larger lesson that constitutional development always depends on political dynamics at least as much as legal argument.

Still, the courts too played an important role in the larger world of constitutional politics, beginning in the 1780s and accelerating after Jefferson's election. In this chapter, the narrative turns to the federal judiciary and the political context in which it worked. Federalists dominated this branch of the federal government during the first decade after the Constitution and continued to do so even after Federalists were swept from elected offices in 1800. When the Jeffersonians took control of the executive and Congress, the Federalist judiciary took up the fight for a Constitution of centralized, national power and, further, for what might be called a legalist Constitution.

Fleshing out the idea of Federalist legalism is central to understanding constitutionalism in the generation after ratification. The idea of legalism describes, first, the Federalist judges' belief that the Constitution embraced core principles of the common law, especially contract and property rights as shaped specifically by the judges who made that law. Relatedly, legalism describes the Federalist judges' belief that the Constitution had entrusted only the federal judiciary, not the elected branches and not the sovereign people, with the final authority to determine the meaning of the Constitution. This legalist Constitution – and law more generally – was the chief bulwark against democratic excess in an age when obsolescent aristocracy could no longer play that role.

Republicans tended to resist both elements of legalism, the ideas that the federal judiciary had the final word on the Constitution and that the Constitution elevated the traditions of the common law over the authority of the sovereign people. The Republican movement, however, contained some diversity of opinion on these matters. Moderate Republicans shared some of the Federalist judiciary's attachment to the common law and venerated the idea of an independent judiciary, even if they did not accept judicial supremacy and sometimes disputed Federalist interpretations of contract rights and the like. These moderates hesitated to oust Federalist judges from office for what they deemed merely political reasons. The radically democratic segments of the movement, however, were skeptical of the vaunted line between law and politics, eager to assert the people's operative sovereignty as against the common law or any other lawyerly obstacle, and impatient with the persistence in office of judges who denied the democratic character of the Constitution. The battle between a legalist Constitution and a democratic Constitution, therefore, was fought within the Republican movement, as well as between the Republicans and the Federalists.

### BUILDING A FEDERALIST JUDICIARY

The first Congress created a modest number of federal courts subordinate to the constitutionally mandated Supreme Court. When President

Washington began to appoint judges, he naturally chose men whom he deemed friends to the new Constitution, which they would be sworn to implement. Ratification had not eliminated the serious tensions within American politics and law, and it seemed prudent and logical to Washington and Adams that appointments go to men who were decisive friends to the infant Constitution. For the nascent opposition, though, the resulting appointments seemed more partisan than logical.

Although Washington's appointees were not members of a modern-style party, because none yet existed, their ideological leanings were often pretty clear. And the intensifying ideological split between Federalists and Republicans across the 1790s only made more obvious the political character of the judiciary. For example, as paraphrased by a Federalist newspaper, Justice William Paterson opened a session of court in New Hampshire with a public reminder of the danger posed by the "Jacobins," that is, the Republican "disorganizers of our happy country, and the only instruments of introducing discontent and dissatisfaction among the well-meaning part of the Community." The report of the jury charge avowed no partisanship but only a veneration for "good government, good order and good laws."[1] Republicans, however, saw such attacks as an abuse of office and an unabashed example of judicial partisanship.

Among Federalist judges few matched Justice Samuel Chase's ideological intensity and partisanship. During the Sedition Crisis, Chase emerged as one of the most detested of the Federalist judges. His sentencing of one Republican rabble-rouser to an eighteen-month jail term represented the most severe sentence among the ten or so convictions under the Sedition Act, all of them directed at Republicans and most of them at the press. Chase frustrated every constitutional argument made by Republican lawyers and refused to let them use the jury as a mechanism to question the constitutionality of the Sedition Act. Chase forbade juries from doing anything more than fact-finding and provided instructions that all but sealed the fate of those unlucky enough to come before him on sedition charges.

By the late 1790s, then, the opposition had all but given up on the federal judiciary as then constituted. If the Federalist courts would not defend the Constitution, as Republicans saw it, then Republicans would

---

[1] "Circuit Court," *The United States Oracle of the Day* (Portsmouth, New Hampshire) May 24, 1800.

resort to a range of political devices for shaping the meaning of the Constitution in defiance of the courts. As described in Chapter 2, the Republican legislatures of Virginia and Kentucky offered their famous Resolutions of 1798–1799 to correct the courts' reading of the First and Tenth Amendments. Although this effort failed to gain the support it sought from other legislatures, it galvanized a popular movement that would triumph in Jefferson's so-called Revolution of 1800. Unrestrained by Madisonian and Jeffersonian notions of elite leadership, populist political organizers had already experimented with the notion that pure democratic will was the ultimate constitutional authority. The Democratic–Republican Societies of the mid-1790s had hinted at the Republican organization that would emerge in 1800. And episodes of popular constitutional assertiveness in defiance of judicial authority had punctuated the 1790s, especially in the Whiskey Rebellion and in Georgia's Yazoo controversy of 1796, in which the people of the state bypassed the courts and rose up to nullify a massive, corrupt land grant by their legislature. The Revolution of 1800, then, manifested the people's determination to control the meaning of the Constitution without regard to the views of the Federalist judiciary.

After the Republican triumph, the Federalists realized that strengthening their hold on the judiciary might be their only means to prevent the Republicans from undoing the hard-won victories of the previous decade. The project of reforming the judiciary had been agitated since shortly after the enactment of the 1789 Judiciary Act and had been given serious legislative attention beginning at least a year before the 1800 election. The culmination of these efforts was the Judiciary Act of 1801. This statute addressed a number of practical problems, including the justices' well-justified desire that circuit-riding be eliminated and that justices no longer sit on the circuit courts, whose decisions they regularly reviewed at the Supreme Court. But the Act also manifested the Federalist design to neutralize "Jacobin" opposition in the states by extending federal power into the localities. Some Federalists regretted that the government had not established a standing army for this purpose. Most, however, looked to a strong judiciary to achieve order and win over the people by demonstrating that it could bring fair and uniform law to every community.

Thus, in the run-up to the election of 1800, Federalist Congressman Theodore Sedgwick argued the case for judicial power to a colleague: "[M]uch may and ought to be done to give efficiency to the government, and to repress the efforts of the Jacobins against it. We ought to spread out the judicial so as to render the justice of the nation acceptable to the people, to aid national economy, to overawe the licentious, and to punish the guilty."[2] After the election, one Federalist paper claimed that, in the absence of a standing army, such an extension of the judiciary had always been part of the Federalist plan for establishing order: "If free governments can ever be maintained without a *standing army* it can only be effected by a firm, independent, and extensive Judiciary." Indeed, according to this paper, the Federalists had long sought "to extend the protecting power of the Judiciary to every part of the Union, and to every case provided in the Constitution" but had been undone by their own "timidity" in the First Congress.[3] In the wake of the Republican triumph of 1800, the paper suggested that the law remained the last hope for the Federalist program: Judicial power would replace the traditional mechanisms that had been employed by European monarchies and English court politicians alike, to defend order against anarchy.

If the 1789 Act had been too timid in its objectives, the 1801 revision manifested a determination to enhance judicial power. Thus the Judiciary Act of 1801 created general federal question jurisdiction without regard to amount in controversy, finally empowering the federal courts to hear any case that turned on federal law. Further, the Act removed minimum value restrictions from the vitally important category of land cases in diversity; that is, land cases between citizens of different states. It also reduced the minimum for other types of diversity cases, created exclusive bankruptcy jurisdiction in the federal courts, and significantly increased the number of cases that defendants could remove from state to federal court, among other expansions of federal jurisdiction. Moreover, this new jurisdiction would be exercised by an expanded judiciary with sixteen new circuit judges, all of whom were expected to be Federalists.

The effect was to transfer control over important public policies from state judges to federal. Federal judges gained the power to adjudicate the rights to millions of acres of disputed lands across many states, including especially Georgia, Virginia, Kentucky, and Pennsylvania and, in doing so, to upend those states' own land policies. Similarly, these changes

---

[2] Congressman Theodore Sedgwick to Rufus King, November 15, 1799, in Maeva Marcus, ed., *The Documentary History of the Supreme Court of the United States, 1789–1800* (1992), 4: 616.
[3] "Consistent Federalist," *Columbian Centinel* (Boston), January 14, 1801.

promised to bring much commercial litigation and thus commercial law under the control of the federal courts. Most Federalists, and some Republicans, undoubtedly believed that such reforms would bring a uniform system of justice and greater protection for the rights of property to many who had been beyond the reach of the courts. Most Republicans, however, saw Federalist policy in more sinister terms: an effort to centralize power further, deprive ordinary Americans of access to local juries sympathetic to their plights, and further limit the authority of state legislatures.

The Act thus became an object of fear and hatred to many of the most outspoken leaders of the Republican opposition. The fact that Federalists had rammed the policy through the lame-duck session only sharpened Republican hostility. The Federalists determined not only to get the Act through before the Republicans took over but also to ensure the appointment of exclusively Federalist judges, no matter what haste and compromise were necessary to fill these life-tenured offices. The Act also increased the number of federal officers such as clerks, attorneys, and marshals. The creation of this swarm of federal "placemen" conjured up the worst images associated with traditional Whig fears of corruption.

The Federalists' lame-duck scramble to secure the judiciary had numerous consequences. For one, it produced the "midnight appointment" of William Marbury. This appointment would provide the factual underpinnings for *Marbury v. Madison*,[4] one of the most famous confrontations between the Federalists and the Republicans, between the judiciary and the elected branches, and between law and democratic politics after the Revolution of 1800.

*Marbury* would not come before the Supreme Court for two more years, but, when it did, it would find a Chief Justice who had personally facilitated the hasty Federalist appointments and received the most important of them himself. A former Virginia congressman, federal diplomat, and executive officer, as well as lawyer and land speculator, John Marshall understood and feared the consequences of the Republican ascendancy for Federalist legalism. In the postelection winter, therefore, as President Adams's Secretary of State and most important advisor, he launched the Federalist strategy of obstructing Republican

---

[4] *Marbury v. Madison*, 5 U.S. 137 (1803).

constitutionalism through judicial action, a strategy that he would direct from the Chief Justice's post for more than thirty years. He served as Adams's aide in making the nominations of the new federal judges, and he ultimately became Adams's choice for Chief Justice. In the last weeks of his term, Adams rushed Marshall's appointment to ensure that the Federalists would hold all six positions on the Court and retain them all even after the new Judiciary Act eventually reduced the number on the Court to five. Jefferson would have no chance to appoint even one justice until two Federalists had left the Court.

Even as Adams rushed Marshall's appointment through to unanimous confirmation in the Senate, moreover, he had Marshall continue as Secretary of State, holding one of the highest posts in the executive branch even after assuming leadership of the judicial branch on February 4. Among the duties that Marshall continued to perform as Secretary was that of delivering the sealed commissions to Adams's numerous judicial appointees. It was his failure in that executive duty with respect to William Marbury that generated the *Marbury* case, which he would so famously decide in his judicial role as Chief Justice.

It is easy and no doubt accurate enough to label the fevered moves by Marshall and the Federalists "partisan." Still, it seems clear that they earnestly considered their steps essential for the protection of the Constitution and the rule of law against wild-eyed, democratic schemes to undermine property, contract, and social order. Thus, in the midst of Adams's struggle to appoint a Chief Justice, his son John Quincy Adams reminded him that "an upright judiciary is the only bulwark that can oppose & restrain the impetuous torrent of division & disorganization with which this Continent is threatened."[5] Charles Cotesworth Pinckney, who had been a Federalist delegate to the Philadelphia Convention in 1788, greeted news of Marshall's nomination happily: "At a time when attempts are making to construe away the energy of our constitution, to unnerve our Government, & to overthrow that system by which we have risen to our present prosperity, it is all important that our supreme Judiciary should be filled by men of elevated talents, sound federal principles & unshaken firmness."[6] As much as the Judiciary Act was a product of political will, Federalists were convinced its passage was not an act of partisanship but done in the service of law and country.

[5] Quoted in Kathryn Turner, "The Appointment of Chief Justice Marshall," *The William and Mary Quarterly*, Third Series, vol. 17, No. 2 (April 1960), 143–163, 148.
[6] Quoted in Turner, "Appointment," 162–163.

Unsurprisingly, few Republicans approved of the Federalists' lame-duck behavior. Talk of repeal emerged almost immediately. Still, many Republicans hesitated because the Act seemed to accomplish some legitimate reforms. Complicating matters further were the constitutional impediments to repeal that moderate members of the Republican coalition identified. As distasteful as Adams's pattern of appointments had been, the appointees now held Article III offices that the Constitution guaranteed as long as they refrained from "high crimes and misdemeanors." Thus, even in the glow of Jefferson's electoral triumph and anger over Federalist overreach, many Republicans were reluctant to abandon the notion of law as a salutary constraint on democratic will.

Not all members of Jefferson's coalition, however, were so concerned about honoring legal principles that might stunt their efforts at reform. Some went so far as to advocate constitutional amendments to limit federal judicial power. Jefferson's fellow Virginian Edmund Pendleton proposed that the judiciary be appointed and removable by Congress. Other radical voices sought to use the impeachment power to rein in Federalist judges or to curb the use of the common law in federal court. Although such proposals gained some traction in some states, they made little progress in Congress. For the moment, the effort to repeal the 1801 Act marked the outer limit of Republican judicial reform.

Jefferson himself exemplified both the legalist and majoritarian approaches to the question of repeal and to the law more generally. He initially bore serious, legalist scruples as to the constitutionality of repeal. But he soon found himself provoked by the filing of a petition in the Supreme Court by Marbury and others. In December of 1801, Marbury asked the Court to compel the Jefferson administration to deliver his commission, which Marshall had left undelivered at the close of the Adams administration. When the Court agreed to hear argument in the next term and presumed to order Secretary of State Madison to appear, Jefferson's remaining scruples disappeared in a wave of indignation. At this moment, Jefferson famously wrote that the Federalists had "retired into the Judiciary as a strong hold ... and from that battery all the works of Republicanism are to be beaten down & erased."[7] Now, he determined

---

[7] "From Thomas Jefferson to John Dickinson, December 19, 1801," *Founders Online*, National Archives, last modified June 29, 2017, http://founders.archives.gov/documents/Jefferson/01-36-02-0090. (Original source: *The Papers of Thomas Jefferson*, vol. 36, *1 December 1801–3 March 1802*, ed. Barbara B. Oberg [Princeton, NJ: Princeton University Press, 2009, 165–166.])

to see the repeal through without regard to constitutional niceties. And the repeal did go through in the new session of Congress, but not without controversy and not without tension within the Republican ranks. Significant numbers of moderates might well have opposed the bill – because of constitutional objections or because the new courts were genuinely useful – but for Jefferson's powerful influence.

Having thrown down a challenge to Jefferson in the early phases of the *Marbury* case in 1801, only to see Congress repeal the 1801 Judiciary Act, the Court soon acquiesced in the constitutional politics of the moment. As will be discussed later, the Court would largely back down in *Marbury*, though salvaging an important rhetorical victory. More relevant here, it quietly accepted the repeal of the Judiciary Act of 1801 in the 1803 case of *Stuart v. Laird*.

In that case, Stuart objected to the jurisdiction of the lower federal court to which his case had been transferred under the repeal statute. He argued that that statute had violated Article III when it eliminated the positions of life-tenured judges. Chief Justice Marshall and others on the Court are known to have considered the 1802 repeal unconstitutional, but with Marshall recusing himself, the Court unanimously accepted the constitutionality of the statute. The opinion was brief and opaque, simply accepting Congress's general power to transfer cases from one court to another, without explicitly addressing the lawyers' extended arguments as to why this particular transfer might be unconstitutional. (The Court also tersely rejected the contention that the repeal's restoration of circuit-riding was unconstitutional. Regardless of the original meaning of the Constitution, Justice Paterson wrote, "practice and acquiescence under it for a period of several years, commencing with the organization of the judicial system, affords an irresistible answer, and has indeed fixed the construction."[8])

When faced with a square test of its power relative to that of Congress and the president, the Court did not stoutly defend the law and constitutional rights as it saw them. Rather, it pragmatically accommodated itself to the dominant politics of the moment. Had the court struck down the repeal statute in defense of its legalist principles, it would have forced a confrontation with a Congress that was already firing up the machinery of impeachment to remove Federalist judges in the name of popular sovereignty.

---

[8] *Stuart v. Laird*, 5 U.S. 299, 309 (1803).

## SEPARATION OF POWERS AND POPULAR SOVEREIGNTY

The construction and reconstruction of the federal judiciary in the Acts of 1789, 1801, and 1802 occurred within the frame of the Constitution's separation of powers. The Constitution created three branches of the federal government and more or less carefully defined the powers of each. In theory, this separation ensured that every exercise of power might be checked by other exercises of power. Different arms of the government could check each other because their functions designedly overlapped: the president might veto legislation; the Senate would deliberate on presidential appointments; the courts would review the acts of the other branches.

The extent of this overlap, however, could never be defined with precision. What, for example, were the obligations of judges under Article III? Were they free to accept assignments from the executive branch? Most of the early Supreme Court Justices concluded that they were and repeatedly accepted such assignments. Chief Justices Jay and Ellsworth both undertook diplomatic missions while on the Court. Some Justices accepted the role of federal pension commissioner during their tenure.

Advisory opinions posed similar difficulties. Would judges overstep their bounds by offering opinions on legal questions before cases raising those questions reached their courts? Or were judges obliged to offer legal opinions when asked, thus participating in the legislative and executive processes? Some of the Justices publicly delivered advisory opinions in 1792 when the constitutionality of the Invalid Pensioners Act was brought into question. And many Justices offered advisory opinions to executive officers and others both formally and informally in a variety of circumstances during the 1790s, apparently with no more qualms than the many state judges who have written formal advisory opinions from that day to this. In 1793, however, the Justices famously declined to offer an advisory opinion, when requested by President Washington, regarding questions of international law and treaty obligations between the United States and France. The Justices' position has sometimes been taken to mean that they deemed themselves constitutionally barred from giving advisory opinions. But, in fact, the Justices seem to have been moved only by a prudent desire to avoid a heated controversy between the Franco-phile Jefferson and the Anglophile Hamilton (and their followers).

With respect to the judiciary's power to review other branches' actions for constitutionality, again some measure of uncertainty existed but no major controversy in the early years under the Constitution. The

1787 North Carolina case of *Bayard v. Singleton*[9] reflected the consensus logic of judicial review even under the state constitutions. A North Carolina court relied on the state's constitution to invalidate a state statute that barred loyalists from trying their claims to forfeited lands. James Iredell, a leading North Carolina lawyer, counsel in *Bayard,* and a future Justice of the U.S. Supreme Court, explained the logic of this judicial power in a newspaper essay of 1786: If all branches of the government, including the judiciary, were bound by a constitution that represented the sovereign people's will, and if a case presented judges with two conflicting laws, one the act of the legislature and the other the act of the sovereign people, then the judiciary must apply the constitution (the act of the people) and disregard the statute (merely the act of the legislature). The judges were not reaching beyond their office to strike down the acts of the legislature, but were simply applying controlling law to the adjudication of the case before them; to do otherwise would be to act unlawfully themselves and violate their judicial oaths. This straightforward argument underlay the broad support for judicial review among the nation's lawyers and judges, including many of the delegates at the Philadelphia Convention. It also purported to show how popular sovereignty and judicial review harmonized rather than conflicted.

During ratification, Federalists assumed the power of judicial review and when necessary defended it, particularly in Hamilton's *Federalist No. 78,* which celebrated the judicial role even as it disclaimed judicial supremacy. Like others before him, Hamilton insisted that judicial review reflected the supremacy of the people over legislators and judges alike, not the supremacy of the judiciary over the legislature. Moreover, as a practical matter, he reminded his readers, judges had the power of neither purse nor sword to enforce their decisions. Enforcement required the support of the executive. The judiciary was therefore "the least dangerous branch," posing little threat to the sovereignty or liberty of the people.

Opposition to the judicial power of constitutional review did appear among the more radical wing of Anti-Federalists. For them, the jury was the proper arbiter of constitutionality, not the judiciary. Other Anti-Federalists looked to the legislature, not the courts, as the primary enforcer of rights. And indeed a legislature or two in the 1780s had tried to discipline courts for finding particular statutes void under their constitutions. These legislatures had supposed that they, not the courts, were

[9]  1 NC 5 (1787).

the most reliable agents of the popular sovereigns. Finally, among the most radical voices, ultimate constitutional judgment might reside in the militia or even the people themselves assembled as the crowd. In the face of all these views, however, judicial review rapidly became an accepted power under the new Constitution, as anticipated by Iredell, Hamilton, and others.

In 1792, for example, a federal circuit court invalidated a Rhode Island stay law under the Contracts Clause. The same year, federal judges considered the federal Invalid Pensioners Act, which imposed certain administrative duties on the circuit courts and made their decisions reviewable by Congress. The judges generally considered the Act an unconstitutional incursion on judicial independence under Article III. Some chose therefore not to perform the statutory duties (although others devised a strained construction of the Act in order to render it valid). In *VanHorne's Lessee v. Dorrance* (1795), Justice Paterson on circuit over-rode a Pennsylvania statute as inconsistent with both the Pennsylvania constitution's guarantee of the jury right and its guarantee of fundamental property rights. In *Ware v. Hylton* (1796), the Supreme Court itself invalidated a Virginia sequestration statute under the Supremacy Clause because the statute conflicted with the Treaty of Paris. The Court also gave full consideration to the constitutionality of the federal carriage tax in *Hylton v. U.S.* (1796), ultimately upholding it on the merits.[10]

This notion of judicial review as a defense of the sovereignty of the people was widely embraced from the beginnings of the new federal government, and few of these early cases raised much of a ruckus. The new Republican ascendancy, however, caused Marshall and the Federalists to fear for the integrity of the law at the hands of the unprincipled democrats now in power. Under Marshall's leadership, consequently, the isolated Federalist judiciary launched its campaign on behalf of law and the judicial power as a counterweight – rather than a complement – to popular sovereignty. In this context, the Federalist judiciary would stretch its acknowledged powers as far as it could get away with. Prudently avoiding confrontation in *Stuart v. Laird*, Marshall and the Court managed to use *Marbury* to commence the campaign for judicial supremacy on constitutional questions. Whereas judicial *review* was embraced by most Republicans as well as virtually all Federalists, judicial *supremacy* was a peculiarly Federalist fetish. Thus, in cases that would not force a

---

[10] *VanHorne's Lessee v. Dorrance*, 2 U.S. 304 (C.C.D.Pa. 1795); *Ware v. Hylton*, 3 US 199 (1796); *Hylton v. U.S.*, 3 U.S. 171 (1796).

losing confrontation with the elected branches, the Court found ways to claim a specially authoritative power over questions of law, as against the other two branches of government and even the "sovereign" people.

The Court's first major vehicle for its legalist ambition after the election turned out to be the 1803 case of *Marbury v. Madison*. Marbury sought a writ of mandamus to compel Secretary of State Madison to deliver his commission as justice of the peace for the District of Columbia. Marshall understood, however, that the Court was unlikely to benefit from issuing a direct order that Madison would ignore. Marshall thus took the indirect route to vindicating the courts' authority to "say what the law is." Striking down the statutory provision that purported to empower the Court to issue a mandamus, he avoided a losing confrontation with Madison and Jefferson. At the same time, however, he made a point of puffing the Court's chest a bit by exercising the power of judicial review. Even more important, he claimed the resulting space to lecture the executive on its legal obligation to deliver the commission to Marbury. The Court thus claimed a special authority over questions of law even when it had no case to decide; that is, even when a decision belonged to the executive alone.

It is possible to argue that, in *Marbury*, Marshall did not claim judicial supremacy but only defended the ordinary, limited power of judicial review; that is, the unavoidable judicial power to "say what the law is"[11] in the course of an adjudication. He never said that the other branches lacked power to interpret the Constitution in the course of their own duties; he only explained his own institution's parallel power and the Court's conclusion that the mandamus statute conflicted with the Constitution. If that were the end of the story, then Marshall could be counted as a "departmentalist" in the same vein as Jefferson, who agreed that judges must interpret the Constitution in the normal course of their duties but also held that the president and Congress – the executive and legislative "departments" – must do the same, with no branch entitled to any greater authority over constitutional meaning than that of any other branch.

However, reading the opinion as a whole, it is clear that Marshall meant to claim special judicial authority on legal questions generally. After all, the main business of the *Marbury* case was not the low-stakes review of the mandamus statute. Rather, the evident purpose of the opinion was to vindicate the Court and the law as against the mere will

---

[11] *Marbury*, 177.

of the president and the Republican Party. Thus, despite the Court's conclusion that it lacked authority to afford a remedy, it explained at length Marbury's legal right to his office and the president's legal obligation to deliver the commission, concluding that, "having this legal title to the office, he has a consequent right to the commission; a refusal to deliver which, is a plain violation of that right" under "the laws of his country."[12] Marshall's justification for his elaborate and forceful dicta was the judicial-supremacist claim that, "The question whether a right has vested or not, is, in its nature, judicial, and must be tried by the judicial authority."[13] The Court's elaborate legal reasoning and its rhetoric of "vested rights" and "legal title to the office" projected a distinctive judicial voice and tone, designed to naturalize a judicial ideology that portrayed the Constitution as law that neither the executive branch nor even a democratic majority could be trusted with or perhaps even understand. Rather, in a republic of laws, the elected branches and the people themselves must take their guidance from the Court. Marshall's opinion thus aimed both to protect the Federalist construction of a judicial fortress – supreme on all questions that could be made out to be "legal" – and to defend the Constitution from the rival claim that majority will was the supreme law.

In the meantime, the radical Republicans went to the opposite, populist extreme, seeking to subordinate the separation of powers to the ultimate authority of the people on questions of constitutional meaning. Giving popular sovereignty an operational meaning never imagined by the Framers or even by Jefferson, they suggested that the final word on every question, be it ever so legal, lay with the people, not the courts or any other branch. Radicals of this stripe came to early prominence in the Georgia Yazoo controversy of 1796. In that episode, the Georgia legislature assumed power to review the constitutionality of a prior legislature's statute – a massive land grant to speculators – without the aid of judicial process and without regard for established principles of contract and property law. That radical offensive would finally make its way to the Court in the *Fletcher* case of 1810, providing Marshall with another chance to vindicate the judiciary as the exclusive oracle of the law. The radicals also played an important role in the repeal of the Judiciary Act, unsuccessfully seeking a constitutional amendment to authorize removal of judges by mere legislative decision. Other radicals resisted even the exercise of judicial review, attacking that power as inconsistent with

[12] *Marbury*, 168.    [13] *Marbury*, 167.

legislative authority and with popular control of the Constitution and laws. Although this position found some modest success at the state level, it never fully prevailed anywhere.

Ohio affords one striking example in which radicals won a temporary victory in limiting judicial power. Ohio was admitted to the Union in 1803 with a constitution that provided for judges to be appointed by the legislature for seven-year terms, removable only by impeachment. Relatively conservative Republicans constituted the initial leadership of the state, but radical Republicans rapidly gained ascendancy in Ohio and would soon challenge the power of judicial review more directly than Congress's Republicans ever dared.

Only three years into statehood, in 1806, the Jefferson County Court of Common Pleas found unconstitutional the so-called Fifty Dollar Act, a jurisdictional statute that forced anyone with a claim smaller than $50 to adjudicate it before a justice of the peace without benefit of a jury. The following year, the Ohio Supreme Court affirmed this ruling in a case called *Rutherford*. In the meantime, the judiciary had also flouted a statute that repealed Ohio's reception of the common law. This statute reflected a strong, popular resentment of judge-made common law in this period. The judges did not find the statute unconstitutional, but they continued to consult the common law on their own authority as a resource for developing rules of decision.

Angered by such deliberate disregard of democratic will, the legislature resolved to discipline the courts. The state Supreme Court's invalidation of the Fifty Dollar Act prompted a legislative resolution declaring that judges lacked the power to "set aside any act of the legislature, by declaring the law unconstitutional . . ."[14] An initial drive for impeachment directed at the state's highest court petered out, but the next elections returned a strong anticourt majority to the lower house. The House then impeached the chief judges of each of the courts that had struck down the Act. Each judge avoided conviction in the Senate by a single vote. Still, some courts declined to treat *Rutherford* as good law, and some of Ohio's elite lawyers, seeking to calm the storm, organized an extraordinary movement to vitiate *Rutherford* by refusing to rely on it in litigation. Meanwhile, the self-styled "Democrats" in the legislature refused to back down, turning to another device to shorten the term of Chief Justice Tod

[14] Quoted in Donald F. Melhorn Jr., *Lest We Be Marshall'd, Judicial Powers and Politics in Ohio, 1806–1812* (Akron, OH: University of Akron Press, 2003) 72. Our account of the battle over judicial review in Ohio generally follows Melhorn.

of the Supreme Court. Tod had been appointed as a replacement justice by the governor amid a general assumption that such appointments would come with a full seven-year term. But the impeachment legislature passed a resolution to substitute a constitutional interpretation that replacements would only serve out the residue of the original term, thus shortening Tod's term by two years and removing him almost immediately.

Some judicial resistance continued here and there, but the ascendant Democratic Republicans appeared to have won the battle. Still, even in Ohio, by the 1820s the practice of judicial review had managed to reassert itself. With the Federalists disintegrating and the new Democratic Party advancing in organization and political dominance, fears of an obstructionist judiciary waned. The result was the practical legitimation of judicial review over time, even as it became mostly marginal to the democratic, party-organized politics of the state. Increasingly, the will of the people – or at least the will of the party – proved much the greatest determinant of the law's content.

A similar story unfolded at the national level, not so much with respect to judicial review – which few challenged in any sustained way – but with respect to the use of impeachment to tame the Federalist judiciary. Like the emergent Ohio Democrats, the radical Republicans in Congress faced the resistance not only of Federalists but also of moderate Republicans, who shared elements of the Federalists' legalist cast of mind. Faced with the solidarity of legalists across parties, the radicals failed to advance a constitutional amendment to bring the judiciary permanently to heel, but they found a bit more success when they turned to impeachment.

The first target was John Pickering of New Hampshire, a notorious drunk who was incompetent to serve by any measure. The use of impeachment as a political tool troubled many, however, including a number of moderate Republicans who doubted that Pickering's deplorable behavior fit the requirement of "high crimes and misdemeanors" for removal from office. The radicals, supported by Jefferson, won over enough members of the Senate to convict Pickering, but the case against their second target, Samuel Chase, was even more challenging.

As a judge, Chase had enthusiastically deployed the Sedition Act in a crusade against Republican newspapermen and had pressed to the limit the prosecution of John Fries, the leader of the short-lived Fries Rebellion, sentencing him to death for treason (though he was ultimately pardoned). More than once in these trials, Chase pressed the case so hard that he drove the defense lawyers to withdraw from representing their clients.

Chase further provoked the Republicans when, in 1803, he delivered a fierce, partisan charge to the Baltimore grand jury, condemning the repeal of the Judiciary Act as well as basic Republican principles of broad suffrage and "equal liberty and equal rights." Thanks to Republican reforms, "Our Republican Constitution will sink into a mobocracy, – the worst of all possible government ..."[15] From that moment on, Jefferson and the radicals were prepared to impeach Chase, and, as soon as Pickering was convicted in March of 1804, they started the wheels in motion.

The problem of course was that moderate Republicans and Federalists insisted that an impeachable offense must be a criminal act, a "high crime" or "misdemeanor" as the Constitution seemed to stipulate. Impeachment, they insisted, should not be used as a political tool. The radicals' strained efforts to characterize Chase's conduct as criminal, compounded by their inclusion of obviously noncriminal charges, drove a wedge between radicals and moderate Republicans.

Meanwhile, Jefferson lost his enthusiasm for the prosecution. Probably, he shared some of the moderates' feeling that the impeachment had become an unnecessary threat to the independence of the federal judiciary, which no longer presented more than an occasional obstacle to Jefferson's goals. More immediately, he saw that his goal of conciliating moderate Federalists and establishing a politics of republican consensus required that he embrace his own more moderate inclinations. This policy was vindicated in Jefferson's 1804 reelection, won with the electoral votes of every state but Delaware and Connecticut, a grand step beyond the narrow victory of 1800 and the merely partisan politics that Jefferson deplored.

Thus, when Chase was tried in 1805, the Senate failed to convict. Still, Chase was humbled, and his remaining years on the bench lacked the partisan bravado that prompted his impeachment. Moreover, Chase's impeachment and a rumored threat to impeach Marshall himself chastened the Federalist judges generally. Even as it showed that Congress might hesitate in the future to intrude into the judicial sphere, it equally established that the judiciary could defend its independence only so long as it plausibly explained its actions as distinctively legal, divorced from politics.

---

[15] Quoted in Richard E. Ellis, *The Jeffersonian Crisis: Courts and Politics in the Young Republic* (New York: Oxford University Press, 1971), 79–80.

The repeal of the Judiciary Act, the impeachments of two federal judges, and similar controversies in some of the states proved important episodes in the settling of the separation of powers. The radicals had sought to substantially dissolve the separation of powers in the sovereignty of the people and their elected representatives. The Federalists had sought to hobble democracy and vindicate judicial supremacy on questions of legal and constitutional meaning. But the most notable victors were Republican moderates, who neutralized the radicals in their own party and managed to rein in the worst excesses of the Federalist judiciary. The postimpeachment settlement on the separation of powers – preserving a distinctive role for judges and law independent from politics and democratic will – did not guarantee a future of apolitical judging, but it established the fundamental language and basic principles of the separation of powers.

## FEDERALISM AND THE COURTS

To turn more directly to the question of federalism in the courts is to turn to the Yazoo controversy and the great case of *Fletcher v. Peck* (1810). As previously noted, Yazoo involved a massive, corrupt land grant by the Georgia legislature, which provoked almost unanimous popular outrage and immediate revocation of the grant by the next-elected Georgia legislature. Fourteen years later, the Supreme Court invalidated the state legislature's revocation statute in the *Fletcher* case, widely deemed a landmark in the history of federalism as the first instance of the Court's striking down a state statute.

*Fletcher* also raised issues of separation of powers, however, much as *Marbury* had, because the question was not just whether the grantees had property and contract rights under the Constitution, but also which branch of government would answer that question. The Yazoo controversy pitted *political and legislative* efforts to settle constitutional questions against *judicial* efforts to claim a monopoly on such questions. More generally, it is important to see that separation of powers and federalism were always intertwined in this period, proponents of a strong judiciary often seeing the courts as the best tools for vindicating national power and common-law principles, and opponents of excessive judicial authority seeing the judges as a constant threat to states' rights and majority will.

By the time *Fletcher* reached the high court, tensions over federalism had become a defining feature of American constitutional debate. The rift that had separated Federalists from Anti-Federalists in 1787–1788 only widened in the decade after the Constitution was ratified and the Bill of Rights adopted. At one extreme stood the radical states' rights theories advanced by Jefferson in the Kentucky Resolutions, building on the confederal theory of republicanism he had adumbrated in the *Summary View* of 1774.[16] At the other stood the Hamiltonian effort to establish a central government powerful enough to anchor an empire.

Chief Justice John Marshall was not a full-fledged, Hamiltonian consolidationist, seeking a British-style regime complete with a standing army and networks of patronage and dependency. Rather, Marshall was the champion of a distinctly legalistic brand of Federalist ideology. Legalism signified for Marshall two main ideas: that civilization rested on fundamental rights of property and contract as developed in the common law, and that the Supreme Court had the final authority to explicate and defend those principles under the Constitution. In his view, the common-law principles of contract and property had undergirded the movement for a new Constitution in 1787 and were incorporated explicitly into the federal Constitution's Contracts Clause. In these respects, it was manifestly the duty of the judiciary to preserve a uniform law without obstruction from individual state governments or popular majorities.

Thus, he was a strong nationalist of a sort but not a consolidationist bent on destroying all state authority; in Marshall's view, state governments would have wide latitude to act within their appropriate spheres of authority demarcated by the Constitution. But states' rights and popular sovereignty did not mean that the people and the states could do whatever they wanted. The Constitution established legal institutions and principles so that even the political branches and the states would be controlled by law. And the law's integrity must be preserved by the expertise and authority of a single legal tribunal, the national Supreme Court, committed to the Constitution and steeped in the common law.

In contrast, the Jeffersonian model of federalism de-emphasized the production of a coherent national law and posited instead the indispensable autonomy of the several republics that constituted the nation. For Jefferson, the state and local governments remained the most authentic organs of the sovereign people. At the foundation of a kind of pyramid of republicanism were the mass of politically equal, white, male citizens, each yielding only so much power over his own life as necessary to maintain civil peace and political equality among the citizenry. As one

[16] Jefferson, *A Summary View of the Rights of British America* (Williamsburg, VA: Clementina Rind, 1774).

moved up the structure of the pyramid, power would be delegated in a limited fashion: local governments yielded only enough power to state government for it to execute its essential functions, those that could not be executed by a government closer to the people. The national government, in turn, might claim from the states only such power as it required to secure peace among the Union's constituent republics and between the Union and the world. While committed to Union, Jeffersonians were not willing to achieve this goal at the expense of the liberty enjoyed by citizens and the states. Jeffersonians were not enemies of a coherent system of law. They did, however, oppose efforts to secure that ideal by creating a powerful central government that would inexorably erode liberty. Therefore, they tended to resist the Marshall Court's accumulation of broad authority, notwithstanding the Court's presence at the only spot in the system from which uniform law might be imparted to the nation.

The point of departure in settling the role of the courts with respect to federalism was the framing and ratification of the Constitution, itself a process of negotiation and compromise resulting in necessary ambiguity. Born of frustration with the Articles of Confederation, the Constitution was a notable step toward consolidation, yet one that Jefferson readily endorsed. It stopped short of extreme consolidation, but it substantially augmented federal power and placed specific limits on the states, most essentially requiring that states refrain from "impairing the obligation of contracts." The Constitution thus arguably imposed traditional principles of contract law on the states. On the other hand, federal power was limited to enumerated categories; nothing in the text incorporated the common law or gave the Supreme Court a monopoly over constitutional meaning; and defenders of states' rights soon secured the Tenth Amendment's reinforcement of that principle. In short, as of 1788, federalism was little more than a flexible principle awaiting practical development.

The Judiciary Act of 1789 appeared to advance the work of consolidation when it established the federal court system as a national arm, intruding into the states, and empowered it to review state court interpretations of federal law. The famous Section 25, for example, granted the Supreme Court jurisdiction to review the judgments of the state courts on federal questions and so enhanced federal judicial control of state institutions and federal law. The provision caused little controversy for a generation, and the Court did occasionally use it to bring state law in line with its vision of the federal Constitution. The Act, however, fell short of creating the imperial establishment that the Anti-Federalists feared, that the Constitution itself arguably permitted, and that the Judiciary Act of 1801 would more closely approach. Reflecting the continuing strength of anticonsolidationist politics, the 1789 Act established only a modest number of federal courts, denied general federal-question jurisdiction to the federal trial courts (although the federal courts did get large and important categories of cases such as admiralty), and imposed strict limits on federal diversity jurisdiction and the Supreme Court's appellate jurisdiction. The ability of the federal courts to reach into the lives of most Americans was therefore somewhat limited, and many cases remained in state courts even when federal law was at issue. The Anti-Federalist fear that citizens would be forced to litigate issues in federal courts hostile to liberty and far from their communities failed to materialize; at least, it never yielded an important political grievance once the Act was functioning.

Defenders of states' rights did, however, react violently when the Court in *Chisholm v. Georgia* (1793)[17] seemed to assert its superiority to a "sovereign" state. Chisholm was a South Carolina resident and creditor of the state of Georgia suing the state for payment. Georgia claimed immunity from suit as a sovereign state. The Court held that Article III's grant of federal jurisdiction in cases "between a State and Citizens of another State" empowered the federal courts to sit in judgment on the states when sued by private parties. This claim of federal judicial power proved highly controversial. Anticipating the issue, some had already argued that, if a mere private person could drag an unwilling state into federal court, the states would "have relinquished all their Sovereignties, and have become mere corporations."[18]

The use of Anti-Federalist rhetoric to oppose the *Chisholm* ruling by some was not surprising. More remarkable was the fact that a Federalist-dominated Congress too rejected the decision, swiftly endorsing the Eleventh Amendment, which was phrased as an implicit rebuke to the judiciary for misunderstanding the original Constitution: "The judicial power of the United States shall not be construed to extend to any suit in law or equity, commenced or prosecuted against one of the United States by citizens of another state, or by citizens or subjects of any foreign state."

---

[17] *Chisholm v. Georgia*, 2 U.S. 419 (1793).

[18] Letter from an Anonymous Correspondent, Philadelphia *Independent Chronicle*, between February 13 and February 19, 1791, reprinted in Marcus, ed., *The Documentary History of the Supreme Court of the United States, 1789–1800*, 5:21.

The states quickly ratified the amendment, overturning *Chisholm* and reaffirming a measure of state sovereign immunity.

A full explanation of the Federalist support for this measure of state autonomy remains elusive. But the evidence suggests a broadly held belief that the 1787 Constitution had implicitly rested on the common-law principle of state sovereign immunity. In fact, in the *Federalist*, Hamilton himself had insisted, "It is inherent in the nature of sovereignty not to be amenable to the suit of an individual without its consent ... [T]here is no color to pretend that the State governments would ... be divested of the privilege of paying their own debts in their own way, free from every constraint but that which flows from the obligations of good faith."[19] Marshall had made the same point in the Virginia ratifying convention: "With respect to disputes between a state and the citizens of another state ... I hope that no gentleman will think that a state will be called at the bar of the federal court. It is not rational to suppose that the sovereign power should be dragged before a court ... If an individual has a just claim against any particular state, is it to be presumed that, on application to its legislature, he will not obtain satisfaction?"[20] *Chisholm* had simply misunderstood the Constitution's presumption of state sovereign immunity, implementing a legalist logic of contract rather than the equally legalist, common-law principle of sovereign immunity.

At the same time, the democratic and localist perspective of the Republicans embraced sovereign immunity as a bulwark against federal consolidation. Like the Judiciary Act before it, the Eleventh Amendment suggested that the legalists and the localists might sometimes agree to see basic principles of private law go unenforced when the alternative was worse. And "worse" might mean consolidation (for the localists), or it might mean violation of a common-law principle like sovereign immunity (for the legalists). Or it might mean something more immediately practical: As it happened, several states at the time, including some Federalist strongholds, faced major lawsuits that the Amendment would allow them to avoid.

Following *Chisholm*, the Supreme Court avoided major controversies over federalism until *Fletcher v. Peck* in 1810.[21] *Fletcher* had its origins in the Yazoo fraud of 1795, in which companies of land speculators bribed

---

[19] *Federalist*, 81, 450.
[20] Jonathan Elliot, ed., *The Debates in the Several State Conventions on the Adoption of the Federal Constitution* (Philadelphia, PA: J. B. Lippincott, 1863), III: 555–556.
[21] *Fletcher v. Peck*, 10 U.S. 87 (1810).

much of the Georgia legislature to execute a huge land sale – most of present-day Alabama and Mississippi – to the companies for a mere $500,000. The speculators' title was thus clouded by the flagrant corruption and also by continuing Indian claims to much of the land, claims that could only be extinguished by the United States. Despite these clouds, the new owners traveled to the northern states and resold their "title" to purchasers who may or may not have been aware of the original fraud. Meanwhile, in Georgia, a political movement arose to invalidate the sale, and in 1796, a newly elected legislature passed "AN ACT declaring null and void a certain usurped act";[22] that is, an act voiding the prior land grant.

Georgia's action – almost unintelligible to us today – asserted the legislature's right to review the constitutionality of legislation, without recourse to the courts and regardless of the federal constitutional protection for contracts. The 1796 Act was not a normal repeal of a statute but a declaration that the 1795 Act had never been law. In this respect, it foreshadowed Jefferson's famous Kentucky Resolutions, which (for all their differences) similarly insisted on a sovereign state's authority to legislatively declare a statute unconstitutional (in that case, the federal Sedition Act) without recourse to the judiciary. The Georgia rescinders (for lack of a better term) might thus have expected the strong support of the Jeffersonian Republican party, defenders of states' rights and extra-judicial constitutional enforcement. But the Georgians had also provocatively challenged some common-law rules of contract. Their actions thus assaulted not just Federalist constitutionalism but also the common-law legalism of many moderate Jeffersonians. For that and other reasons, the Republicans would split badly over the claims of the northern purchasers of the Yazoo lands.

The more-radical Republicans defended Georgia's actions in the language of popular sovereignty and states' rights. For them, such popular constitutional review rested on even firmer footing than did judicial review. The rescinding statute was not a mere legislative act. Rather, it represented the will of the people themselves, who had deputized their representatives to act in a special constitutional capacity in response to exigent circumstances. Local resolutions addressed to a state constitutional convention, declarations of grand juries throughout the state, and popular meetings out-of-doors had specially "invest[ed] this Legislature

---

[22] The Georgia Repeal Act of 1796, reprinted in C. Peter Magrath, *Yazoo: Law and Politics in the New Republic: The Case of Fletcher v. Peck* (New York: Norton, 1967), 127–129.

with conventional powers"; that is, with the powers of the people themselves, as if assembled in convention.[23] The people of Georgia had thus exploited the wide repertoire of "constitutional" options in the early nation to put their sovereignty into practice. In so doing, the people and their delegates in the legislature reviewed the original Act and declared it void – without effect from the moment of its supposed enactment – on the basis of the fraud and other constitutional defects.

This sort of popular constitutional review, however, proved controversial, certainly among Federalists and even among Jeffersonians. Jefferson, Madison, and a moderate minority of the Republican Party would seek a compromise solution, one that would compensate the purchasers of Yazoo land titles in some degree without actually recognizing their titles. Federalists too favored compensation for the grantees, but they more strongly rejected the notion of the people or even legislatures taking questions of legal interpretation into their own hands. Adjudication belonged in courts, just as legislation was delegated to carefully designed legislatures. The people remained sovereign, empowered to elect their representatives and even amend the Constitution. But, for Federalists, "popular sovereignty" had to be bounded by law, by close adherence to judicial reason and the traditions of the common law. In this belief, the Federalists were not far from Jefferson himself, whose First Inaugural insisted "that though the will of the majority is in all cases to prevail, that will, to be rightful, must be reasonable."[24] And they could point to the Constitution of the United States, which placed the judicial power in the courts, not in the people.

The subsequent history of Yazoo, though, demonstrated that constitutional development would rest on the imperatives of political competition and pragmatic compromise, not mainly judicial reasoning. The unwieldy process began immediately after Georgia purported to void the sale and word began to spread that Indian claims might undermine it anyway. A pamphlet by the South Carolina Federalist and participant in the Yazoo speculation, Robert Goodloe Harper,[25] drawing reinforcement from an opinion letter of Alexander Hamilton,[26] made the legalist case

---

[23] Georgia Repeal Act in Magrath, *Yazoo*, 135.

[24] Thomas Jefferson, "First Inaugural Address," in *The Papers of Thomas Jefferson*, vol. 33, 148, 148–152 (1801), *available at* www.princeton.edu/~tjpapers/inaugural/inf inal.html.

[25] Robert Goodloe Harper, *The Case of the Georgia Sales on the Mississippi Considered* (Philadelphia, 1799).

[26] Ibid., Appendix 17, 88–89.

that no legislature could void the enactments of a prior legislature. Rather, "the force, validity, or meaning of a legislative act, is purely a judicial question, and altogether beyond the province of the legislature."[27] Moreover, "[t]his is a fundamental principle of all our constitutions which declare, that the judicial and legislative powers shall be distinct and separate ... As well might the legislature try causes, or hear appeals, as attempt to expound, enforce, or declare void, one of its own acts."[28] Further, even if the merits of the grant were to be considered, Harper's legalist view was that the grants were manifestly contracts and that, "[i]t is an invariable maxim of law, and of natural justice, that one of the parties to a contract, cannot by his own act, exempt himself, from its obligation." Even a state "could no more relieve itself from the obligation, by any act of its own, than an individual, who had signed a bond, could relieve himself from the necessity of payment."[29] By such archetypically legalist arguments – echoing the repudiated *Chisholm* case's subordination of even sovereign states to the courts and the common law – Harper and Hamilton hoped to reassure the public of the validity of the grant and the security of the claims then being sold and resold.

On the opposite side, Abraham Bishop wrote perhaps the most famous anti-Yazoo pamphlet, defending states' rights and the sovereignty of the people in any conflict with the law or the judiciary.[30] Bishop was a Connecticut Republican who evidently purchased a Yazoo claim substantially on credit. As he came to understand the multiple shadows on his title, he wrote the pamphlet as a polemic against the sellers who sought his remaining payments. He asserted, "This is the sovereign independent state of Georgia, having a right to make or repeal their own laws at pleasure, and this right wholly uncontrollable." To him, it was obvious that "a legislature may declare a pretended act void" in any number of circumstances: when pretended to be enacted in the absence of a quorum; when the speaker or president of the body is bribed to misrepresent the outcome of the vote; when necessary votes come from those who have not taken prescribed oaths; and when the act violates the constitution or the votes come from those materially interested in the outcome. Such hypothetical and not so hypothetical circumstances illustrated the point that a state was not the same as a private party to a contract but stood in a

---

[27] Harper, *The Case of the Georgia Sales*, 37.    [28] Ibid., 38.    [29] Ibid.
[30] See Abraham Bishop, *Georgia Speculation Unveiled* (Hartford, CT: Elisha Babcock, 1797).

unique place. It was an independent sovereignty that must be able to control the question of what laws it had enacted and what "pretended acts" it might repudiate as no act of the state at all. "Take this power from a legislature, and where is the sovereignty of the state?"[31]

As Bishop defended states' rights and popular sovereignty, so he dismissed the binding force of the common-law doctrines that Marshall and the Federalists would soon read into the Constitution. Since the Revolution, each state had gained and never relinquished sovereignty, Bishop asserted, and sovereignty trumped "book-principles relating to real estate and to notes" and the legalist notion that "a grant is in its nature irreversible." The very nature of sovereignty precluded the Constitution's subjecting the states to contract law enforceable in federal court: "*an independent power can make, or unmake grants at will; because no power can decide on the morality, equity, or policy of their measures.*" Be legal doctrine what it may, judges and the commercial law had only as much authority as the unreviewable will of the people chose to give them. Even if the sellers had all morality on their side, the fact would remain that the sovereign power on the other side was "beyond their control."[32] Law ultimately emanated from the sovereign will of the people and was premised on ideas of justice that were superior to common-law legalism. Moreover, although Bishop's polemic did not mention it, the Supreme Court's recent failure in *Chisholm* offered Bishop good grounds for treating state sovereignty as a given. The Court had attempted in *Chisholm v. Georgia* to render the states suable in federal court and thus subject to the general law of contracts, only to be soundly undone by the new Eleventh Amendment's affirmation of state sovereignty.

The pamphlets helped set the terms of constitutional debate, but the fate of the Yazoo claimants fell to Congress. In 1802, Congress made the Yazoo problem its own by purchasing Georgia's claims to the disputed lands (much as it had negotiated cession of western lands from several other states). The agreement reserved five million acres of the territory as a fund to satisfy any outstanding claims and promised that the United States would extinguish any Indian title as quickly as practicable. But the Republicans in Congress were divided, both by constitutional principles and by competing views of how to protect Republican political ascendancy against the continuing threat of Federalist aristocracy. Many Republicans might have wanted to support their fellows in Georgia, but many of

[31] Ibid., 11–12.    [32] Ibid., 24–25 (italics in original).

the northern purchasers of the Georgia lands were New England Republicans who expected support from their political allies in Congress.

At the same time, Congress created a commission of cabinet luminaries
(Secretary of State James Madison, Secretary of the Treasury Albert
Gallatin, and Attorney General Levi Lincoln) to investigate the claims to
the territory and propose a resolution. Evidently expressing the views of
the Jefferson administration, the commissioners transmitted their report
to Congress in February 1803. In the report, these moderates avoided
vindicating popular constitutional control and distanced themselves from
the idea that "the Legislature of the State of Georgia was competent" to
void the land grant. At the same time, they expressed "no hesitation" in
agreeing with Georgia that "the title of the claimants cannot be supported" on the merits. Still, the commissioners advocated pragmatic
compromise to serve "the interests of the United States, the tranquility
of those who may hereafter inhabit that territory, and various equitable
considerations which may be urged in favor of most of the present
claimants."[33]

The report thus tried to straddle the positions of different parts of the
Republican Party in the interests of intraparty peace and enabling white
settlement in the southwest. It opened room for political compromise as it
refused to embrace either a legalist defense of the purchasers' titles or a
populist endorsement of the Georgia Legislature's Repeal Act. But compromise would emerge only after years of congressional struggle.

Led by Virginia's John Randolph, the radicals in the House generally
could command a majority of the party but only a minority of the House.
Still, that was enough to thwart compromise session after session. Thus,
the radicals were able to defend a status quo that reflected their constitutional populism. When legislators act "to promote their own private
ends," they proposed to the House, "it is the inalienable right of a
people ... to revoke the authority thus abused, to resume the rights thus
attempted to be bartered, and to abrogate the act thus endeavoring to
betray them."[34] Moreover, the radicals defended an instance of populist
constitutional action in which it seemed genuinely clear that the state's
white men had spoken with virtually one voice. In the congressional

---

[33] James Madison, Albert Gallatin, and Levi Lincoln, Georgia Land Claims, H.R. Doc. No.
7–74 (February 16, 1803), reprinted in Walter Lowrie, ed., *American State Papers, Public
Lands*, vol. 1 (Washington, DC: Duff Green, 1834), 120, 122.

[34] Resolutions introduced by the congressional radicals (though never adopted by the
House) at *Annals of Cong.*, 13 (1804), 1039.

debate, no one disputed that the grand juries and public gatherings that responded to the grant uniformly opposed it and that, indeed, the electorate formally ratified the voiding of the original grant in a provision of the new Georgia Constitution of 1798. Federalists and moderate Republicans thus had to rely on claims that legal doctrine should trump the sovereign will of the people and the state. But Randolph insisted for the radicals that, "Attorneys and judges do not decide the fate of empires."[35] The case might be about land titles, but it did not belong in court. Rather, it belonged in the hands of the people of Georgia.

Exasperated moderate Republicans tried to lower the stakes. They insisted that the proposal did not involve the eternal fate of republicanism in its struggle with Federalist aristocracy. Rather, a compromise would simply reflect that the claimants, including numerous northern Republicans, had just enough color to their legal claims that it behooved the United States to settle and remove the clouds on a vast tract of land.

Debates over the Yazoo claims resurfaced in one Congress after another, but for years the radicals maintained enough strength to prevent any authorization of a settlement. The Yazooists consequently turned their attention to the courts. In fact, the collusive suit of *Fletcher v. Peck* had been pending without action in federal court in Massachusetts since June 1803. The parties were the buyer and seller of claims to substantial Yazoo lands, Fletcher nominally challenging Peck's title. But, in reality, both hoped for a ruling that the claims were good so that Peck could sell and Fletcher could buy with profit to both. But the suit did not move forward in 1803 or for the next several years while Congress wrangled over a possible compromise. By 1806, however, Congress had repeatedly failed to produce a compensation law, and the courts newly looked like the most eligible avenue for the Yazoo claimants. So the *Fletcher* case was finally tried to a pro-Yazoo conclusion. But that was only the first step because only a Supreme Court holding would apply nationwide and have the sort of influence in Congress that the Yazooists wanted.

The case would now go up to the Supreme Court with at least the formal potential to grant the Yazooists the entire, vast tract of land. And when the case got there, it found a Chief Justice who was himself both a seasoned land speculator and a vigorous common-law legalist. Although three of the five justices who would decide the case were Jefferson

---

[35] *Annals of Cong.*, 14 (1805), 1029–1030.

appointees, they generally shared Marshall's legalism and mostly embraced his view of the case.[36]

Marshall's opinion largely recapitulated the legalist arguments that had been made at length by the pro-compromise members of Congress, stressing the sanctity of contracts, the special authority of the judiciary, and the subordinate position of the people's immediate sense of justice. Marshall insisted that the land grant was a contract within the meaning of the federal Contracts Clause. He then offered a disingenuous tribute to state sovereignty by embracing the legislature's original land grant. The Court would not disregard a statute bearing all the forms of a Georgia law, he said. Of course, there was little doubt that, in the most innocent version of events, the 1795 legislators had engaged in massive self-dealing, and further that Georgia had already decided for itself that the 1795 Act was no law, going so far as to embed that determination in its constitution. But, for Marshall, the people of a state had no power to say what its law was. The people, he insisted, could only act through their constitutionally authorized agents, not on their own. The task of declaring the law was for judges, not the people, and no court could recognize a state's attempt to "devest" property rights. Rather, "certain great principles of justice," "those rules which would have regulated the decision of a judicial tribunal," must always govern, and those rules included the rule of equity that protected good faith purchasers, even when sold a defective title. To suppose otherwise, Marshall argued, was to disregard the law and usurp the place of the judiciary. Moreover, recognition of the legislature's voiding of the sale would flout the federal Constitution's "bill of rights for the people of each state"; that is, the Contracts Clause, accompanied by the bans on bills of attainder and ex post facto laws. To Marshall and other Federalists, Georgia's legislature exhibited exactly the vices of the legislatures of the 1780s, the same flouting of established principles of justice that the Constitution had been designed to prevent.

The Yazooists' resounding judicial victory, however, did not put money in their pockets. Various obstacles remained to their claiming and reselling land that was in a distant location and that, in many cases, already had settlers on it, some of them white newcomers and some of them Indian nations long in place. So they returned to Congress once again. There, the Court's opinion no doubt had some influence, but no

---

[36] The Jeffersonian Justice Johnson did write a separate opinion of some interest, departing from Marshall on important points, but Johnson did not substantially deviate from Marshall's legalist approach.

one considered actually implementing the logical remedy implied by the court – recognition of the title of the claimants to the vast area that would soon constitute most of Alabama and Mississippi. Rather, radical Republican orthodoxy continued to impede the progress of a compensation bill until the imperative of facilitating settlement finally overcame that obstruction as well as lingering congressional doubts about the "'strict legality' of the claimants' title."[37] In 1814, Congress at last enacted a compensation law, appropriating the long-reserved five million acres for the purpose of settling the claims. The Yazooists, for their part, unhesitatingly accepted this roughly one-eighth compensation for the "titles" that the Court had impotently recognized.

## CONCLUSION

*Fletcher*'s failure to control the question of the Yazoo claims demonstrated that the Court was just one of several important sources of legal and constitutional meaning, despite its own efforts in *Marbury* and *Fletcher* to claim supremacy on legal questions. Yazoo thus illuminated the range of constitutionalisms available in the generation after ratification. On the Supreme Court and among the Federalists, common-law legalism reigned. The Court deemed itself the only competent and legitimate source of legal interpretation. And it used its special status to sanctify those rights of property and contract that it deemed the core values of the Constitution and indeed the foundation of civilization itself. To Marshall, the importance of *Marbury* and *Fletcher* lay not in their entrenchment of judicial review but in their vindication of a Court-controlled, common-law Constitution to which the people and their representatives must conform.

At the other extreme, the heirs of the radical Anti-Federalists embraced brave acts of popular sovereignty like the repudiation of the land grant by the people of Georgia. No rule of the common law and no court could claim authority superior to that of the people's clearly stated will. They insisted on a populist Constitution that empowered the people to override the doings of their legislatures and their courts alike, determining for themselves when their agents had strayed from their delegated tasks and reserving to themselves the final authority to say what the law was.

---

[37] Magrath, *Yazoo*, 94 (quoting the report of a select committee of the House).

Meanwhile, the moderate, legalist Republicans insisted on a Constitution that neither relied on direct popular control of legal claims nor erased popular will in deference to judicial claims of special expertise. Rather, consistent with Jefferson's departmentalist approach to constitutional interpretation, all branches of government and the people themselves had rightful claims to interpret the Constitution when acting within their legitimate spheres. The people of Georgia might instruct their legislature to disregard an act they disapproved. Marshall and the Court would independently interpret the law and the Constitution when resolving Fletcher's controversy with Peck. But none of that prevented Congress too from stepping in to interpose a statutory settlement of all claims. That settlement became final not because the courts or the people were constitutionally required to accede to Congress's will but because, by 1814, resistance to settlement had faded enough to clear the constitutional path.

The moderate Republicans had also eked out other important wins. Although some would have preferred not to repeal the Federalists' 1801 Judiciary Act, they at least prevented the radicals from bringing the judiciary under immediate legislative supervision. They also prevented the conviction of the impeached Justice Chase, cementing the informal settlement that preserved an independent judiciary as long as that judiciary restrained its political ambitions and stuck to disposing of cases. All of these messy results made clear that the meaning of the Constitution would evolve in fits and starts, not as the working out of a single principle but as the product of a fluid constitutional politics.

Future constitutional controversies, similarly, might be settled by popular movements, by state action, by congressional action, or by the courts, as circumstances dictated. But no dogma of constitutional authority would ever grasp final victory.

# 4

# The Paradoxes of Jeffersonian Constitutionalism

## INTRODUCTION

Looking back two decades after his election in 1800, Thomas Jefferson wrote that his triumph over Adams was "as real a revolution in the principles of our government as that of [17]76 was in its form; not effected indeed by the sword, as that, but by the rational and peaceable instrument of reform, the suffrage of the people."[1] The Republican ascendancy seemed at first to promise the sort of partyless, republican governance that Madison had anticipated in 1787 and even in 1792. At the height of Hamilton's influence, Madison had explained that Hamilton's antirepublican program must ultimately fail because the people's commitment to republicanism was guaranteed. Their "superiority of numbers is so great, their sentiments are so decided, and the practice of making a common cause ... so well understood, that no temperate observer of human affairs [would] be surprised" when eventually they triumphed over Hamilton and the Federalists.[2] Rather than uniting the great body of the people, however, Jefferson's Revolution generated new challenges and revived with a renewed sense of urgency longstanding divisions. Ongoing opposition from the Federalists remained, but so too did latent tensions from within his own Republican movement, rifts that only intensified over time. Indeed, Jefferson's presidency split his own coalition and helped revive the fading fortunes of the Federalists for a

---

[1] Thomas Jefferson to Spencer Roane, September 6, 1819, http://press-pubs.uchicago.edu/founders/documents/a1_8_18s16.html.
[2] James Madison, "A Candid State of Parties," *National Gazette*, September 26, 1792.

time. The tense but ultimately peaceful transfer of power from Adams to Jefferson solved few of the lingering issues that had divided Americans since ratification.

Jefferson firmly believed that his election had given him a mandate from the people. He planned to restore a Constitution premised on states' rights and limited federal power, one that would liberate the white yeomanry – "the chosen people of God, if ever he had a chosen people"[3] – from Hamilton's neo-British state of commerce, manufacturing, and war. In his First Inaugural Address Jefferson imagined an America that was populated by innumerable farmsteads, a "chosen country, with room enough for our descendants to the thousandth and thousandth generation." To remain a virtuous yeoman republic, a confederated "empire for liberty," the nation would spread westward, expanding its geographical boundaries. Hamilton's vision was committed to economic development, Jefferson's to geographical expansion. Even before Jefferson knew that the Louisiana Territory's unimaginable expanses could be incorporated into this empire, he looked westward to achieve his constitutional vision. In his Second Inaugural, following the Louisiana Purchase, he again mused on the nation's destiny and expressly linked western expansion to his vision of republicanism grounded in a states'-rights Constitution: "Who can limit the extent to which the federative principle may operate effectively?" An expansive confederation of republican states would allow America to preserve its agrarian character and escape the baneful consequences of Hamiltonian political economy: class antagonism, "the mobs of great cities," corruption, and political discord.[4]

Predictably, however, the gains of the white democracy were to come at the expense of black Americans and indigenous peoples. The process of incorporating Louisiana into the United States revealed once more the commitment of Jefferson and his supporters to whiteness as much as to states' rights, both of which were central to their constitutional revolution. Not only in Louisiana but also in most of the United States, the years of Republican ascendancy through the War of 1812 would bring a hardening of the racial barriers to participation in civic life.

---

[3] Thomas Jefferson, *Notes on the State of Virginia*, ed. William Peden (Chapel Hill: University of North Carolina Press, 1955), 165.
[4] *The Papers of Thomas Jefferson*, vol. 33: *17 February to 30 April 1801* (Princeton, NJ: Princeton University Press, 2006), 134–152.

Apart from taking advantage of opportunities for geographical expansion, Jefferson's devotion to a Constitution for the white yeomanry demanded that he reduce the federal tax burden on the people. He abandoned Hamilton's efforts to foster a vibrant national, commercial economy, emphasizing instead the "encouragement of agriculture" with "commerce as its handmaid." To achieve his goal of "economy in public expense," he scaled back the size of government and began to pay down the national debt.[5]

The challenges of governance, however, led Jefferson to refine, adapt, and occasionally abandon his constitutional commitments. These challenges came mainly from beyond America's borders. The Louisiana Purchase, for example, moved Jefferson to assume executive powers not clearly granted in the Constitution in the service of his expansive, republican vision. Meanwhile, hostilities between the French and British, with neither permitting the United States to maintain its neutral trade, further diverted Jefferson from the simple program of limited government and fiscal retrenchment that he had imagined. Opposed in principle to the creation of a military establishment, Jefferson resorted to the supposedly more republican policy of commercial coercion, by means of an embargo on American exports. In fact, however, Jefferson thereby assumed federal powers arguably in excess of anything attempted by the Hamiltonians, provoked intense popular opposition in many regions of the country, and revived the political fortunes of the Federalists.

The predictable result was the decision by Jefferson's successor, Madison, to declare the War of 1812. The war inevitably channeled power to the central government and the executive, developments in serious tension with Jeffersonian values. Ultimately, the successes of the war consigned the Federalists to oblivion as a national force and again led many Republicans to believe that national harmony was within reach. Yet, the consensus election of James Monroe in 1816 only papered over the constitutional disagreements of the prewar years. After the war, new divisions came to the fore, in some ways recapitulating those that had once pitted the Republicans against the Federalists. "National Republicans" increasingly looked to deploy federal power in ways reminiscent of the Federalists, while "Old Republicans" and Democratic Republicans defended states' rights and, increasingly, a racialized democracy.

---

[5] Thomas Jefferson, "First Inaugural Address", http://press-pubs.uchicago.edu/founders/documents/v1ch4s33.html.

### THE LOUISIANA PURCHASE AND A WHITE
### REPUBLICAN EMPIRE

At the time Jefferson took office, more than a half-million Americans already lived west of the Appalachian Mountains. For Jefferson, these yeoman settlers were the advance guard of an "empire for liberty," a confederation of agricultural republics to stretch across the continent. The key to implementing his vision of republicanism was the purchase of the mammoth Louisiana Territory in 1803, Jefferson's signal contribution to the making of this empire.

For many in the West, access to the Mississippi River had become crucial to economic prosperity. Pinckney's Treaty (1795) with Spain secured navigation rights down the Mississippi and access to the port of New Orleans, but in 1802 the Spanish closed the port to American shipping and prepared to cede Louisiana back to France. Many in Congress feared that Napoleon Bonaparte harbored a larger plan for reasserting French power in the region. Some Americans, including prominent Federalists, even advocated seizing the city by force, but Jefferson preferred a negotiated settlement. Napoleon surprised the American negotiators by offering to sell the entire territory of Louisiana, presenting Jefferson with an opportunity to double the size of the country. The president's only problem was that the Constitution did not expressly authorize him to purchase new territory.

Jefferson worried that the purchase of Louisiana could be justified only by the type of latitudinarian construction for which he had spent much of the last decade denouncing the Federalists. His advisors and his allies in Congress offered straightforward constitutional arguments to justify the acquisition, but Jefferson was never certain that he could square it with his philosophy of strict construction. For that reason, he contemplated securing an amendment to endow the federal government with express powers to make such acquisitions. The amendment process, however, seemed too slow, especially once word came that Napoleon might withdraw the offer. To secure the future of his yeoman empire, Jefferson chose to cast aside "metaphysical subtleties" and push forward with the purchase.[6]

Opposition to the acquisition came primarily from a group of outspoken New England Federalists. They recast Jefferson's pragmatic

---

[6] Thomas Jefferson to John Breckenridge, August 12, 1803 in *The Papers of Thomas Jefferson*, vol. 41, *11 July–15 November 1803*, ed. Barbara B. Oberg (Princeton, NJ: Princeton University Press, 2014), 184–186.

decision as a hypocritical expansion of federal power. During his long decade in opposition, Jefferson had vigorously opposed loose construction or, as he put it, reduction of the Constitution to "a blank paper by construction." Now President Jefferson appeared willing to stretch the boundaries of the Constitution to serve his own political goals. New England Federalists such as Timothy Pickering, a leading spokesman for the Essex Junto, became the voice of a militant Federalist strain of thought, deeply hostile to Jefferson and the southern slave interest but warmly attached to New England and to commercial interests more generally. Pickering castigated the president for his willingness to "commit every arbitrary act which" his "projects may require." As to the Republicans more generally, Pickering saw only opportunism: "They do not venture to say – they have never said – that the government had a constitutional power to incorporate that new & immense country into the Union." But, he added, "They will not give themselves the trouble to alter the Constitution for that purpose."[7]

Unlike the Federalist program of the 1790s, Jefferson's expansion of the federal treaty power did not trench on the authority of the states. Still, Jefferson had allowed the immediate prospect of political advantage to deflect him from his own best reading of the Constitution, claiming power that necessarily enhanced federal authority. Partisan divisions were evident in the Senate's 24–7 vote to approve the treaty of purchase, as the Republican majority was joined by a lone Federalist vote.[8]

Incorporating Louisiana into an expanding empire for liberty presented further complications and embarrassments for Jefferson, the avowed republican. In the plan he had helped draft for the Northwest Territory two decades earlier, Jefferson had sought to include the inhabitants of new territories as self-governing republican citizens, not subjects. With respect to Louisiana, however, the statute establishing a territorial government gave the people a minimal role in choosing their government officers. Jefferson explained to Secretary of the Treasury Albert Gallatin that officers appointed by the president would introduce basic constitutional liberties gradually and that "as we find the people there riper for receiving these first principles of freedom, congress may from session

---

[7] Thomas Jefferson to Wilson Cary Nicholas, September 7, 1803 in *Papers of Thomas Jefferson*, vol. 41: *11 July to 15 November 1803* (2014), 346.
[8] Timothy Pickering to Rufus King, March 3, 1894 in Lance Banning, *Liberty and Order: The First American Party Struggle*, ed. and with a Preface by Lance Banning (Indianapolis: Liberty Fund, 2004), 313.

to session confirm their enjoyment of them."[9] Secretary of State Madison echoed this view. He acknowledged that the interim plans for Louisiana's government were not consistent with pure "republican theory," but he declared that "every blessing of liberty will be extended to them as soon as they shall be prepared and disposed to receive it."[10] Thus Jefferson and Madison denied that all "men" were equally ready for self-rule and republican government. Francophones in Louisiana required a transition to wean them from the un-republican habits of subject-hood and to adapt their laws and customs to an American, republican model. Indigenous peoples had to undergo an even more radical transformation, abandoning their "savage" state so they could survive and assimilate into American society: "humanity enjoins us to teach them agriculture and the domestic arts; to encourage them to that industry which alone can enable them to maintain their place in existence."[11]

The fate of black Americans posed an entirely different problem. Jefferson believed that free blacks would remain outside of this republican empire in perpetuity. French Louisiana posed a unique challenge to Jefferson's racialist views of republicanism. Not only did the newly acquired territory have a large black population, including numerous free people of color, but it also had evolved a vibrant civic and political culture that included free people of color. Some Eastern politicians and even slaveholders had already imagined that the West could help at least to mitigate the problem of slavery by providing a destination for emancipated blacks. After Gabriel's Rebellion, for example, Governor James Monroe of Virginia broached a plan to relocate emancipated blacks to land in the new Louisiana territory, but the president resolutely opposed it. Indeed, around this time, Jefferson declared that, "I have long since given up the expectation of any early provision for the extinguishment of slavery among us" and adamantly believed that the children of former slaves would never be able to live side by side with the descendants of

[9] Thomas Jefferson to Albert Gallatin, October 29, 1803 available in *The Thomas Jefferson Papers* at the Library of Congress: Series 1: General Correspondence. 1651 to 1827, www.loc.gov/resource/mtj1.029_0387_0387/?st=text.

[10] James Madison to Robert R. Livingston, January 31, 1804 in *The Papers of James Madison, Secretary of State Series*, vol. 6: *1 November 1803–31 March 1804*, ed. Mary A. Hackett, et al. (Charlottesville: University of Virginia Press, 2002).

[11] Thomas Jefferson, *Second Inaugural Address*, March 4, 1805; *Founders Online*, National Archives, last modified June 29, 2017, http://founders.archives.gov/documents/Jefferson/99-01-02-1302.

their one-time masters.[12] He refused to contemplate any scheme that might involve racial mixing or even setting aside some limited amount of land for the exclusive benefit of the formerly enslaved. Rather, Jefferson believed it was necessary "to look forward to distant times, when our rapid multiplication will . . . cover the whole northern, if not the southern continent, with a people speaking the same language, governed in similar forms, & by similar laws." He opposed any policy that would create a racial "blot or mixture on that surface." In this regard, Jefferson's views of Indians contrasted sharply with his attitude toward black Americans. For these "doomed peoples" intermarriage and assimilation was a genuine possibility and perhaps their only hope. The same option would never be available for the problem of black slavery.[13] The West had to be reserved for settlement by whites and those Indians able to assimilate. Rather than solve America's festering race problem, Louisiana would further Jefferson's "empire of liberty" for whites.

Jefferson could never appreciate that New Orleans offered a plausible, alternative model of a multiracial American future. At the time the United States purchased the city from France, one out of six of its 8,000 inhabitants was a free person of color. The city boasted a small but prosperous black elite and was home to a wide range of institutions catering to the city's black population, including schools, churches, and volunteer fire companies and militias. Rather than embrace this multiracial republicanism, Jefferson sought to impose his narrow vision of white republicanism, restricting the rights of the free black population and stemming its growth.

The problem posed by the free black militias in New Orleans illuminated the Jeffersonian quandary on race. Governor William Claiborne informed Secretary of State James Madison that "two large companies of people of Colour" posed a unique challenge to incorporating Louisiana into the American republic. "To re-commission them might be considered as an outrage on the feelings of a part of the Nation, and as opposed to those principles of Policy which the Safety of the Southern States has

---

[12] Thomas Jefferson to William A. Burwell, January 28, 1805, available in *The Thomas Jefferson Papers at the Library of Congress: Series 1: General Correspondence. 1651 to 1827*. www.loc.gov/resource/mtj1.032_0347_0347/?st=text.

[13] "President Thomas Jefferson to Governor James Monroe, 24 November 1801," in Gordon S. Wood, *The Rising Glory of America* (Lebanon, NH: Northeastern University Press, 1990), 365. Jefferson to Nathaniel Niles, March 22, 1801, *The Thomas Jefferson Papers, Series 1. General Correspondence, 1651–1827*. Available online from the Library of Congress at http://memory.loc.gov/ammem/collections/jefferson_papers/index.html.

necessarily established." Alternatively, disbanding these units was equally dangerous. It would "raise an armed enemy in the very heart of the Country." Claiborne proceeded cautiously and eventually reorganized the structure of the militia so that the free black units were incorporated into a structure that placed them firmly under white command. The ultimate compromise on the militia reflected the tension between the region's legacy of multicultural accommodation and the ever-present specter in the white mind of armed black resistance. But the clear goal of Jeffersonian policy was to incorporate the region into the American polity based on principles of racial subordination.[14]

The territorial legislature shared Jefferson's vision of a white republic and diligently enacted laws to implement his policy. No law better symbolized this racist commitment than Section 40 of the new legal code enacted for the region. It stipulated that "free people of colour ought never to insult or strike white people, nor presume to conceive themselves equal to the white." Violation of this law carried a punishment of imprisonment, the exact time to be determined "according to the nature of the offense." Free blacks were prohibited from immigrating into the region, and those not born in Louisiana were ordered to leave or face deportation. Although enforcement of the law was difficult, the official policy was to discourage the growth of the free black population. Meanwhile, free blacks who remained were required to carry passes and observe curfews. In 1812 free black men were stripped of the right to vote.[15]

The racial animus driving this new territorial legislation reflected movements elsewhere in Jeffersonian America. In the first decade of the new century a number of localities, states, and even territories in the Old Northwest, also passed new "Black Laws," which severely limited the rights of free blacks. In 1804, Ohio enacted a law requiring free blacks to obtain "freedom papers" and file them with local county clerks. Two years later, Ohio passed a law requiring free blacks entering the state to post a bond. Additional legislation prohibited interracial marriage and prevented blacks from testifying in proceedings involving whites. Nor was Ohio unique in passing such racist laws. In 1804 Virginia enacted a law requiring manumitted slaves to leave Virginia within a year of gaining

---

[14] William Claiborne to James Madison December 27, 1803 in *Official Letter Books of W. C. C. Claiborne, 1801–1816* (Jackson, MI: State Department of Archives and History, 1917), 313–314.
[15] *A General Digest of the Acts of the Legislature of Louisiana: Passed from the Year 1804 to 1827* (New Orleans, LA: Benjamin Levy, 1828), 40 Acts, 112.

freedom. Illinois passed restrictive legislation in 1819, adding additional disabilities in a revision passed in 1829. In addition to the requirement for bonds and proof of free status, the 1829 legislation prohibited interracial marriage.

Even in places with significant free black communities, such as Philadelphia, the legal status of free blacks was precarious. During economic downturns, members of the African-American community were especially vulnerable to attacks on the few rights they enjoyed. Thus, during an economic slump in 1813, the Pennsylvania legislature began debating their own draconian Black Laws, including a ban on any further immigration of blacks into Pennsylvania, an initiative that was driven in part by white resentment of black competition for jobs. Blacks convicted of crimes would be bound to service and sold out of the state. Finally, some Pennsylvanians sought to impose a system of registration and bonds for good behavior on all free blacks residing in the state.

Philadelphia's black community did not sit by passively as the legislature proposed to strip away their rights. James Forten, a leading figure in the African-American community, wrote his "Letters from a Man of Color" to denounce the new policies in the language of American constitutionalism. He reminded readers that the Pennsylvania state constitution affirmed that "all men are born equally free." It made no mention of invidious distinctions of color and protected the "inherent and indefeasible rights" of all men, including "life and liberty."[16] Fortunately for the black community, the manifold problems of the War of 1812 consumed the attention of the legislature, and the movement to rob free African-Americans of their rights failed in this instance.

The Louisiana Purchase exposed the plasticity of Jefferson's constitutional theory. Although his belief in strict construction was no doubt sincere, he was ultimately controlled by his expansive dream of a confederated nation of white, agrarian republics, spread across the West. This expanding empire for liberty would not be a multiracial society on the model of New Orleans, but would extend the increasingly firm racial hierarchy of American republicanism. The seemingly limitless expanse of the West would provide no refuge for emancipated slaves or free black communities, let alone communities in which whites and blacks might live together in peace. Firm as he was in his condemnation of slavery,

---

[16] Julie Winch, ed., "James Forten, Letters from 'A Man of Colour,'" *William and Mary Quarterly* 64 (2007), Web Supplement for William and Mary Quarterly.

Jefferson was far more committed to the exclusion of black Americans from the promise of America's future.

## THE CHALLENGES OF THE EMBARGO

In 1803, within two weeks of its sale of Louisiana, France was again at war with Britain. Although Jefferson would attempt to keep the United States clear of European hostilities, the conflict had profound effects on the development of Jeffersonian republicanism. First, the policies of Jefferson and Madison resulted in a most un-republican expansion of executive power. Relatedly, they brought a reversal of roles in which Federalists became defenders of states' rights, while Republicans seemed intent on enhancing federal power. Finally, the recurring constitutional conflicts demonstrated that the federal courts could not impose their vision of law on the new nation but would have to contend with the state judiciaries, Congress, state legislatures, state militias, local juries, and the people themselves speaking through petitions, newspapers, and when necessary direct actions out-of-doors.

During the early phases of the new European conflict, American merchants reaped enormous profits by trading with both sides. However, both Britain and France set out to blockade the ports of their adversaries. The United States insisted that neutral nations had a right to carry on nonmilitary trade with both sides, but neither Britain nor France agreed. The British Navy boarded and searched American ships and seized cargoes without providing compensation. Even more galling was the British practice of impressment, forcing merchant seamen to serve in the British navy. Many American sailors had once served in the British Navy but now claimed American citizenship. The British considered these men deserters and impressed 6,000 Americans between 1803 and 1812.

Rather than go to war with the British and French, Jefferson proposed a policy of "peaceable coercion," in part because of his republican commitment to small government and his aversion to a strong military. Starting with the modest 1806 Non-Importation Act and following with the comprehensive Embargo Act of 1807, which purported to bar virtually all export activity, Jefferson tried economic pressure to force both sides to respect the rights of neutrals. The policy proved a dismal failure and the Embargo's impact on American trade was catastrophic. Exports fell from $108 million in 1807 to $22 million in 1808, while smuggling was common. Immensely unpopular in parts of northern Vermont and New York along the Canadian border, in New England, and in many seaport towns throughout the nation, the Embargo actually revived the declining fortunes of the Federalists. Opposition to Jefferson's foreign policy launched a new phase of partisan political conflict.

Amid such broad opposition, enforcement of the Embargo proved imperfect, at best. Smuggling was rampant in many places, and customs officers were often harassed by angry mobs. Even when individuals were prosecuted for criminal acts, juries were reluctant to convict. In New England and parts of New York, defiance of the Embargo turned violent, moving beyond the symbolic humiliation and harassment of government officials. In Castine, Maine, a crowd of women liberated a group of prisoners jailed for smuggling. In Augusta, Maine, a crowd burned down the local jail and freed prisoners prosecuted for violating the Embargo.

This battle against Jefferson's "Dambargo" illustrates the continuing importance of both popular action and federalism to constitutional thought and politics in this period. Although Republicans had seemed the exclusive defenders of federalism when in opposition, defenses of state prerogatives came quickly and easily to Federalists once the Republicans had gained control of the central government. Federalists had never denied that federalism was a basic structural feature of the Constitution, so they readily turned to principles of states' rights when an unprecedented sort of federal power – a set of discriminatory policies targeting a major segment of the economy – was turned against their disproportionately commercial constituency. In Massachusetts, petitions even appropriated elements of the Republican language of 1798, demanding that the state legislature "interpose" to protect the rights of its citizens against Jeffersonian tyranny.

Nor was opposition to the Embargo confined to any one institution or method. Individuals and communities employed a variety of constitutional means to influence government policy. Petitions poured into legislatures, and angry citizens took to the streets to protest, sometimes resorting to armed resistance to federal officials. Juries, local militia units, and crowds gave voice to popular discontents. Some acts of resistance led to court cases regarding federalism and the scope of executive power, which set the independent trajectories of constitutional politics and court-centered law on a collision course.

Federal courts, including the Supreme Court, generally supported the constitutionality of the Embargo, but the actual implementation of these decisions did not so much vindicate federal power and judicial authority as underscore the fragility of both. Interpreting the Constitution was one thing; enforcing rulings that might lead to resistance to judicial authority was quite another. Thus, the Embargo cases suggest a significant gap between the federal courts' assertions of power in the Marshall era, expressed in constitutional doctrine, and the limits of their power in practice. This would not be the first time that constitutional law and political reality existed in tension with one another, nor would it be the last.

One of the key judicial tests of the government's power to enforce the Embargo Act came in the case of *Ex Parte Gilchrist*.[17] The case was triggered by a law that gave sweeping authority to federal customs officials at the local level to detain vessels in port. Any vessel suspected of intending to evade the Embargo could be seized. The statute thus seemed to embrace a vigorous conception of federal power. For his part, President Jefferson tried to make the most of this federal statute, ordering his customs agents to detain all vessels with any cargo that might be in demand in foreign ports, an exceptionally broad notion of contraband. Yet, on the specific facts of the case, Justice William Johnson, a Jefferson appointee to the Supreme Court, found that the president had over-reached. A ship owner from Charleston sought a writ of mandamus to force the customs official to release his ship, and Johnson, while riding circuit, sided with the ship owner, ordering the local customs officials to allow the ship to leave port. The law, Johnson held, gave customs officials, not the president, discretion in detaining ships. Federal power had been vindicated in the abstract, but the ruling actually favored the ship owner. So the courts were relieved from actually enforcing the president's unpopular policy in this instance.

Although it was only a circuit court decision, Johnson's ruling became a minor sensation. Newspapers across the nation offered editorial commentary on the conflict between a Republican justice and a Republican president. Federalists praised the ruling as demonstrating the value of a strong and independent judiciary. The *Charleston Courier* asserted that "the importance and value of an independent judiciary to control the arbitrary or mistaken construction of the laws, by executive officers, cannot be appreciated too highly."[18] Republicans predictably took the opposite view, attacking Federalist support for a powerful judiciary. The Philadelphia *Aurora*, one of the most radical outlets for Jeffersonian ideas, denounced the "monstrous absurdity of what is called the independence of the judiciary." Drawing on a popular antijudge, antilawyer

---

[17] *Ex Parte Gilchrist* 5 *Hughes* 1 (1808).    [18] *Charleston Courier* June 25, 1808.

tradition, the *Aurora* derided the "wretched subterfuges and equivocations" of Johnson's legalistic opinion. It likewise condemned the sophistry of "this subtle class of men" – denouncing judges and lawyers who used their legal skills and knowledge to advance their antidemocratic agenda. The only way to eliminate such examples of judicial tyranny, the paper concluded, was to rein in judicial willfulness and restore power to the people themselves.[19]

Johnson's decision also provoked an unusual, written response from the Administration. Angered over the outcome in *Gilchrist*, Jefferson solicited from his Attorney General Caesar Rodney a public critique of Johnson's decision. Rodney took the predictable, Republican position – especially post-*Marbury* – that judicial power must be exercised with restraint and not trench on the constitutional authority of the other branches. "There does not appear in the Constitution of the United States," Rodney argued "anything which favours an indefinite extension of the jurisdiction of Courts over the ministerial officers within the Executive Department."[20] Rodney did not dispute the judge's obligation to interpret the law in deciding cases, nor the power of judicial review, but he objected to the judiciary's ordering constitutionally coequal executive officers to bow to a court's interpretation of their duties. He disparaged "the *high church* doctrines so fashionable on the bench" that would allow "the judicial power," if unchecked, to "swallow up all the rest. They will become omnipotent." Further, the Federalist delusion of judicial supremacy was now infecting Republican appointees to the bench and had become, Rodney argued in a pungent turn of phrase, "the leprosy of the Bench."[21] Having spread from Federalist to Republican judges, undermining the separation of powers and federalism, the threat to Jefferson's agenda demanded a firm response from the executive.

Justice Johnson, on the other hand, defended his reading of the law as mere execution of his official duty, even as he articulated a broad scope for judicial authority: "of these laws, the Courts are the constitutional

---

[19] The *Aurora*'s attack was reprinted, with critical Federalist commentary, by several anti-administration newspapers, including the *Washington Federalist*, June 16, 1808.

[20] The importance of the *Gilchrist* case prompted a leading legal journal to reprint Rodney's attack and Johnson's response, see *American Law Journal*, vol. 1 (Baltimore, 1808), 429–459.

[21] To Thomas Jefferson from Caesar Augustus Rodney, October 31, 1808, Library of Congress.

expositors, and every department of the government must submit to their exposition."[22] Perhaps Johnson only meant to defend his authority to decide cases, or perhaps he had indeed succumbed to the "leprosy of the bench," tainted by Federalist ideas about judicial supremacy. Either way, the *Gilchrist* controversy testified to the persisting tension between, on the one hand, a Republican belief in the people's sovereign superiority over the judiciary and, on the other hand, the Federalist belief in judicial supremacy on questions of law.

The Embargo controversy, like the Louisiana controversy before it, revealed Jefferson's support for an expansive theory of federal executive power, a commitment that now overshadowed his efforts to shrink the size of the federal government and the national debt produced by Hamiltonian economics. A similarly expansive conception of executive power informed his understanding of the Treason Clause, which Jefferson pursued in the trial of Aaron Burr for his unsanctioned military schemes in the West and invoked again in response to popular resistance to the Embargo in parts of northern Vermont and New York, where smuggling across the Canadian border was widespread. Residents of St. Albans, Vermont, a town about fifteen miles south of the Canadian border, expressed their "astonishment" at the president's determination to treat certain armed clashes with customs officials as acts of treason rather than prosecute them as simple criminal conduct. In their published remonstrance, the "St. Albans Memorial," they reminded the president that "the actions of such desperate persons, driven by economic necessity, could hardly justify proclaiming a state of insurrection or rebellion." Conceding that local residents had engaged in petty smuggling, they insisted that the Constitution's very precise definition of treason could hardly reach such conduct.[23]

The decision to use treason prosecutions to crush opposition to the Embargo was tested in federal court in *United States v. Hoxie*. When an armed group of smugglers in Alburg, Vermont, "rescued" a shipment of "timber which had been seized by the Collector when on its way to Canada," Jefferson was presented with an opportunity to implement his expansive view of treason. In a letter to the Governor of New York, the president conceded that events along the Canadian border "may not be an insurrection in the popular sense of the word," but he insisted that individuals who violently resisted customs officials, federal marshals, or

---

[22] *American Law Journal*, 454.
[23] "Proceedings of the Town of St. Albans," *The Balance*, June 7, 1808.

the militia were "fully within the legal definition of an insurrection." In *Hoxie*, Supreme Court Justice Brockholst Livingston, another Jefferson appointee riding circuit, decisively rejected this broad construction of treason. Livingston pointed first to the "very limited definition" of treason in the Constitution: "Treason against the United States, shall consist only in levying war against them, or in adhering to their enemies, giving them aid and comfort." He then briefly surveyed English common law and recent American precedents, drawing particular attention to the Whiskey Rebellion, the Fries Rebellion, and the Burr conspiracy trial, concluding that the *Hoxie* prosecution was ludicrous. Livingston sardonically observed to the jury, "You are seriously expected to condemn the prisoner, as a traitor, for forcing some lumber from the possession of a collector." Livingston reminded the jury of their sacred obligation to "do justice to your country, the prisoner, and yourselves," and unsurprisingly the jury acquitted Hoxie.[24]

Jefferson could never have predicted the circumstances that would turn his 1800 campaign for limited government and states' rights into a presidency marked by a vigorous expansion of federal power and enhancement of executive authority. Nor could he have anticipated the intensity of the resistance to such constitutional innovations, not only in the courts but also in the state legislatures and in popular action out of doors.

### WAR AND CONSTITUTIONAL CHANGE

Jefferson's policy of peaceable coercion not only failed to compel Britain and France to respect American rights; it damaged the American economy and helped revive Federalist fortunes politically, even as it exacerbated tensions within the Republican coalition. As James Madison assumed the presidency in 1809, therefore, it appeared to many that war was the only way left to reassert American independence and Republican dominance. Many Republicans continued to resist, especially the doctrinaire "Old Republicans," who feared the creation of a large military establishment, new taxes, and a further concentration of power in the central government. The immediate future, however, lay elsewhere as the political center of gravity shifted from old colonial centers of power such as

---

[24] *The Founders' Constitution*, vol. 4, Article 3, Section 3, Clauses 1 and 2, Document 23, http://press-pubs.uchicago.edu/founders/documents/a3_3_1-2s23.html, The University of Chicago Press.

Virginia, to the southwest, in new states such as Kentucky and Tennessee. Congressmen Henry Clay of Kentucky and John C. Calhoun, an upcountry South Carolinian, were the rising stars among the new breed of Republican politicians. In addition to championing a military response to Great Britain, the most aggressive of these "War Hawks" favored a policy of expansion into Indian-inhabited territory, the annexation of Canada, and possible expansion into Florida.

One consequence of Jefferson's effort to shrink government, however, was demilitarization, which left America in a weak posture to take on Great Britain. Clay and Calhoun nevertheless pressed for war, and Madison too concluded that the failure of commercial coercion made war necessary. Still, the unanimous opposition of the pro-British Federalists and the reluctance of old school Republicans delayed a declaration until June of 1812, when Congress voted for war 79 to 49 in the House and 19 to 13 in the Senate. No single line of division accounts for all the votes, but, by 1812, most Americans had come to believe that something akin to a second war for independence was necessary to bring Britain to heel, break British domination of international trade, and cut off British support for hostile Indian populations along the frontier.

Declaring war was constitutionally straightforward, but circumstances made the actual raising of a fighting force constitutionally tricky. On the eve of the War of 1812, America possessed a small standing army and a tiny navy. To meet the sudden manpower needs of war, the government would have to draw on both volunteers and the state militias. A scant four days after Congress declared war on Great Britain, Major General Henry Dearborn requested the governors of Massachusetts, Connecticut, and Rhode Island to supply him with forty-one militia companies. When local Federalists opposed these requests, another showdown over federalism ensued, this time focused on the constitutional limits on federal use of the militia. During ratification, Anti-Federalists had raised the specter of a tyrannical federal government marching militiamen beyond their state borders. For many Federalists, the effort to use state militias to wage an offensive war, not to defend their states, seemed to vindicate this fear.

Massachusetts took the lead in developing a constitutional argument against the use of New England militias. The governor of Massachusetts requested an advisory opinion from his own state's Supreme Judicial Court on the appropriate constitutional uses of the militia in time of war. The judges reasoned that the governor of each state alone retained the authority to decide when to call out the militia. While the president might request that the militia be called out to defend against insurrections or invasions, to use militia troops in any other context required the approval of the governor of the state from which the troops were requested.

Ironically enough, Madison's own writings, specifically *Federalist No. 46*, had developed the idea that the states were constitutionally empowered to resist the president's request to muster their militias. Although it is hard to imagine that Madison went to Philadelphia to endorse this form of state resistance, the repeated attacks of Anti-Federalists on the Constitution's provisions for federal military power led Madison to probe the scope and limits of that power. Writing as Publius, Madison argued that each state retained a residual power to resist unjust aggression from the federal government and that the allocation of power over the militia, divided between the states and the federal government, provided an effective check on federal overreach. The de facto power of the state militias, he argued, should assuage Anti-Federalist worries about the federal government's authority to raise a standing army and call out the militia. Madison conceded this power of state resistance only in response to a doomsday scenario, in which every other form of check and balance had somehow failed to slow the progress of federal tyranny. He did not endorse militia resistance on minor policy disagreements or as an ordinary means of settling constitutional disputes, which would typically be adjudicated by the courts. Yet, a generation later, Federalist state court judges relied on an argument that was essentially neo-Madisonian, endorsing the militia's role as a structural check on federal power.

Madison's administration did not back down. Secretary of War Monroe took the lead in challenging the judges' logic. Monroe declared his own support for the "rights of the individual States" as indispensably necessary for the "existence of our Union, and of free government in these States." Still, in Monroe's view, the judges had carried "the doctrine of State rights further than I have ever known it to be carried in any other instance." This novel theory, he claimed, would leave the nation vulnerable to military attack. Monroe further insisted that there was no right of resistance against the "legitimate authority of the United States," a statement that took on added urgency in light of the unrest during the Embargo and the prospect of further opposition to an unpopular war in New England.[25]

---

[25] "James Monroe to the Chairmen of the Senate Military Committee," February 1815, *The Founders' Constitution*, Volume 3, Article 1, Section 8, Clause 15, Document 18

Nevertheless, for much of "Mr. Madison's War," the New England state militias remained firmly under the control of their governors. As had been the case during the Embargo and throughout Jefferson's presidency, Federalists insisted on the prerogatives of the states. Faced with a central government engaged in policies they viewed as inimical to their interests and subversive of liberty, Federalists in New England found themselves in a position reminiscent of Republicans more than a decade earlier. Similarly, Republicans found themselves uncomfortably insisting on a vigorous exercise of federal power for the good of the nation while continuing to declare their principled attachment to states' rights.

In New England, resistance to Republican power extended to actions by the people in their localities. Towns throughout Massachusetts petitioned their state legislature to "interpose a shield or devise a system by which the liberties of our country may still be preserved." These "memorials" requested a convention of the "northern and commercial states" to address the constitutional issues raised by Republican policy.[26] Many of these issues had been simmering for more than a decade, but two years of war now brought talk of extreme measures, such as secession and direct diplomatic overtures to Great Britain.

In response to the town memorials, Massachusetts's legislature and governor supported a convention of the New England states to meet in Hartford, Connecticut. Not all states sent full delegations, and the Federalists who did travel to Hartford were dominated by moderate voices, not the firebrands of secession. Rather than follow a radical states' rights agenda, the Hartford Convention adopted a platform of more moderate constitutional reforms, including seven proposed amendments that squarely targeted Republican power. The first would have revoked the Constitution's pro-southern, three-fifths compromise, thereby depriving the Republicans of substantial representation in Congress. The second vented displeasure with the Louisiana Purchase and the extension of slavery by proposing a two-thirds vote in Congress, rather than a simple majority, to admit new states. Federalist criticism of Republican foreign policy would be constitutionalized by a prohibition of any shipping

http://press-pubs.uchicago.edu/founders/documents/a1_8_15s18.html, The University of Chicago Press.

[26] "Proclamation on the Embargo, 19 April 1808," *Founders Online*, National Archives, last modified November 26, 2017, http://founders.archives.gov/documents/Jefferson/99-01-02-7861; "From Thomas Jefferson to Daniel D. Tompkins, 15 August 1808," *Founders Online*, National Archives, last modified November 26, 2017, http://founders.archives.gov/documents/Jefferson/99-01-02-8520.

embargo longer than 60 days, by a supermajority requirement for any policy designed to interfere with international trade, and by a similar supermajority requirement to declare war. Further, in a thinly veiled rebuke to the main architect of Jeffersonian economic policy, Albert Gallatin, the Convention would have barred naturalized immigrants from holding civil office or serving in Congress. Finally, the office of president would be limited to a single term, and no president could be elected from the same state in successive terms.

This list was forwarded to the states to begin the formal amendment process, but the timing of the Convention could hardly have been worse. At first, it seemed propitious, coming at the end of a dispiriting, two-year military stalemate that included the burning of the president's residence (a humiliation that also included British troops' ransacking the mansion and feasting on an elegant dinner that had been prepared for President Madison and his wife Dolley Madison). So there had been good reason to think America might be receptive to the Hartford Convention's statements of grievances and reforms. By the time the proposals were published, however, a peace treaty ending the war had been signed in Ghent, Belgium. Even more disastrous for the Federalist revival, though, was the news of a stunning victory by Andrew Jackson and his troops at the Battle of New Orleans on January 8, 1815. Although the Treaty of Ghent had already been signed, Jackson's impressive victory over the British provided cause for national celebration. Indeed, Jackson would ride "The Glorious 8th of January" to a political career that symbolized, if it did not embody, the triumph of the democratic Constitution over the retrograde Federalist constitutionalism of "aristocracy." Overnight, it seemed, the Hartford Convention and the New England Federalists went from hopes of resurgence to political oblivion.

## MADISON'S LIVING CONSTITUTIONALISM, INTERNAL IMPROVEMENTS, AND THE EMERGENCE OF THE NATIONAL REPUBLICANS

Just as the Federalist revival succumbed to a new wave of Republican triumphalism at the close of the War of 1812, some Republicans began to drift in a neo-Federalist direction, especially on matters of political economy. The nation had weathered a number of crises precipitated by the war, sustaining a wartime economy and coping with local and state resistance to federal policy. But these crises would have been less daunting if they had not been exacerbated by continuing Republican hostility to institutions like a standing army, a national bank, and a national system of internal improvements (public infrastructure). The experience of war now led a number of prominent Republicans to jettison elements of Jeffersonian orthodoxy. Dogmatic adherence to strict construction and skepticism of federal power gave way to a more pragmatic view of the Constitution.

Scholars since Henry Adams have suggested the deep irony of constitutional politics in this era as Federalists and Republicans appeared to reverse roles on questions of federal power. But the postures Republicans and Federalists adopted were predictable from the federal structures imposed by the Constitution itself. From the outset, defenses of states' rights were never exclusively the province of Republicans any more than defenses of federal power were the exclusive preserve of Federalists. In 1788, the most nationalist-minded Federalists had to adapt their arguments to Anti-Federalist critiques, acknowledging a limited commitment to states' rights, at least within the sphere of powers clearly reserved to the states by the Constitution. Madison's doomsday scenario in *Federalist No 46* was one dramatic example of such an accommodation. In contrast to Hamilton's more extreme nationalism and statism, Madison had always embraced a federalism that rested on a dynamic, not static, analysis of the balance between federal and state power. To get the balance right in any particular situation required pragmatic adjustments and accommodation of other constitutional actors.

The issue that most urgently compelled Madison's reconsideration of his constitutional convictions was the controversy over rechartering the Bank of the United States in 1811. The original Bank was born amid a fierce debate over policy and constitutional law in 1791, and its charter was now set to expire in 1811. When supporters of the Bank proposed to renew its charter, it was hardly surprising that politicians on both sides of the question would revisit the rhetoric and ideas aired during the first war over the Bank.

Although many of the same ideological issues were put in play, circumstances had changed dramatically. In the decades since its incorporation the Bank had prospered and mostly avoided political controversy. In addition to the Bank's headquarters in Philadelphia, it had opened four branches in 1792 in Baltimore, Boston, Charleston, and New York, which gave it a regional balance and presence that helped win over many staunch opponents. In the next decade, additional branches were added in Norfolk, Washington, Savannah, and New Orleans. The Bank's notes circulated widely as a medium of exchange, and its loans helped fund a variety of economic activities. The Bank also lent the government money and facilitated the government's fiscal dealings with foreign nations, playing a major role in the purchase of Louisiana, for example. Although it did not function exactly like a modern centralized bank (individual branches had a good deal of autonomy), the Bank did attempt to coordinate the activities of all of the branches to pursue a coherent set of fiscal goals.

Given its centrality to the American economy, re-rechartering the Bank might have been an uncomplicated affair. But the connections between the Bank and Hamilton's vision of a fiscal-military state made it an easy target for Republicans of the old school. Many remained hostile to the Bank, partly on the grounds that the power to create such an institution was simply not among those delegated to the federal government by the Constitution. Others opposed it on economic grounds, believing that state banks were more likely to promote economic growth. Finally, some simply attacked the Bank for reasons of political advantage.

Perhaps the two most important exceptions to Republican antipathy to the Bank were Albert Gallatin and James Madison. The former supported the bank for fiscal and economic reasons. Although not an enviable political task in the face of Republican hostility, Gallatin's intellectual task was fairly straightforward. He had only to demonstrate that the Bank had served the nation's economic interests. Madison's challenge was not as easily met. He recognized the utility of the Bank, but he had to explain why an institution he had attacked as unconstitutional in the 1790s had gained legitimacy with the passage of time.

In the 1790s Madison had helped develop an intentionalist theory that looked to the state ratification conventions as dispositive of the Constitution's legal meaning. According to this theory, constitutional meaning lay in the understanding of those who gave the Constitution legal effect through ratification, not in the intent of the Philadelphia framers. This theory of constitutional meaning had never been fully debated, officially sanctioned, or formally ratified, but it represented Madison's best attempt early on to articulate a model of constitutional interpretation consistent with his views of popular sovereignty.

Still, Madison's commitment to this theory had always been tempered by his pragmatic view of the indeterminacies of language and, indeed, the limits of all modes of legal interpretation, particularly when pitted against the will of the people or the politically powerful. Madison thus believed that many contentious issues would not be resolved by recourse to the constitutional text and ratification debates alone. Rather, the meaning of the Constitution would be worked out one case at a time by policy makers and judges using something akin to a common law model of reasoning. Madison described this process as constitutional "liquidation." Writing to Virginia jurist Spencer Roane, Madison noted that it "was foreseen at the birth of the Constitution, that difficulties and differences of opinion might occasionally arise in expounding terms & phrases necessarily used in such a charter," especially the language of federalism that "divide[d] legislation between the General & local Governments." Consequently, "it might require a regular course of practice to liquidate" that language.[27]

The question of the Bank's constitutionality offered the clearest example of "liquidation." For over twenty years, agents of the federal government had done official business with the Bank, implying a kind of tacit constitutional recognition. The Bank had also gained a measure of popular approval, evidenced in its growth and prosperity and the failure of efforts to defund or abolish it. Finally, the courts had treated the Bank as a legal entity in various proceedings. So it seemed that all three branches of government, and perhaps the people themselves, had accepted the Bank's legitimacy as an accomplished fact. Madison thus came to endorse the Bank as well and, in so doing, recognized that the meaning of the Constitution in 1811 could diverge from its meaning in 1791.

Madison's position shocked many Republicans, who deemed it a betrayal of strict construction and a repudiation of the states'-rights principles that had undergirded their opposition to the Federalists since the 1790s. One of the most vociferous critics in the press, writing under the pen name "Tammany," derided Madison's theory of the Constitution as "chameleon-like." Tammany wondered if the Constitution's meaning "changes its hue according to the times and positions in which it may viewed." Madison's answer to this question was clearly yes. Another Republican critic, Harmodius, writing in the *Richmond Enquirer*, the leading southern voice of Republicanism, attacked the very idea that the Constitution might evolve by means of judicial precedents, a central part of Madison's view of constitutional liquidation. Rather than conform to the "changing and uncertain light of precedent," elected officials, including judges, representatives, and even presidents were bound by the

---

[27] "James Madison to Spencer Roane, 2 September 1819," *Founders Online*, National Archives, last modified November 26, 2017, http://founders.archives.gov/documents/Madison/04-01-02-0455.

unchanging "words and spirit of the Constitution."[28] For Tammany and Harmodius, the meaning of the Constitution's text had been fixed at the time of enactment. Madison's view was far less textualist in spirit. In particular, the mature Madison showed a greater willingness to accept an important role for constitutional change outside the formal process of amendment.

When the issue of renewal came before Congress, Republicans were arrayed across a considerable spectrum on how to best deal with the bank question. Congress eventually defeated the renewal bill by a single tie-breaking vote cast by Madison's own Vice President George Clinton, the one-time Anti-Federalist who had grown into an old school Republican. Efforts to gain a temporary reprieve so that the Bank might tie up financial loose ends before ceasing to exist were also rebuffed, and the Bank's charter expired in 1811.

The timing of the Bank's demise could hardly have been worse. The War of 1812 strained the economy, and the absence of a national bank exacerbated the government's fiscal difficulties. Learning grudgingly from these experiences, Congress in 1815 finally drafted a bill to establish a Second Bank of the United States. By the time it reached Madison's desk, the political horse-trading in Congress had produced a plan that Madison deemed so defective as to require a veto. In 1816, after considerable political wrangling, a new bill establishing the Second Bank of the United States passed and was signed by Madison.

For radical Republicans, of course, the new Bank represented a major capitulation to Hamiltonian Federalism. Indeed, Republican hostility to the Bank would continue to fester. A decade later under Andrew Jackson's leadership, a resurgent democratic movement would place opposition to the Bank near the top of its political and constitutional agenda.

In his eighth and final annual message to Congress, Madison took up another element of the neo-Hamiltonian agenda: internal improvements. Madison had come to accept that federal support for internal improvements was vital to the growth and safety of the republic. At the same time, he continued to believe that the federal government lacked the constitutional authority to undertake such an ambitious program without an express constitutional amendment. Although Madison believed the authority to charter a bank had been established by a kind of common-law

---

[28] "Harmodius," *Richmond Enquirer*, December 13, 1810.

constitutionalism, he discerned no similar consensus as to the constitutionality of federally funded internal improvements.

Rather than take Madison up on his invitation to amend the Constitution, Congress rallied around a proposal by John C. Calhoun to fund internal improvements with surplus funds generated by the recently chartered Second Bank of the United States. Calhoun's Bonus Bill was a product of compromise and political expediency. It lacked the coherence and comprehensiveness of an 1808 proposal by then-Secretary of the Treasury Albert Gallatin, which had envisioned a unified network of roads and canals to help tie the nation together. Echoing one of Madison's earliest essays in the 1790s, Gallatin had argued that the survival of the republic required a system of roads and canals to make communication easier and to facilitate commerce. Although Calhoun boasted that his plan would similarly knit the nation together, in reality the plan offered little more than a fund for internal improvements, on which the states might draw. It lacked any cohesive vision or overarching planning mechanism to coordinate the individual projects the states would bring to Congress or to prevent these funds from being used to further parochial interests.

To secure passage of the bill, Calhoun had to accept several changes, including provisions that made the allocation of funding proportional to state population and that required state consent before funds could be spent. These compromises further obstructed the bill's stated goal of a comprehensive, national system of canals and roads. The modified bill would actually have had the opposite effect, providing funds for decidedly local programs. Some members of Congress may have opposed the bill on principle, such as Old Republicans who opposed any policy that smacked of consolidation wherever they found it. Others were driven by narrower political and economic interests. In the end, after a spirited debate and substantial modifications, the bill passed by a mere two votes.

Madison, however, vetoed the Bonus Bill in his last act as president. A vigorous champion of the executive veto, Madison employed it more than any of his predecessors. Still, his veto of the Bonus Bill shocked the bill's two sponsors, Clay and Calhoun. Indeed, Clay remarked that "no circumstance, not even an earthquake that should have swallowed up half this city, could have excited more surprise."[29] Madison feared that the

---

[29] Henry Clay, Speech on Internal Improvements, March 13, 1818, in James F. Hopkins, ed., *The Papers of Henry Clay*, vol. 2 (Lexington: University of Kentucky Press, 1961), 480.

Bonus Bill would establish a dangerous precedent, "giving to Congress a general power of legislation instead of the defined and limited one hitherto understood to belong to them." Faced with such a prospect, he felt he had no choice but to veto the bill.[30]

Indeed, in Madison's view the Bonus Bill violated not only the letter of the law, but also the essential, antipartisan spirit of the Constitution. In a letter to John Adams written shortly after his veto, Madison reiterated a point he had made in his analysis of faction in *Federalist No. 10* almost three decades previously: "The great question ... is, whether checks and balances sufficient for the purposes of order, justice, and the general good, may not be created by a proper division and distribution of power among different bodies, differently constituted, but all deriving their existence from the elective principle..."[31] The system of government created by the Constitution was an effort to create just such a mechanism of government, but the Bonus Bill was not just unconstitutional as a matter of policy; it was inimical to the general good. It was an example of factionalism at its worst. In this sense, the Bonus Bill veto was an entirely fitting coda to Madison's long life in public service and his long public struggle to defend his vision of constitutional government against threats from every direction: Hamiltonian consolidation but also excessive localism, legislative overreach but also popular political passions, and the ever-present threat of factionalism.

### THE RISE AND FALL OF A NATIONAL
### REPUBLICAN CONSENSUS

Madison's successor, James Monroe, was an important transitional figure in American political and constitutional development. Monroe was the last president whose formative years coincided with the American Revolution and the struggle over the Constitution. At a time when most politicians had abandoned their eighteenth-century breeches and silk stockings in favor of the modern fashion of wearing trousers, Monroe continued to dress as an eighteenth-century gentleman, down to the silver buckles on his shoes. More important, he continued to adhere to the antiparty, republican principles of his youth.

---

[30] James D. Richardson, *A Compilation of the Messages and Papers of the Presidents, 1789–1908* (New York: Bureau of National Literature and Art, 1908), I: 585.

[31] Madison to John Adams, May 22, 1817, reprinted in Gaillard Hunt, ed., *The Writings of James Madison: Comprising His Public Papers and His Private Correspondence* (New York: G. P. Putnam's Sons, 1908), VIII: 391.

A skilled political operative and experienced diplomat, Monroe had flirted with Anti-Federalism in 1788 and run against James Madison for a seat in the first Congress, but he soon joined the Republican opposition to Hamilton in the 1790s. In 1808 he emerged as an alternative Republican candidate to Madison for president, a position that temporarily strained relations between the two men. Madison recognized Monroe's talents, however, and, amid worsening tensions with Great Britain, made him secretary of state, a position then seen as a stepping stone to the presidency.

Now in the White House, President Monroe took a cue from Washington, seeking first of all to establish a public persona as an old-fashioned republican statesmen, a president above party. He began by planning a limited, public tour of western and coastal defenses, but the public's enthusiastic reception in one of his earliest stops, Baltimore, led him to reconceive his trip in more ambitious terms. Monroe would take the presidency to the people, making three separate tours of the North, the West, and the South. As many as 50,000 people turned out to greet Monroe in Boston, an impressive number in the heart of Federalist New England. One Boston paper described Monroe's tour as a "demonstration of good feelings" that helped heal old political wounds.[32] The prospect of an era of good feelings, with old party affiliations dissolving into national unity, shone briefly but would not last.

Despite efforts to prop up a new, supra-partisan consensus, Monroe could not forestall the schemes of leading Federalists and Republicans to advance their partisan fortunes. Federalists had hoped that Monroe would use his cabinet appointments to reach out to them, lobbying especially for an appointment of Daniel Webster, one of their rising stars, to the position of attorney general. Republicans rebuffed such nonpartisanship and adamantly opposed such outreach. Despite the president's avowed antipathy to party, he did not in the end move to appoint any Federalists to his cabinet. The president did seek geographical balance and included voices of the Old Republican wing of his own party in addition to supporters of the rising, nationalist strain of Republican thought.

Monroe's political and constitutional ideology combined traditional eighteenth-century republican ideals with some of the more nationalist republican ideas that Madison and others had begun to develop in

[32] *Columbian Centinel,* July 8, 1817.

response to the problems posed by the War of 1812. Monroe used his inaugural to underscore the commonalities uniting Americans – "one great family with a common interest" – and to suggest that a new consensus could harmonize the Republican focus on the "great agricultural interest of the nation" and such Federalist priorities as encouragement of American shipping and "domestic industry." Monroe celebrated "the increased harmony of opinion which pervades our Union." He observed that, "Experience has enlightened us on some questions of essential importance to the country," and he now vowed that preservation of the nation's hard-earned "harmony" would be his highest priority.[33]

A cornerstone of this new synthesis was Monroe's acceptance of Madison's position on the Bonus Bill. A federal program of internal improvements was desirable both to promote prosperity and to enhance national unity, but it could only proceed once the Constitution was amended to expressly give the desired powers to Congress. Echoing sentiments that Madison and others had articulated, Monroe asserted that "the improvement of our country by roads and canals, proceeding always with a constitutional sanction, holds a distinguished place" among the nation's highest priorities and that such improvements would "bind the Union more closely together."[34]

In response to Monroe's reluctance to recognize a current, federal power to undertake internal improvements, a committee of the House of Representatives led by Henry St. George Tucker pressed for a more aggressive interpretation of the Constitution. A distinguished legal scholar from one of Virginia's most eminent families, Tucker represented the postwar spirit of progress and liberation from the most restrictive Republican dogmas. Adopting a position in between the traditional states' rights view of the matter and the more nationalist neo-Hamiltonian position, Tucker argued that, with approval from the states, the federal government could construct and improve roads. At a minimum, post roads and military roads were clearly within the ambit of congressional authority. Tucker pointed to earlier congressional actions, such as authorization of the Cumberland Road in 1806. Rather than embrace the strict construction of the 1790s, Tucker accepted the more pragmatic post-1800 view that a looser construction of federal power was permissible

---

[33] James Monroe, "Inaugural Address, March 4, 1817," *American State Papers, Foreign Relations,* vol. 4 (Washington, Gales and Seaton, 1834), pp. 126–129.
[34] Ibid.

when it did not trench on state power. Moreover, Tucker advocated a prudentialist mode of analysis in which policy considerations were a legitimate part of evaluating constitutionality. Finally, Tucker's report referred to Madison's theory of evolving constitutional meaning as a foundation for a more expansive view of federal power in this area.

Neither Monroe nor Madison accepted the committee's analysis. Indeed, Madison wrote to Monroe, informing him that he took particular exception to "the latitude of construction taken in the report."[35] Monroe too opposed the use of latitudinarian construction to expand Congressional authority to fund internal improvements. The Tucker committee's assertion of an expansive reading of federal power in this area was decisively rejected.

Monroe's leanings to Old Republican orthodoxy in this area were tempered by his desire to find a constitutional means forward on the question of internal improvements. The issue returned in 1822 when Congress passed legislation to maintain the Cumberland Road and to fund future maintenance through a system of gates and tolls. Monroe rejected the advice of his cabinet and vetoed the bill. The main problem with the bill, in his view, was the unconstitutional imposition of gates and tolls, which implied, he thought, a general federal power to build a system of internal improvements (a power qualitatively different from that implied by any of the previous appropriations for the Cumberland Road). On the other hand, Monroe had gone somewhat further than his predecessors, including Madison, in conceding Congressional authority to raise revenue for roads and canals, enter into agreements with states and localities, and even contract with private entities to effectuate specific proposals. What the federal government could not do in the absence of an amendment was act unilaterally to build roads or canals, or take on other direct responsibilities for control of internal improvements. Angered by Monroe's stance, Congress sought, but failed, to override the president's veto.

Following the debacle over the Cumberland Road bill, the president and Congress did find some middle ground, allocating funds with a more narrowly tailored purpose. Thus, Monroe happily signed the General

---

35 "Report, in Part, of the Committee on So Much of the President's Message as Relates to Roads, Canals, and Seminaries of Learning, December 15, 1817," *Niles Weekly Register*, vol. 18 December 27, 1817, at 283. "From James Madison to James Monroe, 9 December 1817," *Founders Online*, National Archives, last modified November 26, 2017, http://founders.archives.gov/documents/Madison/04-01-02-0155.

Survey Act of 1824, which allowed army engineers to survey potential road and canal routes to facilitate military preparedness and the delivery of the mail (objects clearly within the purview of the federal government). But the growing zeal for federal action on internal improvements frightened some traditional republicans. Even something as innocuous as the General Survey Bill prompted concern among states'-rights men like John Randolph. This ardent Old Republican argued that the same authority invoked by Congress for surveying would allow the federal government to "emancipate every slave."[36] Rather than mark a new era of nonpartisan support for modest enhancements of federal power, the passage of the Survey Bill fed the fears of the traditionalist wing of Southern republicans.

Nor were these fears confined to Southern champions of slavery. New York's Martin Van Buren, whose political savvy earned him the nickname the "Little Magician," emerged as a harsh critic of Monroe's drift toward National Republicanism. He believed that Monroe's naïve desire for a partyless politics and a healing of divisions with moderate Federalists implied the destruction of the pure Jeffersonian Republican party. Monroe's disdain for the party mechanisms that had saved the nation in 1800 explained Monroe's simultaneous deviation from republican principles on such matters as internal improvements. Of Monroe, Van Buren lamented that, "It was almost inevitable that efforts to destroy the republican organization should lead to the gradual abandonment of the principles it sustained."[37] Monroe's presidency was distracted by a distinctly eighteenth-century ideal of a partyless republican politics. Not so for Van Buren, the man of the future, who firmly believed that only a restoration of Republican Party organization in the coming elections could ensure the safety of republicanism and the states'-rights Constitution.

CONCLUSION

In the 1790s, the Republicans were a loose coalition of opposition voices, but the election of 1800 facilitated their transformation into an effective political movement. That movement delivered a mandate, as Jefferson saw it, for limited government and states' rights. But Jefferson's election

---

[36] John Randolph, "Speech on Internal Improvements, January 31, 1824," in *Speeches of Mr. Randolph* (Washington: Gales and Seaton, 1824), 25.

[37] Martin Van Buren, *The Autobiography of Martin Van Buren* (Washington, DC: U.S. Government Printing Office, 1920), 303.

had consequences for American constitutionalism that neither he nor other Republicans would have predicted. Jefferson presided over a significant increase of federal power, especially executive power, as manifested chiefly in the Louisiana Purchase and the Embargo. The Federalist opposition fervently opposed both policies, resorting to an almost Jeffersonian language of states' rights, just as Jefferson was embracing an almost Federalist accumulation of federal, executive power. Jefferson and his Federalist opponents were not hypocrites in any simple sense – each side had always embraced flexible combinations of federal power and states' rights. In Jefferson's case the realities of governance ended up pitting his principled commitment to strict construction against the best interests of his "chosen people," the white yeomanry. The Louisiana Purchase promised to realize the dream of a confederated "empire for liberty," sustainable for numberless generations, if only Jefferson would trim his constitutional principles a bit. For its part, the Embargo promised to keep the United States out of the kind of international military entanglement that raised taxes and enhanced both military and executive power at the center, threatening the liberty of the states and the people. In both instances the legitimate constitutional ends justified some flexibility in constitutional means. The executive power necessary to these policies seemed worth it under the circumstances, even if it required just the kind of loose construction of the Constitution that he had condemned in the Federalists.

Worth it or not, however, the Embargo started the Republicans down the road to the War of 1812 and the subsequent emergence of National Republicanism. After the War, President Madison, Jefferson's designated heir, embraced a flexible, evolutionary approach to constitutional interpretation, one that permitted him to accept the constitutionality as well as the policy of the once-despised Bank of the United States. His successor, James Monroe, applied this new Republican flexibility on constitutional meaning to the question of the federal role in internal improvements as well.

Together, these shifts in Republican views inaugurated an important new phase of constitutional politics. A group of loose-constructionist, commercially minded National Republicans vied for preeminence against a group of traditionalist, strict-constructionist, democratic Republicans, who retained their hostility to Hamilton's economic agenda and their attachment to a robust version of states' rights. This latter group would provide the core for a new partisan formation, the Democratic Party of Andrew Jackson and Martin Van Buren, which adopted formal structures of party organization and an ideology that for the first time justified party as a permanent and positive feature of the American constitutional order.

Van Buren, a senator from New York during Monroe's second term, was the key organizer and theorist of this new, party-centered approach to constitutional politics and an early critic of the National Republicans. Where Monroe sought to revive and perpetuate the antipartyism of the Framers and the Founding generation, Van Buren argued that experience had demonstrated that only constant vigilance, sustainable by no means but party organization, could protect the Jeffersonian, states'-rights Constitution from the relentless subterfuges of consolidators, the heirs of the Hamiltonian Federalists. Rather than merge Federalist and Republican ideas, Van Buren would take the lead in refashioning the remnants of the Republican coalition into a new, more disciplined political movement. This democratic movement would lay to rest many of the lingering traces of eighteenth-century republicanism and celebrate a democratic, party-centered, white man's republicanism in its place.

# 5

# The White Democracy

## INTRODUCTION

The administrations of Jefferson, Madison, and Monroe demonstrated the difficulty of implementing the Republican ideology of strict construction and states' rights. The Revolution of 1800 had promised a major redirection of American government after twelve years of Federalist efforts to realize a constitutional vision of centralized power, abetted by a liberal construction of the Constitution. The realities of governance, however, generated a Republican regime that compromised with Federalism on matters like the Bank and internal improvements and arguably outdid the Federalists' accumulations of power on matters like the Louisiana Purchase, the Embargo, and the crisis in international relations that eventuated in the War of 1812. On all these issues, important internal divisions developed within the Republican movement: Those coming to be known as National Republicans pragmatically embraced federal power in some areas. But other elements of the movement – soon to coalesce in the Democratic Party – increasingly saw themselves as defending a Jeffersonian orthodoxy of states' rights and democracy against the administrations' deviations from principle.

A major part of this new democratic orthodoxy was an intensified commitment to the constitutional subordination of black Americans. Southern whites who might have been open to moderate augmentations of federal power insisted instead on a rigid defense of state autonomy, for fear that enhanced federal power could turn to regulating slavery within the states. And many whites in both sections increasingly considered white democracy the central promise of 1800 and indeed of the

Constitution. For them, democracy could not survive any deviation from the Constitution's model of autonomous states, yielding only such power to the "general government" as was strictly required by the Constitution. Moreover, both north and south, these democrats thought that the unprecedented American experiment in large-scale democracy could not sustain the burden of giving full civic rights to anyone but white men. Rather, democratization required not just state autonomy but also the systematic subordination of black Americans, whether free or enslaved, in each of the autonomous states.

This chapter will tell the story of the coalescence of both the ideology and the movement of the white democracy, particularly the crystallization of its commitment to stark racial exclusion and the latter's connection to the principle of state autonomy. Although the framers and ratifiers protected slavery in the Constitution, black Americans did possess some substantial rights in many states at the Founding. The full, explicit racialization of the American constitutional order emerged only gradually over two generations. An emergent notion that white men possessed a constitutional right to hold slaves confronted intermittent antislavery initiatives, until the Missouri Crisis of 1819–1821 placed race and slavery durably at the center of American constitutional politics. In the aftermath of the Missouri Crisis, the champions of white democracy built the Democratic Party to implant their vision permanently in the Constitution.

## THE RIGHT TO HOLD SLAVES: THE FUGITIVE SLAVE CLAUSE

The text of the Constitution did not contain the word *slavery*, but its structure had been shaped by the realities of the institution. Taken together, the three-fifths compromise and the Fugitive Slave Clause (referring to those "held to service" rather than "enslaved") clearly constitutionalized slaveholding rights. Yet, the precise scope and workings of those rights depended on subsequent political development.

Indeed, it was not long after ratification that conflict emerged from the uncertainties of the Fugitive Slave Clause. Although the Constitution guaranteed the reenslavement of escapees, there was no prescribed mechanism for accomplishing this end. In 1791 the governor of Pennsylvania, Thomas Mifflin, sought the extradition of three Virginians who had kidnapped one John Davis and taken him to Virginia. Davis claimed to be a free man, but Virginia refused to turn over the alleged kidnappers. The Constitution specified no legal mechanism to adjudicate the states'

opposing views of a case such as Davis's, where one side asserted a right
to reclaim property and the other a right to protect its free inhabitants. In
response to the Davis case, Congress took up the unfinished business of
the Philadelphia Convention and enacted the Fugitive Slave Act of 1793
to specify the precise obligations of all involved.

Consideration of the fugitive slave bill went through a complex give
and take in Congress before a compromise was finally reached. The
1793 Act ultimately provided that slave-catchers might retake a fugitive
by force, the same as any owner of property might reclaim possession
wherever she or he found the property. It protected free blacks from
kidnapping only by mandating that the slave-catchers take their prisoner
before a state or federal magistrate to present their evidence of the
fugitive's status and obtain a certificate to legalize their removal of the
prisoner from the state. The Act did not specify any standard that
the slave-catchers' proof had to meet, only that it be satisfactory to the
magistrate in an informal hearing. Interference with the process of recovery carried a steep fine of five hundred dollars, a sum that exceeded the
assessed value of most American homes in the period. On the other hand,
the fine applied only to those who could be shown to have intentionally
interfered with the recapture. It thus strongly reaffirmed the principle of
property rights in human beings while minimizing the risk to whites who
stayed out of the way of the slave-catchers.

The language of the Fugitive Slave Clause may have been vague, but
Congress clearly understood the Constitution to recognize the full, conventional property rights of slaveholders and the illegitimacy of any out-
of-state interference in those property rights. Some states tried more
diligently than others to protect the free by way of antikidnapping laws
and the enactment of supplementary procedural protections for a seized
fugitive. But these efforts stood in the shadow of the new federal statute
that deployed institutions of law to vindicate slaveholders' constitutional
rights to hold enslaved persons. Moreover, that new federal statute had
passed with little opposition, by 48–7 in the House and by voice vote in
the Senate. Congress had achieved a widely acceptable compromise on the
particulars of procedure while never doubting the slaveholders' constitutionally guaranteed rights to their human property.

### THE RIGHT TO HOLD SLAVES: SOUTHWESTERN EXPANSION

More controversially, slavery expanded westward in this period with an
alacrity and robustness that would have dismayed those in the founding

generation who hoped that slavery was on an inexorable course of extinction. In the Philadelphia Convention, the slaveholding Virginian George Mason had argued for an immediate end to the international slave trade. He observed that southwestern settlers were already clamoring for slaves and would certainly spread the institution aggressively into the West if international supply lines remained open. But his arguments failed. No doubt, many members of Congress in the 1790s would have liked to confine the institution to the East. But realistically, there was no resisting western demand for slaves. English troops and Spanish colonies remained in the West, and residents in these regions made clear their willingness to trade their loyalty to the United States for protection of their interests in slavery. Whatever eastern legislators might prefer, then, the outcome was dictated by the lucrative cotton market, the established slave economies around Natchez and New Orleans, and the readiness of settlers to secede in defense of their interests. Even when the federal government banned international imports of slaves into the territories, it nevertheless tolerated de facto importation (via a brief, domesticating visit to the port of Charleston, South Carolina) until the general ban on the international trade came into effect in 1808. With time, the demand for slavery generated the idea that southerners had a constitutional right to hold slaves, free of interference from other states or the national government.

This right to hold slaves failed to take hold in the territories north of the Ohio River. There, the Northwest Ordinance of 1787 purported to ban slavery, and the new Congress reenacted the Ordinance in 1789. The Ordinance's enactment at about the same time as the framing of the Constitution suggested to some that the Constitution assumed a federal power to exclude slavery from the territories. But the meaning of the Ordinance was not so clear. The Ordinance was enacted with the votes of South Carolina and Georgia, among other slavery-dependent states, but without apparent debate or controversy over its purported exclusion of slavery. Slavery already existed in the northwest, and the Ordinance never did fully eliminate it, a reality that Congress undoubtedly anticipated. It is all but unimaginable, then, that Congress intended an abrupt, top-down emancipation so casually and with deep south support.

One way of accounting for southern acquiescence in the Ordinance is to recognize the limited value of these territories for slave agriculture. In the period when the Ordinance was being considered, the slaveholding interest was primarily concerned with securing American navigation rights the length of the Mississippi and the capacity to export their crops from New Orleans, then held by the Spanish. As a matter of political bargaining, then, obtaining slaveholding rights in the southwest and the right to export their crops by way of New Orleans would be more than an equivalent for giving up a more or less useless right to slavery in the Northwest.

This compromise can be seen in constitutional terms as a precursor to the Missouri Compromise of 1820, which barred slavery from much of the Louisiana Purchase. In both cases, the slavery-dependent states never frankly conceded the legitimacy of federal authority to restrict slavery from the territories, but were willing in these moments to compromise their constitutional principles to protect their interests. Before the Missouri Crisis, the antislavery interest made nominal efforts to exclude slavery from the Mississippi Territory and to limit its rate of flow into Louisiana, but no controversy before Missouri really forced slaveholders to confront a tenable claim that the general government could exclude slavery from territories that they coveted.

Moreover, north of the Ohio River, the Ordinance did not in fact put an end to such slaveholding as was already established. Nor did it prevent the passage of new laws that discriminated against free blacks, whose second-class status was only a marginal improvement on enslavement. Illinois, for example, barely prevented the full legalization of slavery at statehood and did maintain a system of "apprenticeship" little different from slavery into the 1840s.

In short, the constitutional accommodation of property in humans opened the door to the expansion of slavery westward. In the face of that reality, there grew real uncertainty about whether Congress even had the constitutional authority to control slavery in the West. The Northwest Ordinance suggested that it did, but the circumstances of its enactment and its weak enforcement raised doubts. Maybe the general government lacked that power except when the slaveholding interest was willing to bargain away its constitutional rights for pragmatic gains. Such an argument might be difficult for a constitutional lawyer to accept or even comprehend, but constitutions (and laws, for that matter) ultimately mean what authoritative actors make them mean. And members of Congress necessarily kept their eyes on the facts on the ground as much as on constitutional texts and precedents.

## ANTISLAVERY'S LIMITS

None of this evidence of the Constitution's accommodation of slavery is meant to deny countervailing, antislavery developments. An antislavery movement did slowly grow in the years following the adoption of the Constitution. The American Colonization Society (ACS) did emerge as a nationally prominent, though very conservative, organization, arguably working to roll back slavery. Congress did outlaw the international slave trade at the first constitutionally permissible moment with strong support from every state in the Union (though also with sharp disputes on the particulars of enforcement). So antislavery measures and conviction were important. At every step, however, the obstacles to sustained, national progress proved insurmountable.

In New York, the Revolution prompted the founding of the New York Manumission Society in 1785, which kept basic antislavery principles vital and popular. But even in New York a gradual emancipation law had to wait for the right moment. Gradually, the nonslaveholding electorate grew, and changing circumstances favored the spread of opposition to slavery. By the late 1790s, western New York developed a strong economic interest in maple sugar production, which competed with slave-produced cane sugar. Arguments in favor of the home industry began to incorporate antislavery ideas, and the Federalists saw some momentary partisan advantage in tying the southern-oriented Republicans to the slave-sugar interest. Such episodes were enough finally to put gradual emancipation on the agenda and see it easily through to passage in 1799.

In other northern states as well, Federalists saw a chance to stigmatize their Jeffersonian opponents for their connection to an increasingly unpopular institution. Some went so far as to suggest that the slaveholding core of the Republican Party was not qualified to participate in republican government at all. Echoing arguments that Jefferson had made in *Notes on the State of Virginia* and that George Mason had echoed in the Philadelphia Convention, northern Federalists like Noah Webster argued that "men who from their infancy hold, and those who feel, the rod of tyranny become equally hardened by the exercise of cruelty."[1] Similarly, Massachusetts Federalist Theodore Sedgwick, debating a naturalization bill in Congress in 1795, insisted that "in his opinion the relation of master and slave, generated habits at least as uncongenial with

---

[1] Noah Webster, *Effects of Slavery on Morals and Industry* (Hartford, CT: Hudson and Goodwin, 1793), 18.

the principles of our government, as would exist by not requiring the renunciation of a title [of nobility]."[2]

Such antislavery remarks generally served partisan interests because Federalist strength lay overwhelmingly in the northern states, making it easy for most Federalists to oppose slavery, while northern Jeffersonians bore the burden (as well as the benefits) of being allied to a dominant southern wing firmly tied to slavery. Equally partisan was the abortive campaign of some Federalists to eliminate the Constitution's Three-Fifths Clause, which would have substantially reduced Republican representation in Congress. Some Federalists even flirted with secession in 1803 and again during the War of 1812, seeing the Republican Embargo as tied closely to the slaveholding character of the Republican Party and southerners' disregard for the vital economic interests of the northeastern states. In the words of Newburyport minister Elijah Parish, "Let the southern Heroes fight their own battles, and guard their slumbering pillows against the just vengeance of their lacerated slaves ..."[3]

Of course, most Federalists stopped far short of advocating secession or national abolitionist legislation. Indeed, for all that northern Federalists opposed slavery, they remained committed to an orderly, hierarchical, and usually racist structure of society. Most had little doubt that blacks should generally remain at the bottom of that hierarchy, deferring to their white, educated, affluent betters. The northern Jeffersonians responded to Federalist antislavery offensives generally by disavowing slavery too (notwithstanding their southern ties), such that it became easy to pass emancipation legislation or, in the northwestern states and territories, to resist fledgling proslavery movements, even amid entrenched racism.

In the Deep South, these principles of liberty had limited impact, given the centrality of slavery to both culture and economy. But in the upper south, in states like Virginia and Maryland, there briefly appeared to be some room for antislavery. Revolution principles and the post-Revolution development of Quaker, Baptist, and Methodist theology combined to produce a short period of liberalized manumission laws. Under these laws, thousands were liberated before Virginia tightened its manumission laws in 1806. In Maryland, manumission remained legally available but

---

[2] Quoted in in Rachel Hope Cleves, "'Hurtful to the State': The Political Morality of Federalist Antislavery," in John Craig Hammond and Matthew Mason, eds., *Contesting Slavery: The Politics of Bondage and Freedom in the New American Nation* (Charlottesville: University of Virginia Press, 2011), 211, 212.

[3] Quoted in Cleves, 211, 218.

decreasingly popular. The earnest but ineffective antislavery sentiments among some southern slaveholders had strong roots in religion and philosophy, but they were not sufficiently joined to a popular economic or partisan interest to gain meaningful political traction. Moreover, a fear of slave insurrection infected most southerners. Jefferson's *Notes on the State of Virginia* had expressed this anxiety long before, and it was often invoked to cripple antislavery as a political force.

Even the termination of the international slave trade failed to erode domestic slavery, despite some initial hopes. Many slaveholders embraced the end of the international slave trade. This step could be advertised as a sincere manifestation of antislavery feeling, even as it actually served slaveholding interests in some ways: first, by mitigating the threat of insurrection, because it limited the growth of the enslaved population while suggesting no relaxation of rigor as to those already enslaved; and, second, by reducing supply and thus enhancing the price for large slave-holders' excess slaves, while threatening no one's vested property rights in enslaved workers.

The Constitution left the international slave trade to the states until 1808, but the states themselves mostly kept the trade closed, the exceptions being Georgia until 1798 and South Carolina's reopening of the traffic from 1803 to 1807. But the closing of the trade at the first opportunity seemed to most a vital step toward vindicating the nation's reputation as a land of liberty and justice. Thus the slaveholding Jefferson's 1806 message to Congress recommended prompt enactment of a measure that would "withdraw the citizens of the United States from all further participation in those violations of human rights which have been so long continued on the unoffending inhabitants of Africa."[4] For abolitionists, it was a mere first step but a vital one toward full emancipation. For those slaveholders who condemned slavery but lacked the will to abolish it, termination of the trade meant disengagement from a horrific crime and at least the possibility that slavery might slowly, somehow fade away.

The end of the international slave trade encouraged dreams of an organic end to slavery by way of "diffusion." According to this theory, the density of slavery everywhere would decline as supply dwindled and as many of the enslaved were taken west, even as the western migration

---

[4] Quoted in Matthew E. Mason, "Slavery Overshadowed: Congress Debates Prohibiting the Atlantic Slave Trade to the United States, 1806–1807," *Journal of the Early Republic* 20 (Spring 2000): 59–81, 63.

increased the sheer number of states embracing slavery. Facing a diminished threat of racial violence and spreading the cost of an ultimate emancipation among a large, dispersed population, increasing numbers of states might follow the northern example and consider a policy of gradual emancipation. Such diffusion, according to Jefferson, would "proportionally facilitate . . . emancipation by dividing the burthen on a great number of coadjutors."[5] His fellow slaveholder Madison shared this view, believing that diffusion was "not only best for the nation, but most favorable to slaves, both as to their prospects for emancipation, and as to their condition in the meantime."[6] Some southern Republicans thus advocated an end to slavery, but in a gradualist manner that would protect white interests and pose no threat to the stability of southern society.

Of course, in theory it was possible to go further than this Jeffersonian view. The Constitution had clearly contemplated the government's power to regulate and ban the international slave trade, presumably as a matter of regulating international commerce. Logically, therefore, it might also regulate interstate commerce in enslaved persons, as it regulated other interstate commerce. Such an argument was exceedingly rare in public life before the War of 1812, but became a fixture afterward. By way of the Commerce Clause, then, and through the judicious exercise of other national powers (for example, the national government's facilitation of colonization), the federal government might gradually pursue a general emancipation. From such a perspective, the termination of the international slave trade counted as a profoundly important first step, even as that enactment itself did little to erode slavery or even to slow its expansion into the West.

In fact, however, no substantial federal move against slavery followed the demise of the international slave trade. Even liberal-minded slaveholders did not see the closing of the trade as the beginning of – but closer to the sum of – federal action touching the future of slavery. Some were open to federal support for colonization, but generally they insisted that the national government must permit westward expansion of slavery and must leave the course of gradual emancipation to the slaveholding states themselves.

---

[5] Quoted in Lacy K. Ford, Jr., *Deliver Us from Evil: The Slavery Question in the Old South* (New York: Oxford University Press, 2009), 74.
[6] Quoted in Ford, *Deliver Us from Evil*, 74.

Thus in most respects those who favored some ultimate termination of slavery actually tended to join the firmer defenders of slavery on most questions of actual policy, including the details of the new ban on the slave trade. In the debates on the act banning the African trade, southerners disputed the power of the national government to interfere with the internal police of the states, including their regulation of slavery. And they made sure that the final bill provided for illegally imported Africans to be handed over to state governments, not emancipated. Liberal southerners might have genuinely longed for an emancipation, but for the foreseeable future they remained committed to preserving the enslaved as constitutional property and preserving the slaveholders' rights as property owners. This position followed logically enough from a Constitution that guaranteed state control of even the international slave trade for a generation, that explicitly recognized slave-owners' rights in the Fugitive Slave Clause, and that denied federal authority to step inside a state and reform that state's law of slave property.

### FEDERAL POWER AND COLONIZATION
### OF BLACK AMERICANS

Before the 1830s, antislavery societies of limited impact existed north and south, but no sustained antislavery movement emerged. Instead, the most prominent institution of antislavery sentiment, the American Colonization Society (ACS), achieved little more than self-defeating provocation of southern radicals. The ACS's efforts to enlist the federal government in the cause of antislavery – however conservatively and ineffectually – contributed to a fierce southern reaction in defense of radical state autonomy and slaveholding rights under the Constitution.

Founded in Washington, DC, at the close of 1816, the ACS sought explicitly to initiate a program of deportation of free blacks, not abolition. But its implicit goals were less clear. It proved attractive to some in the deep south who wanted the allegedly troublesome and dangerous population of free blacks removed. But, as one moved northward, the real purposes of the ACS seemed to expand. Deportation of free blacks to an African colony could encourage emancipations by those slaveholders who would never choose to set their slaves free into American society. Although no one thought that such voluntary emancipations could end slavery in any foreseeable future, many thought that federal financial assistance for colonization could give the program some impact, enough to materially advance the amelioration of slavery and/or the "whitening" of at least the upper south states. And, although no one could articulate the end game, many in the north – including some state legislatures – were willing to say out loud that the ultimate goal of colonization should be a final, general emancipation and a draining of blacks from American society. Thus, although the ACS avowed only the transsectional, racist project of removing free blacks, the ambiguities of its ultimate purposes and its persistent petitions for federal involvement only deepened regional divisions on slavery.

At the time of the founding of the ACS, probably a large majority of the nation continued to hope that slavery could be put on the road to peaceful extinction. Certainly, leading colonizationists believed well into the 1820s that many slaveholders regretted the curse of slavery and dreamed of an ultimate emancipation. The rapid elimination of slavery in a few northern states, the enactment of gradual emancipation in the rest, the ostensible barring of slavery from the northwestern territories by federal power, and the federal termination of the African slave trade all encouraged the hope that abolition might arrive through some combination of federal power, state power, and private action. In states with larger enslaved populations, these same developments joined with the theory of diffusion and the idea of colonization to keep the dream alive. And so the ACS, although declining to avow complete emancipation as a goal, emerged as the first national institution that, according to many of its proponents and opponents, might define slavery's path to extinction.

But the constitutional significance of the ACS lay primarily in its lobbying for federal appropriations for colonization. The use of federal power raised constitutional questions and posed political challenges, triggering southern fears that such policies would embolden those who sought to implement a more robust plan of using federal power against slavery. Embarking on the ambitious plan for colonization envisioned by the ACS would not only have been costly but also would have required a significant expansion of federal power. Thus, despite the modesty of the ACS's initial appeals for federal support, slavery-protective southerners were not necessarily wrong to fear the federalization of the ACS program, especially when they noted among the ACS's founders such advocates of national power as Henry Clay and Daniel Webster. These men would support enhanced national power for any number of purposes, not just colonization. But leading southern spokesmen quickly discerned the possible, antislavery implications of such federal power. Thus, already in 1818 North Carolina's Congressman Nathaniel Macon advised one correspondent to "examine the constitution of the U.S. .... and then tell me if congress can establish banks, make roads and canals, whether they cannot free all the Slaves in the U.S."[7]

Over the next decade, Macon's trepidation bloomed into a broader southern insistence that a hard line be drawn against those expansions of federal power that might threaten the autonomy and security of the slavery-dependent states. But the controversies over the ACS and the prospect of federal action against slavery drew their urgency in large part from the Missouri Crisis, to which we now turn.

### THE MISSOURI CRISIS AND SLAVERY IN THE WEST

The tension between slavery and freedom had been built into the Constitution in 1787, and the issue emerged intermittently in the decades that followed. Still, antislavery efforts were ad hoc and ineffective, despite the efforts of earnest antislavery minorities in Congress. No sustained public debate on the issue occurred before 1819, despite the 1816 founding of the ACS. Fearing western secession in the years before the War of 1812, the federal government accommodated southwestern settlers' demand for slavery. The resulting entrenchment of slave societies in the southwest meant that, by the time the question of statehood came up, there was no practical alternative to admitting Mississippi, Alabama, and Louisiana as slave states. Accordingly, only modest dissents were heard to those admissions. The same looked to be true of Missouri until that territory actually applied for admission.

The extended debate on the admission of Missouri, 1819–1821, was different from its predecessors. The outcome may have been the same, but this time antislavery forces fought vigorously, demanding that the nation take the turn toward freedom that they believed the Constitution required. The protectors of slavery responded with equal force, and the nation experienced its first sustained debate on the status of slavery under the Constitution.

Although slavery had managed to expand throughout the southwest and linger in the northwest during this period, the constitutional powers of the national government with respect to slavery remained unclear. Before the War of 1812, the belief was still widely held that America's destiny was a future without slavery and that the national government

---

[7] Quoted in Mason, *Slavery and Politics in the Early American Republic* (Chapel Hill: University of North Carolina Press, 2006), 162.

might play a role in steering the nation toward such a future. South Carolina's polemicists were not yet turning out fierce threats of disunion should the national government ever act on an antislavery motive. The struggle to reconcile southwestern settlers' claims of slaveholding "rights" with the establishment of a path to ultimate emancipation remained nascent.

But after the War of 1812 important circumstances changed. The nation came out of the war with a more powerful national government but a West that had entrenched slavery ever deeper. And the history of federal action regarding slavery had yielded more than one possible understanding of federal power: on the one hand, an understanding that would vindicate the rights of white holders of human property and bar the national government from regulating that property, and, on the other, an understanding that would empower Congress to employ its commerce powers as well as its authority over the territories to keep the national compass pointed toward freedom. At this moment, the Missouri Controversy erupted – not without warning but as the first chance for emancipationists to reestablish the direction of constitutional development, free from the distorting pressures of European threats on the Atlantic and in the West.

The northern states had already seen a postwar flowering of antislavery societies and antislavery literature. Northern printing presses churned out a steady supply of antislavery tracts and pamphlets. Newspapers devoted more attention to the cause of gradual abolition and colonization. Eventually, abolitionists even expanded their print efforts to include almanacs, songbooks, children's books, and jigsaw puzzles.

In Congress, there were isolated and abortive efforts to halt the expansion of the institution. Rep. Arthur Livermore futilely sought in 1818 to amend the Constitution to prohibit slavery "in any State hereafter admitted into the Union."[8] And, at about the same time, New York's James Tallmadge led a failed effort to prevent the admission of Illinois as long as its proposed constitution protected its systems of quasi-slavery and kept the door open to legalization of slavery as such.

Just as some northerners sought to reclaim the constitutional promise of ultimate emancipation, slaveholders in the coastal states mounted

---

[8] Quoted in John Craig Hammond, "'Uncontrollable Necessity:' The Local Politics, Geo-Politics, and Sectional Politics of Slavery Expansion," in Hammond and Mason, eds., *Contesting Slavery*, 138–160, 150.

increasingly rigid defenses of state autonomy, suppressing their erstwhile hope for a path to emancipation. The passage of years had brought such a quantity of slaveholder migration to the west, such a business in slave sales to the south and west, such entrenchment of the slave economy amid the temporizing language of eventual emancipation, that eastern slave-holders found themselves committed to the protection of slavery from the least federal intervention. Increasingly, southerners united behind the Constitution's supposed commitment of the problem fully to the states. No matter that no state south of New Jersey had produced significant progress toward emancipation, slaveholders insisted that slavery was the states' problem to deal with free from out-of-state pressure.

And so arose the battle over Missouri, which posed the question of whether Congress had power to bar slavery from an entering state or from a territory or, indeed, to act from an antislavery motive at all. But the two-year Missouri Crisis would not settle that question. Rather, the effect of the congressional battle was to crystallize a conflict between a North and a South, where prior conflicts over slavery had primarily pitted eastern states against western. Now, an increasingly cohesive North would claim a federal power to restrict slavery and attempt to redirect the country toward ultimate emancipation. The battle similarly produced a cohesive South in which federal power to restrict slavery was widely thought unconstitutional. This southern attitude reflected for some a deepening commitment to the permanence of slavery. For others, it reflected a determination that emancipation must come only by the work of the slaveholding states themselves, free from federal pressure. In the long aftermath of the Missouri Crisis, it would become clear that the constitutional scope of federal power over slavery would be deter-mined haltingly by the politics of North and South and by continuing developments in the West, not by any court and not by any single compromise.

The Missouri controversy began in early 1819. New York's James Tallmadge offered an amendment to a Missouri statehood bill that would have barred the further growth of slavery in that state and imposed a scheme of gradual emancipation for all enslaved persons born after the state's admission. Timothy Fuller of Massachusetts joined Tallmadge and articulated a stark argument for the antislavery character of the Consti-tution. He claimed that a federal prohibition of slavery in an entering state was actually required by the Constitution's command that Congress ensure the republican character of each state. Tallmadge's amendment, he argued, required no more "than that [Missouri's] constitution shall be republican," pointing to Article IV, Section 4.[9] Slavery lingered in many states out of sheer necessity, lest even greater evils result from hasty emancipation. But that did not imply any compatibility between slavery and republican government or any need to read the Constitution as slavery-protective.

Southern defenders of slavery countered that the Constitution in fact barred Congress from requiring an entering state to exclude slavery. Bridling at the notion that their home states failed the constitutional test of republicanism, they noted that the Constitution obviously embraced slavery as an institution that each state might permit or not as it saw fit. Moreover, they refused any longer to acknowledge the evil of slavery before affirming their customary position that the problem of slavery belonged to each state on its own.

This initial storm caused the failure of the Missouri bill in 1819, as the House narrowly endorsed the restriction of slavery while the Senate refused to go along. The debate resumed early in 1820, animated by a division among three groups: first, those who understood the Constitution as an antislavery document, accommodating it where unavoidable but prioritizing liberty and specifically providing for the abolition of the international slave trade as well as plenary congressional power over the territories; second, those who understood the Constitution as slavery-protective, unambiguously recognizing slave property in the Fugitive Slave Clause and elsewhere, and creating a federal structure that denied the national government any regulatory authority on the issue; and a third group, ultimately successful, that mainly wanted a pragmatic compromise that would see Missouri admitted and sectional hostility dampened.

In the Senate, this last group sought compromise by amending the House bill that would have restricted slavery in Missouri. The Senate removed all restrictions on slavery in Missouri but compensated with a federal ban on slavery in all other territories above the 36° 30' line. In the House, no such integrated compromise was possible because too many southerners would refuse to vote for the 36° 30' restriction and too many northerners would refuse to vote for Missouri's admission as a slave state. Instead, under the leadership of Henry Clay, the Senate's compromise was split into two separate recommendations to the House from a conference committee. First, Clay managed to produce a bare majority in the House for the Senate's removal of the slavery restriction on Missouri, by

[9] Quoted in Robert Pierce Forbes, *The Missouri Compromise and Its Aftermath* (Chapel Hill: University of North Carolina Press, 2007), 38.

combining a unanimous South and just enough northern members (mainly those won over by the South's agreement to admit Maine as a free state). But of course that group could not simultaneously generate a majority for the other half of the "compromise," the barring of slavery from other western territories. So Clay presented that amendment separately, finding a majority that comprised nearly all of the voting northern members and just over half of the southern votes. Although the restriction attracted a sizable number of southern votes, the vote hardly amounted to a compromise. Rather, the votes reveal a small majority of the southern members and a handful of northerners who might've been willing to support an integrated compromise but a large majority of the House that was not. Only by clever parliamentary maneuver, then, was a "compromise" extracted from the House.[10] But this sort of resolution – hardly an auspicious birth for what some would later insist was a "sacred" compromise – could not reliably settle any constitutional questions.

A majority of southern members of the House voted for the slavery ban north of 36° 30' without explanation, thus indicating a willingness to compromise without saying anything as to constitutional principle. But the southerners who spoke out on the question reliably insisted that Congress lacked constitutional power to impose such a ban. This view was shared even by James Madison, who wrote to a correspondent in late 1819 that the authorization by the Territories Clause to

make all needful rules and regulations respecting the Territory or other property belonging to the U. S. ... cannot well be extended beyond a power over the Territory as property, & a power to make the provisions really needful or necessary for the Govt of Settlers until ripe for admission as States into the Union. It may be inferred that Congress did not regard the interdict of slavery among the needful regulations contemplated by the constitution; since in none of the Territorial Governments created by them, is such an interdict found.[11]

---

[10] The final maneuvering in the House can be followed at Annals of Congress, 16th Congress, 1st Session, 1586–1587; the larger story is concisely told by Sean Wilentz, "Jeffersonian Democracy and the Origins of Political Antislavery in the United States: The Missouri Crisis Revisited," *The Journal of the Historical Society* IV:3 (Fall, 2004), 381–382 and throughout.

[11] Madison's argument here seems to ignore the precedent of the Northwest Ordinance, but Madison later in the letter attributes the ordinance to the Confederation Congress, the body that actually created the Northwest Territory as a legal entity before the writing of the new Constitution, and further questions its constitutionality. James Madison to Robert Walsh Jr., November 27, 1819, Founders Online, National Archives (http://founders.archives.gov/documents/Madison/04-01-02-0504, ver. 2013-06-26). Source: *The Papers of James Madison*, Retirement Series, vol. 1, *4 March 1817–31 January 1820*,

Therefore, insofar as the compromise rested on southern votes for a slavery ban in some territories, those votes can be understood as a pragmatic "waiver" of slaveholders' claimed constitutional rights – and arguably worthless rights, at that, because the land north and west of Missouri was often thought inhospitable to slavery. Moreover, if time proved those lands desirable to slaveholders (as it did by the 1850s), southerners could confidently (and accurately) expect that the necessity of organizing those territories and admitting states would provide occasions for renegotiation of slaveholders' rights. A large number of the southern members, perhaps most of them, continued to believe that the Constitution prohibited congressional interference with slaveholding in the territories and in entering states. By contrast, a large number of northern members, perhaps most of them, continued to believe that the federal government had the constitutional obligation to halt the expansion of slavery and perhaps to encourage its ultimate termination.

In sum, it is doubtful that any compromise accomplished in the Missouri Crisis was as solid or as sacred as its defenders would later claim. Instead, it represented an ad hoc maneuver that subsequent politicians tried to sanctify as a protector of durable sectional peace, even as many foresaw the truth that it would hold only until the pressures of settlement, organization, and admission raised again the question of slaveholders' rights. Although the Missouri controversy created a North and a South that had never before crystallized as such – presaging the eventual violent end of the slaveholding republic – the minority compromisers were the victors for the time being. The Missouri Compromise removed enough immediate irritants from the national scene to provide space for those who would build a transsectional Democratic Party to keep slavery off the national agenda.

But there was an important epilogue to the story of the Compromise that illuminated the firmly racist constitutional politics on the immediate horizon. The famous compromise of March, 1820 had not actually completed the admission of Missouri. It had authorized the formation of a state constitution with a promise of admission once completed. But, when Missouri submitted a constitution that categorically excluded the immigration of free blacks, some northern members of Congress again objected. This issue, however, would not galvanize the North the way worries about slavery's expansion had. The original opposition to

ed. David B. Mattern, J. C. A. Stagg, Mary Parke Johnson, and Anne Mandeville Colony (Charlottesville: University of Virginia Press, 2009), 553–559.

Missouri's admission had been led by relatively idealistic antislavery types. Citing the Declaration of Independence and the Constitution, they bridled at accommodation of race-based slavery within a republican order. The dominant northern view going forward, however, was very different. The foreseeable future belonged to the party-building advocates of white democracy, many of whom did not want slavery where they lived or in the common territories but had no compunctions about allying themselves with other states' slaveholders and rendering blacks a subordinated caste.

So Congress finessed Missouri's exclusion of free blacks by fitting a fig leaf over it. Congress accepted the state's constitution on the condition that Missouri affirm that it would not be interpreted to violate the constitutional rights of American citizens. Congress could hardly have demanded anything more explicit because a number of other states, including some in the North, already had equivalent legal bars on the entry of blacks. Moreover, these bars were of a piece with an erosion of the civil rights of free blacks generally in these years.

Finally, the Missouri Crisis dramatically sharpened southern sensitivity to the growth of federal power. The ACS soon renewed its petitions for federal appropriations at the same time that so-called National Republicans defended the Bank of the United States and agitated for federal internal improvements and protective tariffs, all of which could seem like threats to slavery after the Missouri Crisis. Thus, in an 1825 pamphlet, one Whitemarsh Seabrook claimed that the ACS sought in effect to convert the federal government into an emancipationist organization. He argued that even discussion of emancipation in the public councils – as demanded by ACS requests for federal appropriations – would undermine slaves' belief in the permanence of their enslavement and encourage them to resist by any and all means. Indeed, he explicitly blamed such discussions for the Denmark Vesey slave conspiracy of 1822, which had reputedly contemplated a massive, violent slave revolt: "Did not the unreflecting zeal of the North and the East and the injudicious speeches on the Missouri question animate Vesey in his Hellish efforts?"[12]

By 1827, after more than a decade of loose-constructionist administrations under Monroe and John Quincy Adams, the ACS again sought federal appropriations for the limited purpose of colonizing free blacks.

[12] Quoted in Ford, *Deliver Us from Evil*, 306.

Slave-state reaction only grew sharper. South Carolinian Robert Turnbull's influential series of essays known as "The Crisis" linked the proposed appropriations to other desires of constitutionally nationalist politicians – the Bank of the United States, protective tariffs, and federal funding of internal improvements – as threats to "the 'LIVES, liberties and properties' of the WHITE people of the Southern States." The power to pursue any of these policies would have established Congress's power over "the whole domestic policy of South-Carolina" and any other state it chose. And of course the chief "domestic policy" with which he was concerned was slavery, "the LIFE BLOOD of the State." Turnbull did not defend slavery as a positive good and seemed to accept that dominant opinion regretted slavery as an unfortunate inheritance. But the state's lifeblood was its lifeblood, and "if there be an evil in slavery, the evil is ours." Congress, he insisted, had no authority "to legislate, directly or indirectly, on the subject of slavery." Moreover, the mere discussion of even so modest a step as funding the voluntary departure of free blacks went beyond constitutional bounds: "To countenance the American Colonization Society, will be to proceed upon the principle, that slavery is a rank weed in our land ... It will be a declaration of WAR, and MUST be treated and resisted as such." Further, "Discussion will be equivalent to an act of emancipation, for it will universally inspire amongst the slaves, that hope."[13]

Moreover, Turnbull and his like were not necessarily wrong to suggest that the main effect of the ACS's efforts would be to encourage an enslaved class to pursue its own emancipation by its own means. The ACS had no plan to solve the slavery conundrum other than a largely unaffordable and unworkable scheme to pursue a vaguely defined program of colonization, seen in different lights in different regions. Nor did any other advocates of eventual emancipation, north or south, present any plan that could be accepted by the southern slaveholding establishment. With so little prospect of actual emancipation by peaceful means, southern slaveholders justifiably feared that agitation of futile schemes to end slavery might encourage the enslaved to take their fates into their own hands.

Increasingly, therefore, Turnbull's views would become post-Missouri, southern orthodoxy. The conviction only grew that Congress had no power to act on the premise of slavery's being an evil. Nor, therefore,

[13] Quoted in Forbes, *The Missouri Compromise*, 223–226.

did it have the right even to discuss the future of slavery in the states. The House famously embraced this orthodoxy in the Gag Rule of 1836, by which it refused even to consider antislavery petitions. As late as 1827, there hardly existed a national antislavery movement, but the anemic ACS had helped to prompt great constitutional clarity in the post-Missouri South. Slavery might not be a positive good, but the challenge of slavery must remain fully within the control of the states.

In short, the Missouri Crisis crystallized a North and a South in conflict over questions of federal power generally, sharpened by the southern conviction that those questions bore especially heavily on the security of slaveholding. And that conflict was exacerbated by the movement of the National Republicans in the 1820s to enhance federal power in a neo-Federalist program of national economic development. National Republican leaders like Kentucky's Henry Clay sought to assuage southern fears by insisting that the Missouri Compromise secured slaveholding interests and that the ACS represented no threat. But resurgent democrats insisted that only rolling back federal power could secure the white democracy, as well as each state's domestic arrangements.

## THE NEW YORK CONVENTION AND THE EMERGENCE OF THE WHITE DEMOCRACY

Henry Clay, soon to be the leading figure of the Whig party, emerged from the Missouri Crisis as the celebrated engineer of compromise, at least to some. But the engineer of the nation's constitutional politics after Missouri was Martin Van Buren of New York. Having learned the danger of even discussing slavery at the national level, Van Buren defended the Constitution as neither pro- nor antislavery but a Constitution of white democracy and therefore state autonomy. The principle of states' rights was essential to democracy for two reasons: first, because an active, distant government would always misuse the delegated power of the sovereign people ("the democracy"), and second, because the post–Missouri Union could only survive the tensions over slavery by leaving that issue to each state's internal politics.

Even when hostile to slavery's expansion into the western territories, northern Democrats were generally indifferent to the fate of the enslaved in other states. They cared only about the ascendancy of the white man, freed from all political inequalities rooted in station and class. Their aggressive subordination of black Americans in the name of equality and liberty seems oxymoronic to the modern mind and indeed to some contemporaries. But the emergent Democrats believed that such subordination was essential to the democratic order promised by the Constitution. If one state achieved that subordination via slavery and another without slavery, each state should be content to allow the other to do as it thought best. The point was simply to preserve equality and sovereignty in the white, male democracy of each state.

If states' rights and white democracy went hand in hand, the defenders of this arrangement claimed that extending full civic participation beyond white men would be dangerous to the survival of the Constitution itself. When condemning the Federalists' elitist constitutionalism, the new democrats celebrated "equality" and rejected "distinctions," often using the old language of "the aristocracy" – now constitutionally obsolete – and "the democracy," their label for the sovereign people undivided. They explicitly rejected the British notion of estates in favor of an equality that was "universal" for "the democracy" of white men. Simultaneously, they ascribed separate and constitutionally subordinate places to blacks, as well as women and Indians, who would undermine democracy itself if admitted to public life.

This understanding of democracy was reflected in Missouri's formal exclusion of black migrants with congressional acquiescence, described earlier, as well as in the legal restrictions on blacks across the North (as well as the South) in the years after the War of 1812. Connecticut, for example, denied the franchise to any new black voters in its 1818 Constitution. Pennsylvania may have been a pioneer of gradual emancipation in 1780 and something of a refuge for free blacks in this period, but in 1837 the ascendancy of the Democratic Party coincided with the disfranchisement of the state's black population in its new constitution. According to one survey of the northern states, as of 1830 six denied blacks the vote altogether, and three barred blacks from testifying against whites or even immigrating to the state. Blacks were generally, though not universally, excluded from duty on juries and in militias. The civil rights of blacks in the North varied across time and space, but nowhere could blacks count on full equality with whites. And, more to the point, the ascendancy of democratic ideology and the expansion of political rights among white men in the Jacksonian period rested on an explicitly racist understanding of civic capacity, not on a truly universalist egalitarianism.

The complicated dynamics at work in producing white democracy are revealed in the New York Constitutional Convention of 1821, a critical episode in which the legal foundations for the Van Burenite ascendancy were established. The move to revise New York's revolutionary-era constitution formed part of a wave of democratic constitutional reform from after the War of 1812 to the 1840s. Under the leadership of Martin Van Buren and his Bucktail faction of New York democrats, this Convention decisively marked the end of old-style republican ideology in New York and the rise of a self-consciously democratic politics.

In the state's 1777 Constitution, New York had established property requirements for voting that applied equally to white and black voters. Even after the beginning of the Revolution, the distinction between the propertied and the poor remained more salient than the distinction between white and black with respect to the suffrage. The New York electorate remained a propertied club, though a club that rapidly grew to encompass well over half of the adult, white, male population, along with a far smaller proportion of the black population.

But in the two generations that followed, cultural shifts deprived the aristocrat and the gentleman of all claim to distinctive constitutional status. In the wake of the War of 1812, persistent factional maneuvering among New York's republicans led finally to the "Bucktail" faction's push for a new constitution. The Bucktails claimed to speak for the expanding ranks of white men who lacked freeholds, including farmers in the west of the state not yet in possession of deeds and the growing working-class population of New York City. They also exploited long-standing hostility to the Council of Appointment and the Council of Revision, two increasingly anachronistic institutions, reminiscent of the eighteenth-century English model in which offices and officeholders might reside in more than one branch at a time.

The ascendancy of democracy in New York and in the convention was reflected in the statute calling the convention, which used greatly liberalized rules for the suffrage and for eligibility to serve as a delegate. The statute required no freehold but only tax-paying, militia service, or labor on the roads.[14] And this expanded electorate chose delegations overwhelmingly committed to democratic reform, as one member early in the proceedings noted: "It is a fact not to be disguised, that a towering majority of this Convention represent the interests, feelings, and views of the friends of democratic government."[15] Van Buren's democratic Bucktail faction dominated the delegate elections so completely that the Bucktails often fragmented into factions in the convention, yielding

---

[14] Nathaniel H. Carter and William L. Stone, reporters, *Reports of the Proceedings and Debates of the Convention of 1821* (Albany, NY: E. and E. Hosford, 1821), 22–23.
[15] Ibid., 50 (Mr. Livingston).

frequent controversies among those otherwise in agreement on the principle of white democracy. In the end a large majority of the convention approved a dramatically democratized suffrage provision, though of course with a racist cast. This provision closely approximated universal, white, male suffrage, and it explicitly disfranchised nearly all black New Yorkers.

But why? What was the link between democratization, with all its rhetoric of universal equality, and the deliberate exclusion of so many potential voters on the basis of race? The convention's constitutionalization of democracy required a radical break from traditional property qualifications, and it turned out that that break could not be readily accomplished without drawing in the question of race. Delegates often hesitated to abandon the inherited idea that the suffrage was a privilege, deserved only by those who could use it responsibly and independently. On this basis, these democrats rejected property as a marker of civic responsibility but substituted race and gender, denying the suffrage to women, Indians, and nearly all black New Yorkers. There may have been a handful of democrats in the convention who actually wanted to do away with the racial qualification. But even amid the ascendancy of self-conscious democracy the great majority insisted that being black should severely limit one's access to the vote. And the entire body seemed to treat the exclusion of women as a simple matter of common sense (as was made explicit in a handful of unchallenged remarks).

The convention's debate on the suffrage began with the presentation of a report by the chair of the relevant committee, Nathan Sanford of New York City. Sanford immediately targeted the lingering, Anglophilic constitutional ideas that lay in the way of democracy. He announced that the committee had sought "to abolish all existing distinctions, and make the right of voting uniform."[16] And these oppressive "distinctions" were those derived from "British precedents": "In England, they have their three estates, which must always have their separate interests represented. Here there is but one estate – the people."[17]

This framing of the convention as a mechanism by which the democracy would slough off the remaining elements of the British balanced constitution would recur at various places in the proceedings, especially when the tiny Federalist minority and a few conservative Republicans repeatedly initiated rearguard actions against democratic reform. Thus,

---

[16] Ibid., 178.    [17] Ibid., 178.

after a general property qualification failed to gain significant support, Chief Justice Ambrose Spencer proposed such a qualification just for electors of the Senate, so as to preserve a "balanced" rather than a purely democratic government. Only by preserving different "geniuses" in the two legislative houses, one of them specifically resting on the landed interest, could a proper balance be achieved. This reference to the British notion of a balanced constitution again prompted a leading democrat's statement of American exceptionalism. Erastus Root accepted that a monarchy might require a balanced constitution: "In such governments there are different *orders* as lords and commons in England; different *estates*, as in the diets of Sweden, Denmark, and Germany." But America was a new thing under the sun: "We are all of the same estate – all commoners; nor, until we have privileged orders, and aristocratic estates to defend can this argument [for a balanced constitution] apply."[18]

Root thus joined Sanford in throwing over old-school distinctions, marginalizing the remnant of aristocracy, and naming the democracy as the only legitimate "estate." But every democrat, as it turned out, was eager to enshrine one or another distinction in the constitution rather than fully "make the right of voting uniform." Indeed, Sanford had not finished his opening remarks before he introduced a principle by which new distinctions were sustained: "The principle of the scheme now proposed is that those who bear the burthens of the state, should choose those that rule it."[19] Thus the report proposed not quite universal suffrage but enfranchisement of all those who paid taxes, served in the militia, or worked on the roads – "bear[ing] the burthens of the state."

A further committee restriction, which Sanford did not mention, was race. The committee report had limited the suffrage explicitly to "white" men. (Perhaps Sanford did not mention the exclusion of free blacks because he could not quite square that blanket disfranchisement with his principle of enfranchising those who bear the burdens of the state.) This restriction was eagerly picked up by the next speaker, committee member John Ross of Genesee, who celebrated the proposed constitution's racism. Despite his acceptance of blacks' "natural equality," Ross thought them no part of the New York democracy. They were "seldom, if ever, required to share in the common burthens or defence of the state." But, more than that, "they are a peculiar people, incapable, in my judgment, of exercising that privilege with any sort of discretion, prudence, or

---

[18] Ibid., 223.    [19] Ibid., 178.

independence. They have no just conceptions of civil liberty. They know not how to appreciate it and are consequently indifferent to its preservation."[20] Here, he compared blacks to aliens and minors, who could not vote responsibly, and to women and "aborigines," who were axiomatically excluded without a word of discussion by the convention.[21]

This passage proved typical of racist democrats' arguments, mixing exaggerations and falsehoods about the degree to which blacks were asked to pay taxes or defend the state with plain, racist expressions of contempt for blacks' civic capacity. The antiracist Federalist Peter Jay warned such avowed democrats against deliberately entrenching "a large, a perpetual, a degraded, and a discontented *caste*, in the midst of our population."[22] But the firmest racists did not see the tension between their celebrations of equality and their arbitrary exclusions, even as that tension seems to have opened the door to the democrats' smaller but notable restrictions on white male suffrage.

Apart from Jay, hardly any whites in the convention expressed much regard for the civic capacities of blacks. But, unlike the white democrats, Federalists expressed about the same, traditional contempt for propertyless whites as for propertyless blacks. If one adhered to the traditional notion that property-holding was essential to civic participation, then one's racism added little to one's engrained notions of republican civics. Thus it was not hard to accept that the exceptional black property-holder might vote (especially because the black vote generally went Federalist) when the vast majority of black citizens were excluded, as were many poor whites. Racist Federalists did seem to hold the line against black officeholding, but their racism produced no compelling sentiment that the few propertied blacks must also be disfranchised.

In the eyes of the traditionally disfranchised groups of poor white men, however, racist exclusions of blacks were widely thought essential. The fact was that poor whites and propertied whites generally agreed that poor black voters were civically incompetent, lacking the character to do anything but disgrace the polls if given the chance. For the Federalists and other conservatives, such civic irresponsibility was first a product of the same economic dependency that disqualified poor whites, but it was also a matter of race. For white democrats, however, their own claim to the suffrage regardless of property had to rest exclusively on a racial distinction, that black voters' inevitable dishonoring of the suffrage was a matter

[20] Ibid., 180.    [21] Ibid., 181.    [22] Ibid., 201.

of race, not economic condition. It was essential, then, for white democrats to distinguish themselves from blacks, insisting against the Federalists' smug contempt that poor whites generally possessed full civic competence and would honor the suffrage, whereas everyone knew that blacks could not.

As white men in the United States ventured out on a democratic limb, nervously defying the inherited dogma that the people could not govern themselves, they assumed that the branch would fall if weighted with allegedly feckless black men as well. Only by establishing this racial distinction did whites believe they could go forward with untested democratic reforms in confidence that those reforms would escape the fatal scenes of electoral disgrace predicted by the Federalists. If American democracy were to succeed in a world of otherwise hierarchical constitutional structures, most white democrats believed, it must protect itself against infection from within in the form of grossly irresponsible voters. Nearly all whites agreed that the irresponsible included at least the vast majority of blacks, but, while Federalists could protect their republican vision from this class simply through a traditional property qualification, principled white democrats could find no way to do so except by direct constitutionalization of their racist assessment of blacks' civic incapacity. It's not necessarily that white democrats somehow *needed* a class below them, as some modern scholars have suggested.[23] Rather, they simply believed there *was* a class beneath them, one that almost all whites believed dangerous to the fragile democratic experiment.

Democrats deployed an unvarnished racism in defense of the racial exclusion. Thus, for Samuel Young, "The minds of the blacks are not competent to vote. They are too much degraded to estimate the value, or exercise with fidelity and discretion that important right... Their vote would be at the call of the richest purchaser." He would, "emancipate and protect them; but withhold that privilege [of voting] which they will inevitably abuse." And the proof lay in "your jails and penitentiaries," which were filled with "the very race, whom it is now proposed to cloth with the power of deciding upon your political rights."[24] Thus did Young

---

[23] See, e.g., Paul Finkelman, *Slavery and the Founders: Race and Liberty in the Age of Jefferson*, 2nd ed. (New York: M. E. Sharpe, 2001), 126–127. We do not mean to deny that this racial dynamic may have been a factor, but the focus here is on the constitutional logic, such as it was. Finkelman's chapter 5 is a valuable survey of the ways in which Federalist racism made more room for black rights than did Jeffersonian Republican racism.

[24] Ibid., 191.

and other democrats seek to restrict the vote to "those who understand the worth of that privilege" and deny it to those who were "degraded, dependant, and unfit to exercise it."[25]

But every time the democrats defended the exclusion of blacks on such grounds of dependency and irresponsibility, they found themselves vulnerable. The conservative Chief Justice Ambrose Spencer declared himself content to see blacks excluded but insisted that those whites who could qualify only via the militia or road work were equally dependent types and that to enfranchise any of these would only hand their votes over to their employers.[26] As long as the white democrats insisted that blacks' dependency and incompetence disqualified them, they only forced themselves to explain why the most dependent and degraded of whites were somehow qualified.

Van Buren's own answer was that the most civically marginal whites should *not* gain the suffrage. Thus Van Buren opposed qualification by mere labor on the roads, explaining his position in a way that again suggested a concern with black membership in the democracy. He insisted that a road-work qualification would "undervalue this precious privilege so far as to confer it with an undiscriminating hand upon every one black or white who would be kind enough to condescend to accept it." And later the same day, the convention agreed for the moment to withdraw the suffrage from those who could qualify only by road labor.

When the convention turned to the taxpaying qualification, however, it demonstrated a thoroughgoing commitment to white democracy even beyond that of Van Buren. The Revolution principle of "no taxation without representation" led a majority of the delegates to defend a right of taxpayer suffrage that would extend in principle even to black taxpayers. But the racism of the convention ran so deep that ultimately it chose to relieve nearly all blacks of taxpaying rather than permit them to vote. In the final compromise, only the few blacks in possession of a $250 freehold would be permitted to vote (and required to pay taxes). Then, having freed itself of the danger of black suffrage – even the suffrage of those who had long borne the "burthens of the state" – the convention went on to enfranchise not only taxpayers but also white men who served in the militia or worked on the roads as well, extending the suffrage to the great bulk of the white democracy.

[25] Ibid., 190 (Mr. Radcliffe); see also Mr. Root at 185–186.    [26] Ibid., 195–197.

Not every delegate was happy with the proposal. The racial liberal Ezekiel Bacon of Oneida objected that admission of a few blacks to the suffrage did not change the fact that this provision constituted a virtually complete disfranchisement of black New Yorkers, and he thought the convention should have the courage to say so explicitly. This preoccupation with indulging a prejudice had so contorted the convention's deliberations as to leave the democrats insisting that property "conferred neither talents, integrity, or independence" in the white man while somehow supposing that a freehold was the only thing that "imparted them all" to the black man.[27]

Olney Briggs of Schoharie spoke for the most vicious racists in declaring that he "wished to make the constitution consistent in all its parts. The black man was a degraded member of society and would therefore be always ready to sell his vote; nor would real estate make him a better man. The whites can never take them to their bosoms."[28] When Peter Jay rose again to lay the blame for any degradation in blacks at the door of white men and to condemn any unequal treatment of blacks in the constitution,[29] Briggs let loose the reins. Resorting to the language of "monkey" and "baboon," he insisted that there was no place for blacks at all in the constitution.[30]

But more pragmatic racists prevailed. Van Buren had opposed giving the vote to the road-workers before but now supported the compromise. Admitting to lingering concerns with this close approach to universal suffrage, he intimated that it was part of a compromise that would prevent the convention's thoughtlessly sliding all the way to universal suffrage. And to avoid such a catastrophe, he would support the whole package.

But why would universal suffrage be such a catastrophe to Van Buren? This time, he did not explicitly invoke race, but there could be little doubt that it remained an important consideration. According to Van Buren, universal suffrage would produce an electorate unfit to vote, especially in New York City where it would add about 11,000 voters beyond the very liberal suffrage allowed in the election for convention delegates. And "the character of the increased number of votes would be such as would render their elections rather a curse than a blessing; which would drive from the

---

[27] Ibid., 369.  [28] Ibid., 364.  [29] Ibid., 364.  [30] Ibid., 365.

polls all sober minded people; and such ... was the united opinion, or nearly so, of the delegation from that city."[31]

So who were the 11,000 potential voters whose "character" would subvert the democratic experiment? It appears from assertions in the convention[32] and from census figures that about 2,500 of the new voters would have been black citizens, who were excluded from the militia by federal law and who generally had no taxable property. The remaining thousands must have been those untaxable white New Yorkers who also did not serve in the militia (and apparently had no opportunity to do road work). These people, according to Van Buren, "have no interest in the government."[33] Together, the blacks and the noncontributing whites, many of them recent immigrants, would undermine elections by "driv[ing] from the polls all sober minded people."[34] Van Buren may have spearheaded the organization of the democracy in America, but he had grown up in a Federalist stronghold, was acutely aware of the experimental quality of American republicanism and its democratic trajectory, and remained concerned that, for all his and others' talk of universal equality, the experiment could fall under the weight of the civically irresponsible. Needing to draw a line between the qualified and the unqualified, he insisted that the vast majority of whites could come to the polls but that only a tiny number of blacks could be tolerated.

The convention thus adopted a close approximation of white democracy. The vast majority of white men would qualify. The black community would be overwhelmingly excluded, along with the small stratum of the white community whose civic character fell to the level of the typical black person. Finally, black persons were generally exempted from taxation to cement and justify their civic exile, excepting only those few with substantial freeholds, presumably because their votes would be too few to matter but their property too large to leave untaxed.

---

[31] Ibid., 367. It is also important to recognize that Van Buren's position, and that of other strategic thinkers among the democrats, was driven in part by a recognition that the black population tended to vote Federalist and that New York City was an electoral stronghold of DeWitt Clinton, the great personality of New York politics and the nemesis of the democratic organizers. So the retreat from full white democracy was partly driven by electoral calculation. But it is equally important to recognize that the hostility to Clinton arose from his refusal to accept the principle of party regularity and his readiness to cooperate with Federalists, thus, in Van Buren's mind, proving himself a threat not just to one party's electoral fortunes but to the democratic experiment itself. It was therefore imperative to marginalize Clinton by whatever means necessary before the principles of white democracy could be fully implemented.

[32] See Ibid., 198 (Mr. Radcliff).     [33] Ibid., 368.     [34] Ibid., 367.

On this score, Ezekiel Bacon made one last, universalist plea to the white democrats. "One of our first general principles," he argued, "is, that we recognize no distinct casts or orders of men, having distinct and fixed personal or political rights."[35] But this argument simply misconceived the "general principles" of most of the convention's democrats. They had made it clear that the reduction of black New Yorkers virtually to a caste was a primary principle of the white democracy's own emergence from constitutional subordination. Indeed, a failure to exclude the bulk of black New York from "democratic" elections would threaten to undermine democracy from the start. The last of New York's enslaved population would be emancipated in 1828, but the convention ensured that black New Yorkers' civic subordination was written into the fundamental law of democracy. And, in 1826, as the day approached when the last enslaved blacks would be released into mere disfranchisement, white New York enfranchised the remainder of the white, male democracy. On the eve of the Democratic Party's ascendancy, it gained confidence that democracy could survive "universal suffrage" as long as universal meant white and male.

## CONCLUSION

The legal entrenchment of white democracy in New York reflected a national trend in the Jacksonian era. Nearly all states embraced something approaching universal white, manhood suffrage in the first half of the nineteenth century. At the same time, only a few states failed to disfranchise blacks, who had held at least a formal right to vote in most states in the 1790s. And every state admitted after 1819 confined the suffrage to white men. Outside of Federalist- and then Whig-leaning New England, the constitutionalization of the "democratic" experiment everywhere meant the enfranchisement of the white democracy.

This almost complete whitening of the electorate fit seamlessly with Van Buren's larger strategy for securing the hegemony of the democracy nationally, given that one of the two great sections of the nation was built on racialized slavery. Van Buren famously built the new Democratic Party as a reconstructed alliance between "the planters of the south and the plain republicans of the north."[36] That states'-rights alliance had

---

[35] Ibid., 369.
[36] Martin Van Buren to Thomas A. Ritchie, January 13, 1827 (http://vanburenpapers.org/letter/martin-van-buren-to-thomas-a-ritchie-13-january-1827/).

deteriorated after the War of 1812. One-time strict constructionists like James Monroe and other "National Republicans" succumbed to postwar temptations to build the power of the national government and pursue economic policies that demanded loose construction of the Constitution. Meanwhile, northern and southern republicans allowed controversies over slavery to breed exaggerated sectional fears, momentarily losing sight of the white, states'-rights republicanism that united them. Many a northern, white democrat harbored doubts about the democratic quality of the southern states and their planter classes, just as many a southerner developed doubts about northerners' commitment to state autonomy on slavery. But no one expected a near-term end to slaveholding, and northern and southern republicans soon reunited on a platform of racial exclusion, states' rights, and democratic party organization. Northern white democrats widely embraced an alliance with the slaveholders of the South. In both sections, after all, democracy came preloaded with the imperative necessity of managing a subordinated and dangerous race that might, if emancipated and enfranchised, cause the destruction of the democratic experiment altogether.

The 1820s thus brought two major constitutional developments with respect to race and slavery. First, the Missouri Crisis generated a durably sectional constitutional politics. It pitted a newly self-conscious North and South against each other on the question of the national government's powers regarding slavery, especially with respect to the western territories. Second, at the same time and partly in reaction to the new sectionalism, the white democracies of the North cemented black subordination and allied themselves with the slaveholding democracies of the South. The state democracies thus generated a national Democratic party that highlighted the transsectional bonds of white democracy. The ideological bonds that united these democrats were constitutional equality among white men and a commitment to Jeffersonian states' rights. States' rights served two purposes. It protected local equality against the intrusions of a distant government dominated by special interests ("aristocracy"). And it protected each state's independent reconciliation of racial subordination and democratization. The leading figure in the institutional and ideological crystallization of this transsectional alliance was New York's Martin Van Buren, whose de facto remodeling of the Federal Constitution will be a primary concern of our concluding chapter.

For purposes of this chapter, it is essential to recognize that the renewed alliance rested on a northern Democratic commitment to respect the southern states' autonomy on slavery questions. In effect, the

Democratic Party endorsed the South's core constitutional position that the national government could not act out of a motive to undermine slavery in any degree. But it also accepted the Missouri Compromise's exclusion of slavery from a large swath of federal territory. This arguably ambiguous position on slavery was congenial enough to northern Democrats because, on the one hand, most were not actively opposed to slavery in the South. And, on the other hand, the Missouri Compromise purported to keep slavery out of attractive western territories without threatening the South's vital interests. Northern Democrats generally harbored a thorough racism that informed not only their indifference to Southern slavery but also their hostility to living amid blacks themselves, whether free or enslaved, in the East or in the West. The emergent Democratic Party thus conceived of itself as the transsectional white democracy, encompassing two very different approaches to racial discipline but imagining that its commitment to Jeffersonian states' rights would prevent any open conflict between those approaches.

# 6

# The Marshall Court, the Indian Nations, and the Democratic Ascendancy

## INTRODUCTION

By 1838, the white democracy would be ascendant. Through the tool of party organization, Martin Van Buren and his allies would cement their reinvention of the 1787 Constitution as a charter of radical democracy, white supremacy, and states' rights. And the party would marginalize the Supreme Court and other sources of centralization and minority power. As Van Buren inherited Jefferson's project of white democratization, his movement also inherited the ceaseless opposition of John Marshall, who aimed to substitute Federalist legalism for the sovereignty of the people's will. Marshall's Constitution of common-law conservatism and judicial supremacy threatened to block the radically democratic understanding of the Constitution soon to be embodied in the Democratic Party and increasingly endorsed by the electorate.

To explain Van Buren's fear of an always looming aristocracy, it is important to understand the great cases of the postwar Marshall Court. In these cases, Marshall and his brethren sought to vindicate the supremacy of law and thus of the judiciary – especially the Supreme Court itself – with respect to the meaning of the federal Constitution. These cases included crucially *Martin v. Hunter's Lessee* (1816) and *Cohens v. Virginia* (1821), which generated an expansive federal jurisdiction, empowering the federal courts to vindicate broad congressional power and to impose uniform, Federalist law, thus shrinking the scope of state power. Also central to this project were cases that defined the common law of contracts as a critical source of constitutional meaning. In these cases, the Court could impose uniform, national law and limit the power of state legislatures, regardless of the will of democratic majorities. These cases built on the familiar case of *Fletcher v. Peck* (1810) and included *Dartmouth College v. Woodward* (1819), *Sturges v. Crowninshield* (1819), and *Ogden v. Saunders* (1827). Of a piece with these cases were others that protected the powerful Bank of the United States from interference by the state legislatures, including *McCulloch v. Maryland* (1819) and *Osborn v. Bank of the United States* (1824).

But the Court actively intervened not just in cases of economic policy but also in cases regarding race and the Constitution. In this period, such cases rarely touched slavery or the constitutional rights of black Americans; instead, the famous cases of *Johnson v. M'Intosh* (1823), *Cherokee Nation v. Georgia* (1831), and *Worcester v. Georgia* (1832) addressed the constitutional status and rights of the Indian nations. Again, the Court moved to vindicate federal authority, to limit the rights of the states, and to insist on its own authority to dictate the structure of the law – now including a defense of Indian rights against the grasping ambitions of the white democracy.

Although most of these cases have remained centerpieces of the constitutional history of the early nation, they actually yielded limited success in their own time. The dominant institution in developing and steering constitutional meaning in this period would prove to be the emergent Democratic Party of Jackson and Van Buren, not the Court. Indeed, the party of white democracy was built substantially in response to the overreaching of the Court and the resurgent consolidationism of National Republicans like Henry Clay and President John Quincy Adams, as described in Chapter 4.

## THE MARSHALL COURT

The postwar shift by James Madison and the National Republicans in the direction of strong national power – especially the chartering of the Second Bank of the United States and the campaign for a national system of internal improvements – fit neatly with a new run of Supreme Court cases defending national authority. Those cases, in turn, provoked a new phase of states' rights resistance (some of it described in Chapter 5) that would soon feed the emergent Democratic Party. At the Court, the first postwar step in the direction of the Federalist vision came in the 1816 case of *Martin v. Hunter's Lessee*,[1] which took an expansive view of the jurisdiction of the federal courts.

In *Martin*, the Court had previously determined title to some Virginia lands, based in part on federal questions arising out of a treaty with England. In so doing, it had relied on §25 of the Judiciary Act, which granted the Supreme Court the power to review state court decisions when those decisions turned on federal law. In this case, the Court had reversed the Virginia Court of Appeals, but the Virginia court had refused to obey the Supreme Court's mandate. Startlingly, it denied the national Court's authority to revise the judicial decisions of a sovereign state. Now provoked, Associate Justice Joseph Story, a Madison appointee but Marshall's chief ally on the Court, wrote the Court's opinion vindicating its own superiority over state courts. For Story, federal law must be clear and uniform, free from the biases of parochial state courts.

The Court did not, however, send a mandate back to the recalcitrant Virginia court. Section 25 authorized the Court to execute the judgment itself when the state court failed to do so, and so the Court did. The opinion thus appeared to be a vindication of federal judicial authority.

The Jeffersonian Justice William Johnson, however, interpreted §25 and the Court's action differently, deeming them consistent with a states'-rights conceptualization of the Constitution. Johnson's concurrence agreed that uniformity in federal law was critically important and that the state courts ought to defer to Supreme Court judgments on federal questions. Unlike Story, however, he considered it essential to preserve the sovereignty of the states and the formal independence of their judiciaries from the authority of the national Court. And he believed that the Court's holding, properly understood, was consistent with that independence. Thus, noted Johnson, "the Court disavows all intention to decide on the right to issue compulsory process to the State courts, thus leaving us ... supreme over persons and cases as far as our judicial powers extend, but not asserting any compulsory control over the State tribunals."[2] That is, the Court might legitimately impose a new judgment on the parties, but it could not send a mandate to a state court any more than it could send one to a British or French court that might find itself considering a point of American law. Uniformity in federal law would, however, be preserved by comity, rooted in "the profound, uniform, and unaffected respect which this Court has always exhibited for State decisions" and thus the equal

[1] 14 U.S. 304 (1816).    [2] 14 U.S., at 362.

respect owed by the state courts to the federal Court. Moreover, the Court could generally expect the state courts to defer: "in this Court, every State in the Union is represented ... and when decisions take place which nothing but a spirit to give ground and harmonize can reconcile, ours is the superior claim upon the comity of the State tribunals."[3] In short, a Union of multiple, parallel sovereigns could not be held together strictly by law but required that good judgment and good will find a route to peaceful resolutions where law might not.

In contrast, Story's majority made a fetish of lawyerly logic, as if a closely reasoned pronouncement of the state courts' inferiority would settle the matter. Story thus declared in *Martin* that, "From the very nature of things, the absolute right of decision, in the last resort, must rest somewhere ...,"[4] even though Johnson had explained how the principle of comity refuted that very principle. Story deemed the federal courts the essential bulwark of republicanism, imparting legalistic logic to an imperfectly written Constitution and defending common law justice against the impulsiveness of untamed democracy. The law was a creation of reason, informed by experience, speaking through judges across generations. This combination of faith in reason and a conservatism nurtured by the common law led Story to mistrust the elected branches of government and embrace judicial supremacy where possible.

For his part, Johnson treated the Constitution less as a source of law, concentrating power in a single supreme bench, and more as a tool for achieving a kind of republican liberty, dependent on a practical diffusion of power. The Constitution's meaning was to be ascertained not just by legal logic and judicial mandates but by the good will required to manage a system of parallel sovereignties in permanent tension. If this view remained a minority perspective in the Supreme Court, its vindication by judges like Johnson helped sustain it as the ascendant view of the Constitution in Jacksonian politics.

Thus Van Buren, an accomplished lawyer as well as a brilliant politician, similarly insisted that the state and federal courts had no coercive relationship to each other. As creatures of different sovereigns, neither could compel action by the other. The Supremacy Clause might bind the state courts to the Constitution, but it did not bind them to the authority of the Supreme Court:

---

[3] 14 U.S., at 364–365.    [4] 14 U.S., at 345.

To confer upon [the United States Supreme Court], the anomalous authority of issuing writs of error to the highest courts of other States confessedly sovereign, and which in all such matters might well be regarded as foreign States, – courts which were not established by the Federal Government, and between which and it there existed no judicial relations, – commanding those courts to send it for reexamination, reversal, or affirmance, the record of judgments and decrees which had neither been made under Federal authority nor by judges in any sense amenable to it for the discharge of their official duties, was an idea never broached in the Federal Convention, or in the slightest degree alluded to in the Constitution it adopted.[5]

The Court reaffirmed and extended its formal authority over state courts in *Cohens v. Virginia*[6] five years later. During those five years, the postwar spirit of nationalism had begun to fracture in reaction to the Missouri Crisis and the Court's *McCulloch* decision (to be discussed next). Amid a vibrant resurgence of states'-rights activism, Virginia used *Cohens* to deny again the Court's power to control the judgments of state courts. *Cohens* added the wrinkle that the state itself was a party to the case as the prosecutor of a criminal offense. The Cohen brothers had been convicted in Virginia state court of selling lottery tickets, but they defended on the basis of a claimed federal authorization to sell the tickets. The salient issue in the case was whether the Supreme Court even had jurisdiction to review the state conviction.

In this question of jurisdiction, Marshall saw the very survival of the Union at stake. He worried that individual states might actually defy known federal law, not just indulge in diverse interpretations. Counsel argued that in the event of such political resistance courts would have little capacity to rectify the situation anyway. But Marshall insisted that courts were actually central to the reassertion of discipline on rebellious states. Moreover, Marshall argued that the Court's authority over state courts applied even when a state was a party to a case, despite the Eleventh Amendment's seeming vindication of state sovereignty. Indeed, he seemed to read the amendment practically out of existence, arguing that, "The mere circumstance that a State is a party gives jurisdiction to the Court."[7] For Marshall, there was no principle of state sovereign immunity in the Constitution, only a principle of national supremacy and national legal uniformity.

---

[5] Martin Van Buren, *Inquiry into the Origin and Course of Political Parties in the United States* (New York: Hurd and Houghton, 1867), 301.
[6] 19 U.S. 264 (1821).     [7] 19 U.S., at 383.

While these two cases asserted broad jurisdictional reach for the federal courts, the landmark case of *McCulloch v. Maryland*[8] concurrently legitimated wide-ranging Congressional power, to the detriment of the states. In that case, Maryland had attempted to impose a modest tax on the Baltimore branch of the Bank of the United States. Two main questions animated the case: whether Congress had the power to charter corporations in the first place and, if it did, whether a state could nevertheless impose a reasonable tax on the corporation's activities within Maryland (as it might tax any other activity in the state).

Marshall, however, began with a declaration of federal judicial supremacy and a determination to crush states'-rights extremism. He characterized the case as involving not just an arguable conflict of state and federal statutes but an underlying constitutional dispute that might "remain a source of hostile legislation, perhaps, of hostility of a still more serious nature." Raising the stakes to the point of possible political violence, Marshall insisted that if the question were to be decided peacefully, "by this tribunal alone can the decision be made. On the Supreme Court of the United States has the Constitution of our country devolved this important duty."[9]

Yet, somewhat discordantly, Marshall himself revealed how this very constitutional question might be resolved *not* by judicial fiat but by practical, political construction, with little role for the Court at all. Congress had chartered a federal bank twice, and courts had acquiesced. As Marshall observed, it was now late in the game to question "the practice of the Government" and indeed so late that "[i]t would require no ordinary share of intrepidity to assert that a measure adopted under these circumstances was a bold and plain usurpation to which the Constitution gave no countenance."[10] Indeed, he might have further noted that it was Madison who had both strongly opposed the chartering of the First Bank and then presided over the chartering of the Second Bank in 1816, having learned the lessons of experience and acquiesced in the political "liquidation" of the Bank question over time.

But Marshall was eager to disclaim such deference to the coordinate practice of other institutions. Rather, the meaning of the Constitution rested on the wholly independent arguments of judicial logic that dominated the opinion: first, that the Constitution must be taken to have allowed Congress a wide range of tools, including the tool of

---

[8] 17 U.S. 316 (1819).     [9] 17 U.S., at 400–401.     [10] 17 U.S., at 401–402.

bank-incorporation, to accomplish its explicitly delegated purposes; and, second, that a rigid judicial principle of federal supremacy, not case-specific accommodation of federal and state power, must control the constitutionality of a state tax on the Bank. In particular, Marshall embraced the arbitrary principle that a state's general right to impose reasonable taxes must stop wherever it touches federal interests.

On the first question, the constitutionality of the Bank's incorporation, Marshall offered a superficially impressive piece of logic. As the Necessary and Proper Clause made clear, the federal government could never operate without assuming some measure of implied powers. And, for Marshall, incorporation was the very model of an implied power. It was not "like the power of making war or levying taxes or of regulating commerce, a great substantive and independent power." Rather, it was a mere "means by which other objects are accomplished."[11] Except that, of course, all of the explicitly delegated powers mentioned by Marshall were also means to ends. The powers to make war, levy taxes, and regulate commerce did not exist for their own sakes but for further ends, such as peace, prosperity, and the general welfare. Had the Framers wanted Congress also to have the power of incorporation, they might well have specified that power.

Even more important, at the time the Constitution was written, the power to charter corporations was deeply controversial because it was a means by which portions of the people's sovereignty were given away to private actors. Indeed, Marshall's opinion admitted that incorporation "appertain[ed] to sovereignty,"[12] yet ignored the argument that the Convention would therefore have enumerated that power if it had meant to grant it at all. Incorporation had been traditionally understood as a grant of a limited sovereignty to private actors who were entrusted with the achievement of a distinctly public purpose and granted special, quasi-aristocratic privileges in exchange. As Madison had noted in the original 1791 Bank debate, "The power of granting Charters ... is a great and important power, and ought not to be exercised, without we find ourselves expressly authorised to grant them ... They are a powerful machine, which have always been found competent to effect objects on principles, in a great measure independent of the people." Thus, if the Constitution had been meant to authorize congressional acts of incorporation, Madison argued, it would certainly have specified that power:

[11]  17 U.S., at 411.      [12]  17 U.S., at 411.

"[I]f it was thought necessary to specify in the constitution [certain] minute powers, it would follow that more important powers would have been *explicitly* granted had they been contemplated."[13]

Madison had since been won over to the Bank's side by considerations of policy and political development. But Marshall abjured such prudential views of constitutional development and insisted on an easy, if vacuous, judicial logic: "The power of creating a corporation is never used for its own sake, but for the purpose of effecting something else. No sufficient reason is therefore perceived why it may not pass as incidental to those powers which are expressly given ..."[14]

On the second question, whether Maryland's particular tax violated the Constitution, Marshall evinced a similar legalism. Maryland's arguments were powerful: No constitutional provision precluded a state's taxing the activities of a federally chartered corporation (just as it might tax those of any other corporation or any natural person). And Maryland's lawyers pointed out that the Bank was not in fact an arm of the federal government but a profit-seeking entity, whose stock was held mostly in private hands. To deny Maryland the right to tax this corporation, therefore, was to constrain a central feature of any state's sovereignty without any clear warrant in the Constitution for doing so.

For Marshall, however, it was necessary to crush the states'-rights resistance, and to that end it was necessary to vindicate judicial supremacy. Even complex, indeterminate, political issues would be reduced to judicial questions so that the Supreme Court might resolve them with finality in favor of federal authority. Thus, for example, Marshall would not truck with a case-by-case test of the reasonableness of state taxation. Nor would he trust in Congress's ready ability to control the question of state taxation of the Bank by legislation, if Congress deemed action necessary. Instead, he took the question wholly into the Court's hands and focused on the single principle of federal supremacy. The conflicting principle of state sovereignty – vindicated in the Tenth Amendment and presumably including the states' essential power to tax for revenue – would not be balanced with federal supremacy but altogether subordinated.

Maryland, in contrast, defended a political understanding of constitutional federalism. The state argued that federal supremacy and state

---

[13] Madison's speech on the Bank Bill, February 8, 1791: https://founders.archives.gov/documents/Madison/01–13–02–0284.

[14] 17 U.S., at 411.

sovereignty were both embraced in the Constitution and that an acceptable balance between the two could be achieved through a combination of republican politics and occasional judicial policing at the extremes. The Bank was a "trading corporation" whose chief purpose was profit to itself and its mostly private shareholders; taxing a private corporation was an utterly conventional exercise of state power. Indeed, such power was the "highest attribute of sovereignty." Presumably, no such trading corporation should be allowed to face down a state and "claim the immunities of sovereignty." Moreover, Maryland had taken no steps to undermine federal policy. Rather, it had only required "that the bank ... shall be submitted to the jurisdiction and laws of the State, in the same manner with other corporations and other property, without ruining the institution; or destroying its national uses." In short, a balancing of federal supremacy and state sovereignty should permit Maryland to impose a reasonable tax on any corporation, including the Bank.

Of course, it would not always be easy to locate the line between a moderate exercise of the traditional powers of a state government and aggressive attacks on federal supremacy. But like Justice Johnson in the *Martin* case, Maryland insisted that the grand constitutional questions of federalism simply required comity and "confidence" – or, to put it another way, politics: "all our relations in society, depend upon a reasonable confidence in each other. It is peculiarly the basis of our confederation ... If the two governments are to regard each other as enemies, seeking opportunities of injury and distress, they will not long continue friends."[15]

Indeed, Maryland relied on Alexander Hamilton himself in *The Federalist* to support this sort of constitutional accommodation. Addressing a similar question of federalism, whether the unlimited federal power of taxation would crowd out the concurrent state power to tax, Hamilton had defended concurrent powers with all their inevitable tensions. Resolution of the tension between federal supremacy and state sovereignty must rest in politics, on "the prudence and firmness of the people; who, as they will hold the scales in their own hands, it is to be hoped, will always take care to preserve the constitutional equilibrium between the General and the State Governments. Upon this ground, which is evidently the true one, it will not be difficult to obviate the objections which have been made

[15] All of the quotations from Maryland's argument come from Richard E. Ellis, *Aggressive Nationalism: McCulloch v. Maryland and the Foundation of Federal Authority in the Young Republic* (New York: Oxford University Press, 2007), 81–85.

to an indefinite power of taxation in the United States."[16] Marshall, in contrast, sought judicial supremacy on even the highly indeterminate constitutional questions that Hamilton and many others entrusted to republican politics.

Marshall was driven to his holding partly by habits of mind that favored legalism and judicial supremacy and partly by a genuine fear that a metastasizing states' rights ideology was on the verge of destroying the Union. And the Court's subsequent Bank case, *Osborn v. Bank of the United States*,[17] vindicated all his fears. In the teeth of the *McCulloch* holding, Ohio enacted a $50,000 tax on the Ohio branch of the Bank and collected it by force. Unlike the Maryland statute, this tax looked like an effort to chase the Bank out of the state. Even a dissenting Justice Johnson shared the Chief Justice's fears: "[A] state of things has now grown up in some of the States which renders all the protection necessary that the general government can give to this Bank."[18] But, unlike Marshall, Johnson denied that the good policy of protecting the Bank justified the Court's bending the meaning of the Constitution to make itself the Bank's protector.

Marshall held in *Osborn* that the Constitution authorized Congress to extend federal jurisdiction to any case whatsoever in which the Bank was a party, based on the Constitution's grant of federal jurisdiction for any case "arising under" federal law. Thus the federal courts could reach even a run-of-the-mill contract dispute, which was highly unlikely to raise a question of federal law, just because the Bank was a party. Because virtually any case had the theoretical potential to generate a federal question, Johnson noted, Marshall's opinion threatened a radical shift of power from state to federal courts.

The sequence of great Marshall Court cases establishing broad congressional power concluded with *Gibbons v. Ogden*,[19] a legally simple case that Marshall saw as another attack on the very foundations of the constitution. The Court had no trouble holding that a federal regulation of commerce vitiated a conflicting state statute, as the very language of the Constitution made obvious. The constitutionality of the law in question was not the noteworthy aspect of the case; it was Marshall's terror of the states'-rights extremism that could bring such a settled matter to the Supreme Court in the first place. The Chief Justice defended the tedious length of his opinion by claiming that the supremacy of federal law was

---

[16] *The Federalist* No. 31.    [17] *Osborn v. Bank of the United States*, 22 U.S. 738 (1824).
[18] 22 U.S., at 871–872.    [19] 22 U.S. 1 (1824).

under attack. The principles involved were "nearly self-evident." But the threat posed by the partisans of states' rights was of such magnitude "that we should assume nothing." "Powerful and ingenious minds" were at work to "so entangle and perplex the understanding as to obscure principles which were before thought quite plain ..."[20] He could not permit any life to remain in the radicals' persistent attacks on federal supremacy.

If Marshall and his Court relentlessly subordinated state authority to federal, they equally subordinated state regulation to common-law property and contract rights. The breadth of this project was indicated back in the *Fletcher* case of 1810, which read the Contracts Clause to hold states to the same common law rules of contract as private parties. In that case, the Court had treated Georgia like any private citizen, subject to the federal courts' reading of the common law, not as a sovereign state remedying the wholesale corruption of its legislature.

The later case of *Dartmouth College v. Woodward*[21] lacked the drama of legislative corruption but raised a similar question of contract and prompted similar efforts by Marshall and the Court to constitutionalize the common law and property rights at the expense of state policy. In *Dartmouth College*, the state of New Hampshire had legislatively modified the college's corporate charter, which had been granted to private parties by the Crown before the Revolution. Opinions by Marshall, Story, and Associate Justice Bushrod Washington confidently insisted that the grant was a "contract" protectable by the Constitution, finding a sufficient "consideration" under the common law in the grantees' commitment to pursue the educational goals embodied in the charter itself and in the reliance of donors to the corporation on the perpetuity of the charter. But it was just as natural to see the charter as a unilateral grant or a delegation of a defined measure of sovereignty, not a contract, especially because the transaction lacked conventional consideration like the money payments to Georgia in the Yazoo legislation. And, even if the grant were deemed a contract, the contract had long since been executed. The New Hampshire legislature's modification of the charter seemed at worst an interference in or taking of the property rights for a public purpose. Thus, whether the charter was ever a contract or not, it would be easy enough to suppose that the state could modify the charter in the public interest at any time.

[20] 22 U.S., at 221–222.    [21] 17 U.S. 518 (1819).

However plausible that view, though, the Court opted to extend the protection of private rights through the Contracts Clause. In so doing, it again constricted the right of each state to pursue the public interest as it saw fit, even though the Constitution contained as explicit a protection of states' rights as it did contract rights. That same year, in *Sturges v. Crowninshield*,[22] the Court further decided that the long tradition of states' enacting laws to relieve the debts of the bankrupt or the insolvent could not survive the Contracts Clause. Those laws purported to discharge contractual debts, thus violating the common law's principles of contract, now constitutionalized by the Court. (On the other hand, the *federal* government could enact such laws because it had been explicitly granted that power by the Constitution.) Once again, the Court came to the rescue of common law rights of contract and property at the expense of state policies.

A few years later, in *Ogden v. Saunders*,[23] the Court would concede to the states the power to enact a discharge law if applicable only to future contracts. Because contracts took their legal authority from state law in the first place, they could operate only as that very law, including its discharge provisions, prescribed at the time of contracting. But, for Marshall, even this prospective limitation on private parties' contract rights was too much. Dissenting for the only time in his career, he defended the notion that the Contracts Clause protected a presocial notion of contractual rights: "Individuals do not derive from government their right to contract, but bring that right with them into society."[24] For him, the Contracts Clause embraced a natural right to contract as understood in the common law, regardless of any state's preference for a different contract regime conducive to its own vision of the public interest.

In sum, the Marshall Court's opinions on questions of federal jurisdiction, federal legislative power, and the constitutional law of contract consistently promoted federal power and national uniformity, all at the expense of state autonomy and the modest legal diversity that might be expected in a compound republic. This legalistic, judicial-supremacist, and centralizing view of the Constitution did not go unchallenged. But the challenge came more from without than within the courts. As the next sections will demonstrate, the Marshall Court extended its legalist and centralizing tendencies also to landmark cases on the constitutional status

---

[22] 17 U.S. 122 (1819).   [23] 25 U.S. 213 (1827).   [24] 25 U.S., at 346.

and rights of the Indian nations. There, it encountered the fierce and effective resistance of the white democracy.

## CONSTITUTIONAL POLITICS AND THE INDIAN NATIONS

The essential background for the Marshall Court's Indian cases is the political history of state and federal relations with the indigenous peoples. For any particular stretch of Indian-claimed territory within the borders of an American state, the common law and the Constitution offered no clear answer to the questions of landownership and sovereignty. Conflict reigned between indigenous hunting nations, which claimed far more land than they seemed (to whites) actually to occupy, and a nation of European settlers looking to extend the reach of agriculture and "civilization." At times, the Supreme Court made valiant efforts to define Indian status by legal argument. But the constitutional politics of Indian status ensured that the law of the agricultural Europeans (however much they hunted) would define a subordinate constitutional position for the indigenous hunting civilizations, even those that actually cultivated the land quite extensively. The conflict was always likely to turn on the law of the stronger nation, a law that would predictably naturalize its own people's constitutional superiority.

Legal arguments informed settler actions from the start of the colonial projects, but in fact colonists took possession of new lands by whatever means promised to be most effective. Sometimes that meant private purchase, sometimes treaty, sometimes conquest. The colonists were equipped with theories that told them that the Indians were somewhere between "brutes," who might be justly conquered, and civilized peoples who had nevertheless failed to recognize individual property rights and cultivate the land as God intended. They had no basis for complaint, therefore, if the colonists took possession of such land as had been left uncultivated, underutilized, and thus effectively unclaimed. Some colonial leaders insisted that all acquisition must be done by purchase, and the colonists did generally choose to take possession via purchase or treaty rather than enter into potentially violent conflicts. But they sometimes resorted to violence and justified acquisition by conquest, often by reference to the superior rights of Christians or by the claim that Indians lacked any system of landownership that the colonists were bound to respect. No single justification predominated, however. Early land transfers rested on a miscellany of commingled justifications.

Although many sales of land by Indians were voluntary, many increasingly occurred in the context of relentless white pressure westward and a ruthless determination by settlers on the ground to take the land they wanted. Often illegally, settlers pushed beyond old boundaries, establishing farms on apparently unused lands. These practices had both ecological and political consequences, including the thinning of game on which some Indian nations had long depended, the disruption of old ecosystems, and even provocation of wars by which the colonists could take yet more land as putatively justifiable spoils.

A veneer of legality was important to the European settlers, however, and the evident incompatibility between European and Indian societies left a stark choice between, on the one hand, respecting unfamiliar and inefficient modes of land use and, on the other hand, insisting on and legalizing the extension of "civilization." Indian societies tended to be much more mobile and less tied to European-style property rights in land. As colonial populations grew, it was difficult for the settlers to accept that vast, apparently unsettled lands were off limits to agriculture. They came to realize that agricultural settlement – including the clearing of woodlands, an influx of farm animals, and a measure of hunting by the newly arrived population – disrupted Indian modes of survival. Still, their belief in the superiority of European civilization and cultivation practices justified for them the displacement of Indian peoples and practices.

If western settlers turned out to be important constitutional actors simply by creating facts on the ground, so too did land speculators in search of windfalls. Gazing at the vast, seemingly chaotic area west of European settlement, private speculators sought to buy millions of acres from Indians in the hope that their title would be recognized in white courts and purchased by white settlers at a fantastic profit. Among many such deals were the private purchases in 1773 and 1775 of two large tracts of land in modern-day Illinois, in apparent violation of a royal proclamation that Indian land was to be obtained only by treaty. The purchasers' agents would press their land claims before Congress and the courts repeatedly after the Revolution and ultimately yield the landmark case of *Johnson v. M'Intosh* (to be discussed later). This was the first of a series of Supreme Court cases between 1823 and 1832 that directly confronted the question of the constitutional status of the Indian nations.

The durable contours of that question were suggested by the Articles of Confederation in 1781. Article IX announced that Congress would possess the "exclusive right and power of ... regulating the trade and managing all affairs with the Indians, not members of any of the States, provided that the legislative right of any State within its own limits be not infringed or violated." On the one hand, the grant of "exclusive right and power" to the federal government seemed to imply that the Indian nations were foreign sovereign entities with whom only Congress would deal, not the states. On the other hand, the preservation of the "legislative right of any State within its own limits" had the potential to swallow up both Indian sovereignty and much of the exclusive federal power, as Madison recognized soon after. This provision thus foreshadowed all of the coming years of conflict and ambiguity as between, on the one hand, federal control over all Indian relations on a model of foreign affairs and, on the other hand, each state's right to treat all Indians and Indian lands within the state's perimeter as wholly subject to state sovereignty.

This lack of clarity would be exacerbated by the conflict of European and Indian powers in the West. The Indians themselves, of course, comprised many nations contending among themselves for power and territory amid pressures from multiple European powers. Those powers included the Spanish, who schemed to lure the southwest away from the American confederacy. The British too remained a military and political presence in the West until the War of 1812. At the same time, the Americans hardly presented a united front. As federal emissaries tried to exercise exclusive authority in Indian affairs, negotiators for Georgia and other individual states asserted their own putatively sovereign rights to execute treaties with Indians and send settlers into Indian lands. Moreover, those settlers often pushed westward without much regard even for state policy, let alone federal. From the perspective of the West, therefore, it was quite hard to tell which power would actually emerge in control of this or that region, and very few actions by any of these powers had much of the flavor of legality as opposed to raw power.

The first federal effort to establish a framework of American sovereignty in the West emerged in 1783–1784. In those years, Congress tried to claim all land to the Mississippi River by virtue of the American triumph in the Revolution and the Treaty of Paris. At the same time, Congress was willing to go through the motions of gradually purchasing the lands as white settlers moved west. Thus, federal treaty commissioners in 1784–1785 effectively dictated treaties that delivered most of modern-day Ohio to the United States for modest compensation. But, dictate as they liked to those Indians willing to cooperate, the relevant nations did not widely accept the legitimacy of the treaties. Similarly, in the south, the federal Treaties of Hopewell in late 1785 (with the Cherokees) and early 1786 (with the Choctaws and Chickasaws) tried to establish clear boundaries. But confusion reigned as the state governments of Georgia and North Carolina were already making their own treaties and claiming sovereignty over the same lands. Amid the swirl of contenders for power in the trans-Appalachian West, the treaties settled little. Instead, frontier war broke out north and south in 1786, and settlers continued to press westward. Occasional U.S. military efforts proved futile and only further contributed to the general uncertainty.

Learning its lesson the hard way, the federal government in 1787 accepted that it lacked the strength to simply claim the West, but it did not abandon its determination to control that land nonetheless. Changing course, Congress embraced a committee report of August 9 that accepted both the justice of the Indians' land claims and the incompetence of the United States military to divest the Indians of their lands and sovereignty. The report concluded that relations with the Indians should henceforth be matters of peace, regular trade, and fair purchase of any lands. The Northwest Ordinance of July 1787 similarly declared that Indian land should be acquired only in "good faith" with Indian "consent." Still, the Ordinance made clear its expectation that all of the land in the territories would ultimately come into white hands. The very point of the Ordinance, after all, was to organize for white settlement vast lands all the way to the Mississippi, which would ultimately be divided into states and "remain forever a part of this Confederacy." Perhaps members of Congress really meant to operate only in "good faith," but the Ordinance read much more like a polite declaration that Indian land rights would soon expire.

The other great event of 1787, of course, was the drafting of the new American Constitution. This document said little about the Indian nations, but it did announce exclusive federal control over "commerce . . . with the Indian tribes." It also abandoned the Articles' explicit reservation of state legislative rights over Indians within state boundaries. For some, this constitutional language indicated that the federal government had exclusive authority to deal with the Indian nations as foreign nations, whose lands could be acquired only through federal treaty. But the limitation of the provision to regulation of "commerce" perpetuated a measure of ambiguity, and little in the founding documents shed light on the precise balance of authority between the federal and state governments on Indian affairs.

It seems that little more was said in the ratification debates on Indian questions, and the new government's centralizing bent soon generated a federal Indian policy that might be the best indicator we have of the

Framers' vision. Secretary of War Henry Knox played the leading role. His report of June 15, 1789, sought to establish a policy of orderly westward settlement guided by the federal government and informed by a fair and humane policy toward the Indians. On the one hand, he seemed to vindicate Indian rights: "The Indians being the prior occupants, possess the right of the soil. It cannot be taken from them unless by their free consent, or by the right of conquest in case of a just war. To dispossess them on any other principle, would be a gross violation of the fundamental laws of nature, and of that distributive justice which is the glory of a nation."[25] Yet dispossession is exactly what he anticipated. He firmly expected a pattern of Indian land sales under a kind of American pressure that he evidently deemed consistent with "justice": "As the settlements of the whites shall approach near to the Indian boundaries established by treaties, the game will be diminished, and the lands being valuable to the Indians only as hunting grounds, they will be willing to sell further tracts for small considerations." He thus anticipated that gradually "the Indians will ... be reduced to a very small number."[26] But what if the Indians understood these dynamics as well as Knox and ceased selling? Would that be cause for "just war" or other methods to ensure continued cessions? Knox did not say, but an affirmative answer would not be long in coming.

Knox's subsequent report with respect to the southern Indians articulated the same policy but also confronted the especially aggressive white settlement and states'-rights radicalism in that region. The excessive pressure from southern whites prompted him to sharpen the argument that western expansion must remain within disciplined, federal management. He argued that "the independent nations and tribes of Indians ought to be considered as foreign nations, not as the subjects of any particular State."[27] Thus Indian affairs must remain within the federal treaty power and taken entirely out of the hands of the states, even if the states would retain preemption rights with respect to any Indian land ultimately ceded within their boundaries.

For some, this internationalist framing seemed the commonsense approach. After all, the indigenous peoples had occupied these lands as

[25] Quoted in Reginald Horsman, *Expansion and American Indian Policy, 1783–1812* (East Lansing: Michigan State University Press, 1967), 55.
[26] Quoted in Ibid., 56.    [27] Quoted in Ibid., 57.

independent societies for numerous generations, had fought numerous wars with the colonizers, and had concluded even more treaties. But the states themselves had emerged from colonial status into full sovereign statehood, limited only by the terms of their alliance under the Articles of Confederation and then by the indeterminate provisions of the new Constitution. Old habits die hard, and many states were reluctant to give up any of their claims to full sovereignty within their own borders, borders that some states – especially Georgia and North Carolina – believed still to extend west into modern-day Alabama, Mississippi, and Tennessee. So, Knox's reports notwithstanding, Georgia and North Carolina continued to carry out their own policies of western settlement without regard for the Treaty of Hopewell or other federal efforts to control the boundaries of white settlement.

Back in the north, the 1789 Treaties of Fort Harmar further reflected the new federal policy. These treaties reaffirmed the previous cessions of much of Ohio but added more compensation for the Indians, indicating a new federal recognition of Indian ownership. Many Indians, however, resisted these cessions and further rejected the United States' claim to preemption rights, as any sovereign nation would, insisting on their right to sell to whoever they chose, whenever they chose.

The American bargaining position became stronger as the new nation built its military forces in earnest. At the same time, Indian resistance took the form of a confederation of tribes in the Ohio area. Fighting in the northwest continued until the 1794 American victory at the Battle of Fallen Timbers, which compelled capitulation to federal terms and opened Ohio to wide settlement by whites. No doubt, Knox and other federal policymakers considered that justice had been done in this instance, but the goal of peaceful expansion by fair purchase of Indian lands was, to say the least, elusive.

The opening of Ohio could be portrayed as a success in the campaign to maintain federal rather than state control of American expansion into the Indian west. So could the concluding of the 1794 Jay Treaty, which called for withdrawal of British troops from the American northwest, and the 1795 Pinckney Treaty, which established the American boundary with Spanish holdings and required both governments to restrain "their" respective Indians. Gradually, it seemed, the chaos in the west was giving way to American federal sovereignty. Meanwhile, from 1790 to 1799, Congress passed every three years a new Trade and Intercourse Act to regulate white interactions with Indians, clarifying the boundaries between the United States and the Indian nations, criminalizing white settlement in Indian lands, banning again private purchases of Indian lands, and authorizing the president to use force against illegal settlers, among other things.

None of this accumulation of law for the West, however, established the sort of orderly and gradual program of acquisitions that the Federalist government in Washington desired. As emergent Republicans back east resisted the Federalist program of centralization, so frontier whites respected none of the federal boundary lines as legitimate restraints on their claims to local, apparently unsettled land.

Rather than turn its energies to the futile task of rolling back illegal white settlements, the federal government simply followed every treaty's guarantee of absolute Indian rights with new pressure to sell. The often unscrupulous means of negotiation employed in the Federalist administrations of the 1790s were brought near to perfection under Jefferson. Jefferson carried into office an overriding belief that the great yeoman republic was destined to expand to the west. He also believed that the Indians had full capacity to assimilate into "civilized" society but little right to maintain their way of living in the way of white migration. And he had a strong commitment to the forms of legality but an equal readiness to blink the realities by which putatively legal purchases were accomplished. Thus Jefferson explicitly promised that the 1795 Treaty of Greenville, guaranteeing Indian rights to northern lands west of Ohio, would be scrupulously respected, but he also ordered the American territorial governor of Indiana, William Henry Harrison, to press constantly for new cessions. Harrison was aided by white settlers' persistent encroachment on Indian lands. And he freely employed proven techniques for bringing the Indians around: fostering Indian debts to white traders, outright bribery of key Indians, and constant entreaties to sell even after repeated rejections. Harrison thus succeeded in obtaining numerous tracts of land for the United States (including areas that contained the speculator lands that would generate *Johnson v. M'Intosh*).

All of these federal efforts arguably implemented the Framers' vision that the nation's Indian affairs would be federal matters, just like relations with other nations and relations among the states. Of course, western expansion of white settlement was anticipated, but it was to be accomplished in an orderly and legal way, via treaty and purchase. The national interest would require that foreign nations and private parties be denied the right to acquire land from the Indians, but in all other respects the Indian nations were to be regarded as sovereign and therefore immune to regulation by the states.

The states, however, did not always accept the federal approach. Georgia, in particular, resisted any federal effort to limit its sovereignty or its citizens' rights to move westward. And Georgia's resistance generated more than one landmark of the early nation's legal history. As the question of Indian rights entered the Supreme Court, then, the Justices were acutely aware of the lessons of constitutional politics: that the question remained unsettled whether the indigenous peoples were foreign nations or mere subjects of the United States or something else; that the division of power between the state and federal governments with respect to the Indian peoples remained equally uncertain; that Americans widely deemed Indians an alien, nomadic civilization inherently at odds with the higher, agricultural civilization of Euro-Americans; and that western, white settlers were probably the main constitutional actors in the situation, giving force to the dominant view among whites that the Indians must ultimately give way.

## THE INDIAN NATIONS IN AND OUT
## OF THE SUPREME COURT

The constitutional politics described earlier proceeded almost entirely without the intervention of the Supreme Court, but the Court did gradually and tentatively find its way to the center of the issue, beginning with the endlessly illuminating case of *Fletcher v. Peck*. In that 1810 case, Marshall's effort to constitutionalize the common law of contract ran into multiple complications. Apart from those discussed previously, he had to confront the question of whether Georgia even had the property rights in Indian lands that the legislative grant purported to sell. The 1795 Georgia Legislature granted vast tracts to private companies in fee simple, notwithstanding that Indian nations had long resided on them and continued to claim full rights to them. The state could have chosen to grant only its well-established preemption right, but the legislature evidently believed that it already possessed sovereignty over all the land within its borders.

Writing for the Court, Marshall acknowledged the difficulties raised by the grant's "fee simple" language: "[A] decision that [Georgia was] seised in fee, might ... be construed" to mean that those who had bought Yazoo lands could evict Indians from the land – "maintain an ejectment for them" – notwithstanding federal recognition of Indian occupancy rights. He finessed the problem by affirming that the "Indian title" was "certainly to be respected" – thus undercutting private ejectment claims against the Indians – but holding that this "title" was somehow not "absolutely repugnant" to the state's simultaneous claim to fee simple ownership. By this unexplained assertion, he cleared the way to his most immediate goal, an expansive reading of the Contracts Clause and judicial power, but at the price of some confusion about Indian status and state sovereignty.[28]

Johnson in dissent, however, abjured these manipulations and denied Georgia's claim to fee simple ownership of the lands, because the relevant Indian tribes remained sovereign nations. Observing that matters of conflicting national rights were "more fitted for a diplomatic or legislative than a judicial inquiry," he nevertheless deemed Indian rights clear, based on "innumerable treaties formed with them ... and the uniform practice of acknowledging their right of soil, by purchasing from them, and restraining all persons from encroaching upon their territory." Consequently, Georgia's legal claim to the lands was only a preemption right. And even that was wholly "dependent on a purchase or conquest to be made by the United States" sometime in the future.[29] The Indians might lack a couple of important attributes of sovereignty, but those that they retained precluded Georgia's encroachments until the federal government should act.

The Court would not return to the question of the Indians' sovereignty until the 1823 case of *Johnson v. M'Intosh*,[30] which again suggested substantial sovereignty in indigenous peoples. *Johnson* was not really a constitutional case and did not make a holding as to Indian sovereignty, but its rejection of the property claims of white speculators, who had bought land directly from an Indian tribe a few years before the Revolution, seemed to rest on a recognition of Indian sovereignty. As a sovereign nation, Marshall suggested, the tribe obviously had the authority to sell land to foreigners as it chose, according to the terms of its own laws, as it equally had the sovereign authority to annul such sales. At the same time, it lacked authority to bind a different sovereign, the United States, to recognize the speculators' putative title. The Court thus rejected the speculators' property claim because it derived from the law of a foreign sovereign that could not bind an American court.

More important, for our purposes, the Court had to confront the claim that the doctrine of "discovery" stripped the Indian nations of full title to their lands and thus the ability to transfer those lands to speculators or to anyone but the United States. *Johnson* is famous for its acceptance of this

[28] 10 U.S., at 142–143.    [29] 10 U.S., at 146–147.    [30] 21 U.S. 543 (1823).

racist doctrine. However, accounts of the case are not always clear on the function of the doctrine in Marshall's opinion, which actually sought to defend a measure of Indian rights.

The essential context is the wide supposition among whites that their character as Christians and farmers rendered them more advanced than the Indian nations on the ladder of civilization. The European newcomers generally presumed that a Christian, agricultural society was both superior to and incompatible with an Indian society that they supposed not only heathen but also nomadic and oriented to hunting (a characteristic that was more and less true of different Indian nations). On the basis of such prejudices, the discovery doctrine held "that discovery gave exclusive title to those who made it"; that is, to those Christian, agricultural nations who first encountered the indigenous nations and their land.

Marshall made clear his distaste for this doctrine, taking some solace in the fact that it did not go so far as peremptory dispossession of the Indians but only gave the European intruders preemption rights. Now explaining the position he had taken in *Fletcher* thirteen years before, Marshall noted that the original inhabitants "were admitted to be the rightful occupants of the soil, with a legal as well as just claim to retain possession of it." Still, the doctrine of discovery gave the Europeans "ultimate dominion" and thus a form of "title."[31] Marshall openly recognized the "extravagance" of the discovery doctrine, giving legal color to American claims that were plainly driven by an arbitrary and militant assertion of white superiority. But he also recognized that, by 1823, it was too late for the judiciary, at least, to substitute its own notions of justice for the principles and practices that underlay white landholding throughout the states.

Here, the arch-legalist Marshall freely explained how law rests on and gradually sanitizes the violence that inaugurates any "legal" order and that establishes durable hierarchies of values and peoples. He acknowledged how "extravagant the pretension of converting the discovery of an inhabited country into conquest may appear." Yet, he observed, the maintenance of such a principle over time, such that "a country has been acquired and held under it" and "the great mass of the community originates in it," makes it "the law of the land."

The same was true of the preemption right that derived from the discovery principle: "However this restriction may be opposed to natural right, and to the usages of civilized nations, yet if it be indispensable to

---

[31] 21 U.S., at 574.

that system under which the country has been settled, and be adapted to the actual condition of the two peoples, it may perhaps be supported by reason, and certainly cannot be rejected by courts of justice."[32]

This was no full-throated defense of European dispossession of the Indian nations but a frank acknowledgment of reality. One might (or might not) credit Marshall with a genuine regret that he could not do more to protect the Indian nations against white encroachment. But by 1823, the most he could do was to reiterate as solemnly as possible the Indian right to inhabit and control their remaining lands for as long as they could resist white pressure for treaties of cession.

Marshall's analysis of the private claim in *Johnson*, then, proceeded from an assumption of as much Indian sovereignty as he could plausibly recognize under the circumstances. But Marshall's rhetorical efforts mattered little to the actual case because the relevant lands had been ceded to the United States. After cession, Indian law no longer applied, and recognition (or not) of any titles to land in that territory became subject entirely to American law. Because the treaty of cession had not reserved the title of the speculators and because British and American law had consistently barred the private purchase of Indian lands, at least since 1763, American law was never bound to recognize the private purchase of Indian lands.

*Johnson*'s rhetorical endorsement of Indian sovereignty appeared just as the coming Democratic ascendancy was gathering its early strength. In some states, the Jacksonian Democrats primarily attacked national economic initiatives like internal improvements and a protective tariff; in other states, they defended slavery against the least hint of federal action; but in Georgia they increasingly focused on their claim to sovereignty over Indian lands, notwithstanding federal treaties. In the wake of the Yazoo scandal, Georgia in 1802 had ceded all its Yazoo land claims to the United States for $1.25 million and a federal promise to extinguish Indian title as soon as practicable. By the 1820s, the rising tide of states' rights and the failure of the federal government to fulfill its obligation to extinguish the Indian title lent new power to the state's assertions of sovereignty over Indians and their lands.

Georgia had never allowed much breathing room to the Cherokees (the primary Indian holders of land within Georgia's boundaries), but a new phase of aggression began in 1827. Statutes in the late 1820s purported to

---

[32]  21 U.S., at 591–592.

extend Georgia law over all persons and lands inside Georgia's borders and further purported to annex all Cherokee lands over time. These statutes together rejected all Cherokee pretensions to sovereignty.

Andrew Jackson's election to the presidency in 1828 sent the clear message that the Georgia Cherokees and other tribes must be removed to make way for white settlers. The new Congress rapidly enacted the Indian Removal Act of 1830, which authorized the president to negotiate the "voluntary" removal of the eastern Indian tribes to lands west of the Mississippi. The Cherokees thus understood that two of the three federal branches had turned firmly against them. Notwithstanding significant, minority support for their cause in Congress and in the North, only the Supreme Court appeared in any position to preserve their rights.

The Cherokees hired former Attorney General William Wirt, who began to search for a test case. Wirt latched on to the 1830 prosecution of one George Tassel, a Cherokee accused of killing another Indian within Cherokee boundaries. Extension of Georgia's criminal jurisdiction over Tassel for this act clearly violated Cherokee sovereignty if anything could. But Tassel's case never made it to the Supreme Court. Rather, his lawyer's efforts to get the state conviction certified to the Court and Wirt's securing of a writ of error both proved fruitless. Georgian authorities simply refused to recognize the authority of the Court to address Georgia's internal affairs at all. Instead, Georgia swiftly executed Tassel and silently dared the Court to reclaim its authority over the Constitution.

The Cherokees and Wirt next sued Georgia itself to enjoin its extension of its sovereignty into Cherokee lands and affairs.[33] Even to invoke the Court's jurisdiction, however, the Cherokees had to demonstrate that they counted as a "foreign state," since Article III of the Constitution granted the Court original jurisdiction over "controversies between a state or the citizens thereof, and foreign states." Marshall was sympathetic to the Cherokees but ultimately denied that the founders had the Indian tribes in mind when they adopted Article III. By denying jurisdiction, he temporized on the question of the Cherokees' substantive rights, perhaps aware that the political ascendancy of the Jacksonians severely limited the Court's practical authority.

Justice Johnson concurred in dismissing the case, reaffirming a position he had first adumbrated in *Fletcher v. Peck*. In *Fletcher*, Johnson had deemed the question of Indian status political or diplomatic rather than

---

[33] *Cherokee Nation v. Georgia*, 30 U.S. 1 (1831).

judicial, but the question there had been an unavoidable aspect of an otherwise eminently judicial question of contract. In *Cherokee Nation v. Georgia*, however, there was no technical question of law clearly appropriate to judicial disposition. The suit was just a contrived effort to have the judiciary restrain the political branches. After all, the Cherokee Nation claimed to be a foreign state facing physical invasion under the authority of Georgia statutes; it thus effectively asked the Court to enjoin a war. Similarly, the Cherokee request to quiet title in their favor clashed with their claim to be a foreign state because a U.S. court could never have such authority over foreign territory. The Court further could not command the enforcement of federal treaties or the federal criminal laws that barred trespass on Indian land. Enforcement of treaties and prosecution of criminal laws were discretionary to the executive. In sum, the Cherokees' constitutional complaint, well-founded or not, was properly directed to the constitutional conscience and politics of the nation, not to its constitutional law.

Justice Baldwin added his view that Georgia had full sovereignty over all lands and people within its borders. For Baldwin, the key evidence was the hopelessly one-sided terms of the 1785 Treaty of Hopewell, in which the Cherokee tribe "transferr[ed] to a foreign government the regulation of its trade and the management of all their affairs at their pleasure." If the Cherokees ever qualified as a nation, therefore, that status "was surrendered by the treaty of Hopewell,"[34] before the drafting of the Constitution.

In contrast, Justice Thompson's dissent (joined by Story) argued that the Cherokees' history of compromised sovereignty was not inconsistent with membership in the community of nations. The history showed that, before and after the adoption of the Constitution, American governments had dealt with the Cherokees as a foreign, sovereign state: "Whenever wars have taken place, they have been followed by regular treaties of peace ...; the Indian Nation always preserving its distinct and separate national character." The states and the United States might claim preemption rights in their land, but "the right of occupancy is still admitted to remain in them, accompanied with the right of self-government according to their own usages and customs."[35] Thompson canvassed the history through the 1810s to show that all departments of the government had indeed dealt with the Cherokees as a sovereign nation, not as a

---

[34] 30 U.S., at 39.    [35] 30 U.S., at 54–55.

band of persons merged into the American population. Finally, while admitting that the Court might not be in a position to give the Cherokees all the relief they sought, Thompson declared that certain actions of the state of Georgia were readily subject to injunction, such as the statutorily authorized appropriation of gold mines and other lands.

In the following year, 1832, the Cherokees finally got a case on the merits before the Court. In *Worcester v. Georgia*,[36] Georgia prosecuted a missionary for violating a statute that prohibited white persons from living in Indian territory without a license. Worcester and his allies in The American Board of Commissioners for Foreign Missions believed in the Cherokees' status as a sovereign nation and decided to defy the Georgia statute, hoping for a judicial declaration of the unconstitutionality of Georgia's incursions on Cherokee sovereignty. After conviction in state court, Worcester obtained a writ of error from the U.S. Supreme Court. Georgia predictably flouted the Court's authority on this matter and refused to appear at all. The argument at the Court was, therefore, a one-sided affair, although everyone understood Georgia's position.

None of the opinions wasted much ink on the indeterminate text of the Constitution. The Commerce Clause allocated to the federal government the power to "regulate commerce . . . with the Indian tribes" but did not otherwise restrict the states. Little else in the Constitution spoke clearly to the Indians' status. No provision clearly delineated the scope of Indian sovereignty or territorial integrity within the boundaries of a state, nor the precise dividing line between each state's independent police power and the federal power to regulate "commerce" with "Indian tribes."

Marshall's opinion for the Court, now effectively inviting Georgia's and Jackson's defiance, joined Thompson's previous opinion in vindicating the constitutional and legal rights of the Cherokees. Marshall endorsed Worcester's claim that the statute under which he was prosecuted conflicted with federal treaties, with the Constitution's commitment of Indian affairs exclusively to the federal government, and with federal statutes. He began by reviewing his previously expressed contempt for the doctrine of discovery, that mere "sailing along the coast" of a distant land could confer on the sailors' country "a rightful property in the soil, from the Atlantic to the Pacific, or rightful dominion over the numerous people who occupied it."[37] Equally, he dismissed the arbitrary insistence that "nature, or the great Creator of all things" decreed the

[36] 31 U.S. 515 (1832).     [37] 31 U.S., at 543.

subjection of "hunters and fishermen" to the rule of "agriculturists and manufacturers."[38] He recognized that arbitrary conquest slowly generates law that legitimates the new structure of power, granting "rights, which, after possession, are conceded by the world, and which can never be controverted by those on whom they descend."[39] Still, the "legal" principle that grew from "discovery" was not dispossession of the "aboriginal inhabitants," nor vitiation of their sovereignty. It was only a restriction on their right to sell their land, whenever they should choose to do so.[40]

The arbitrariness of the legal reasoning here should be as obvious to the reader as it was to Marshall. The same principle that would allow discovery magically to generate a preemption right could as easily have generated a right to dispossession of the Indians at will. Marshall's effort to draw reliable law out of a frequently violent history had a purpose, to draw a line after all these generations that might preserve the residue of Indian civilization and autonomy after so much had disappeared under white pressure and violence. As in *Johnson v. M'Intosh*, Marshall recognized the fundamental lawlessness underlying the white colonizing of North America, yet sought to tease a genuinely legal regime for the future out of a history of violence.

And it was a valiant effort. The history of relations with the Indian nations yielded much evidence that whites had considered those nations sovereign entities: "The King purchased their lands when they were willing to sell, at a price they were willing to take, but never coerced a surrender of them." Further, the king bought alliances with indigenous nations "but never intruded into the interior of their affairs or interfered with their self-government."[41] Great Britain "considered them as nations capable of maintaining the relations of peace and war; of governing themselves, under her protection; and she made treaties with them the obligation of which she acknowledged."[42] Such was "the settled state of things when the war of our revolution commenced."[43] And such was the view perpetuated after the Revolution by the new United States, Marshall asserted, citing the numerous treaties after the Revolution with various tribes, including the Cherokees.

But this history was a good deal more ambiguous than Marshall let on. The determination to expand westward was always the most salient imperative among whites. Duplicity, corruption, and violence were at

---

[38] 31 U.S., at 543.    [39] 31 U.S., at 543.    [40] 31 U.S., at 544.    [41] 31 U.S., at 547.
[42] 31 U.S., at 548–549.    [43] 31 U.S., at 549.

least as common as good faith purchase. A white belief in the superiority of farmers and Christians over hunters and heathens was at least as central to white American civilization as were avowals of respect for law and Indian sovereignty. The Constitution, in its long historical context, did not unambiguously embrace Indian sovereignty.

Indeed, it was not Marshall's opinion but Justice McLean's lucid concurrence that explained the grim future for the Indian nations under the white Constitution, as well as the limits of the Court's role. On the question of Indian rights, McLean accurately considered removal of the Indians from the path of white settlement inevitable, not because there was any law to that effect but as a matter of history and current constitutional politics. On the separate federalism question, however, he did claim that clear law gave the federal government – not the states – exclusive authority to manage Indian policy generally and Indian removal in particular.

As to the first question, the rights and status of the indigenous peoples, McLean frankly accepted that Indian rights were simply not a matter of law but of the relative strength of clashing civilizations, one centered on hunting and the other on agriculture. Beginning with the first European settlements, the indigenous nations and the new arrivals could both point to the "law of nature, which is paramount to all other laws" and which "gives the right to every nation to the enjoyment of a reasonable extent of country." Thus the newcomers could fairly resist the native monopolization of sprawling hunting lands at the expense of agriculture: "In this view, perhaps, our ancestors, when they first migrated to this country, might have taken possession of a limited extent of the domain, had they been sufficiently powerful, without negotiation or purchase from the native Indians." But they lacked such power, and so the acquisition "of their lands was never assumed except upon the basis of contract and on the payment of a valuable consideration."[44] The practice of purchasing rather than simply claiming Indian land for white use – a practice cleansed of much of its coercion by McLean – proceeded not from legal principle but from expediency and calculations of relative power. Consequently, McLean thought judges had little basis to opine on the remaining scope of the Cherokees' sovereignty.

On the separate question of state versus federal power, however, McLean identified clear law. Here, McLean noted a tradition of limited

[44] 31 U.S., at 579–580.

Indian "sovereignty," but his argument aimed not so much to recognize Indian rights judicially as to vindicate the federal government's exclusive power to manage the removal of the Indians. It was true that "more than forty years" of federal treaty-making with the Indians had settled the constitutional status of the Indians as "a separate and distinct people, and as being vested with rights which constitute them a State, or separate community . . ."[45] But their constitutional status as a distinct people only meant that they were subject to the federal government's power over foreign affairs rather than the states' internal police powers, not that they had any enforceable rights. And, especially in the wake of Jackson's election, the trajectory of federal policy was clear.

With one eye on the Jackson administration, McLean sketched out the constitutional reality:

The exercise of the power of self-government by the Indians, within a State is undoubtedly contemplated to be temporary. This is shown by the settled policy of the government, in the extinguishment of their title, and especially by the compact with the State of Georgia. . . [A] sound national policy does require that the Indian tribes within our States should exchange their territories, upon equitable principles, or eventually consent to become amalgamated in our political communities.[46]

McLean had started his argument by observing the incompatibility of white and Indian communities in close proximity. Their cultures and economies were so incompatible that there was no readily available law for determining their relative rights. Rather, the question was one of power. He now finished by insisting that nothing had changed except the relative power of the two sides. These legally anomalous peoples would be moved out of the way of white settlement, and the only question for the law was the allocation of power among whites – between the state governments and the federal – not between white and Indian communities.

On that question, the fate of the Indians was a negligible consideration for McLean, but the fate of the Union seemed genuinely in the balance. Like Marshall in *McCulloch* and related cases, McLean sought to defend federal power against the looming threat of a radical states'-rights ideology, now animating both Georgia's aggressions against the Cherokees and South Carolina's simultaneous Nullification Movement.

[45] 31 U.S., at 583.    [46] 31 U.S., at 593.

In response to National Republican efforts to enhance and deploy national power in new ways, political leaders in South Carolina had revived the language and ideas of "nullification," which had appeared in Jefferson's Kentucky Resolutions more than a generation earlier. South Carolinians were not the only southerners to resist both a protective tariff inimical to slave-holding interests and the slavery-threatening concentration of national power that went with it. But only South Carolina fully embraced the radical position that a state might nullify federal law within its boundaries, and only South Carolina was prepared openly to consider secession.

Indeed, as the nullification crisis intensified, Georgia sought a way to de-escalate its Cherokee crisis without backing down, knowing that Jackson would not tolerate nullification or threats of secession, even if he was sympathetic to Georgia on Indian matters. Thus, while the Georgia trial court refused to obey the Court's command that Worcester be freed, Georgia's leaders accepted a way out of the confrontation suggested by Martin Van Buren and other members of his New York political machine. Van Buren and his allies were in the process of building a transsectional party of the white democracy, and they recognized the danger in Georgia's radicalism and South Carolina's near-secessionism. So these northern Democrats suggested that Worcester ask for a pardon without insisting on his innocence. By granting the request, the governor would moot the legal case, before the Supreme Court could order U.S. marshals to free Worcester. Georgia's defiance of the Court would be vindicated even as it separated itself from South Carolina's secessionism. For his part, Worcester was induced to accept the pardon by the consideration that further defiance would lead to wide southern sympathy with the nullifiers and thus the possibility of disunion. Georgia had once again defied the Supreme Court's constitutional pronouncements, and, with the Jacksonians in the ascendancy nationally, the Cherokees' fate was sealed.

## CONCLUSION

The Marshall Court's Indian cases fit neatly with the rest of the Court's postwar jurisprudence. *Martin, McCulloch, Dartmouth College*, and the rest of the cases surveyed in the first half of this chapter constituted a judicial effort to defend the Union, judicial supremacy, and common law principles against states' rights and raw democratic will. For Marshall, Story, and the Court, the United States could be a republic of laws only if the Constitution were read to empower the Supreme Court to defend a consistent body of national law, derived substantially from the common law. Only such a Court could prevent the chaos of states' rights and political control of the Constitution. The Indian cases too moved the Court to resist state sovereignty and deploy law to control democratic will. The Court further sought in these cases to curb the stark racism of the white democracy. As a whole, then, the postwar Marshall Court deployed ambitious claims of judicial power to oppose every major principle of the white democracy.

The Court's efforts, however, met with little success. Rather, the operative meaning of the Constitution depended on political and cultural development much more than on constitutional text, established doctrine, and judicial pronouncements. Especially in the Indian cases, the relevant political and cultural history was ambiguous and ambivalent. It began with arguably justified settlements of small numbers of white people on the edges of a vast continent, well populated by indigenous peoples but lightly occupied by European standards. In the absence of a familiar structure of government and landownership among the Indians, these initial settlements could claim some justification in the terms offered by Justice McLean, merely seeking a fair share of underused land on which to subsist. Over time, however, white settlement increasingly interfered with Indian economies and traditions. White-Indian relations came to embody a fundamental clash of cultures and economic systems, in which white Americans came gradually to dominate in numbers and power. When the Cherokees resorted to the Supreme Court in the 1830s, they well knew that it was a last resort, a desperate effort to appeal to the nation's conscience more than its law. And their momentary triumph in that venue represented a late effort to slow the ascent of a Constitution of states' rights, white democracy, and a subordinated federal judiciary.

That effort failed. When Jackson and the white democracy swept into power in 1829, the Constitution became what they insisted it was, a charter of power for the majority of white men in each state. The new, democratic Constitution displayed its power when Georgia defied the Supreme Court decision in *Worcester*. President Jackson himself never had occasion to defy the *Worcester* Court, but his commitment to the removal of the Cherokees was clear. Even some of the Cherokees' firmest allies in national politics began to conclude that the best path now was to accept the inevitability of removal and seek the best terms possible. The Court had said its piece, but the actual allocation of powers and rights among the federal, state, and Cherokee governments would be deter-mined anywhere but in court. The Jackson administration's willingness to conclude the Treaty of New Echota with a pro-removal minority of the Cherokees, Georgia's persistent pressure on the ground (including the temporary jailing of the Cherokee leader John Ross as he led the resistance to the treaty), and the Senate's willingness to ratify an obviously fraudulent treaty – all of these acts and more determined the effective meaning of the Constitution for Indian–white relations. When the Cherokees were in fact physically removed from Georgia in 1838, it helped to signal the ascendancy of the white democracy's remade Constitution, as well as the marginalization of the Supreme Court.

# Conclusion: The Constitutional Triumph and Failure of the Democratic Party

## THE AMERICAN CONSTITUTION FROM
## THE FEDERALISTS TO JACKSON

The great Marshall Court cases after 1815 supported the postwar ambitions of National Republicanism, construing Congress's power expansively, asserting exclusive judicial control over the meaning of the Constitution, and battling the emerging democratic, states'-rights interpretation of the Constitution. The Marshall Court failed, however, and the decisive rise of the Jacksonian Democrats not only humbled the Court and the National Republicans but also signified the transformation of the Federalist Constitution of 1787 itself.

To refer to the Federalist Constitution is not to say that all supporters of the Constitution in 1787 shared the same Federalist understanding of that document and its intended effects. But, as this book has argued, the advocates for the new Constitution broadly shared the goal of a republic of laws under elite leadership and, crucially, a substantial enhancement of power at the center. For Madison and his ilk, the 1780s had exposed American imbecility in foreign affairs, a self-defeating attachment to the undiminished sovereignty of each state, and a short-sighted, quasi-democratic, special-interest politics. Advocates of the new Constitution sought to save republicanism by enhancing federal power and insulating that power from popular whims by lodging it in a distant, governing elite, controlled less by the electorate than by built-in checks and balances. The intended result was not necessarily Marshall-style judicial supremacy. Madison, for example, embraced judicial review but presciently declared that the judges would never be strong enough to resist a determined political majority. Nevertheless, the Framers hoped that the new governing structure would re-infuse republican governance with "justice" and law.

The 1790s exposed serious differences among the original champions of the Constitution. Three terms of Federalist presidents revealed that certain tensions were built into American constitutional politics, particularly the tension between centralized power and states' rights and the tension between republican elitism and democratic will. Neither ratification of the Constitution, nor the unanimous election of George Washington, nor twelve years of Federalist rule could provide a durable consensus on such fundamental matters as the line between state and federal powers and the balance between elite leadership and democratic control. The subsequent Republican regimes under Jefferson and Madison only confirmed that real problems of governance would continually reinvigorate these tensions. Moreover, the split between the Republican dominance of the elected branches and the Federalist retention of most federal judicial offices after 1800 brought into high relief the tension between (emergent) democracy and the republican traditions of the law, a tension that would remain acute all the way to the Jacksonian ascendancy.

If the Constitution remained always subject to widely divergent interpretations, it did have clear effect in channeling the struggles over constitutional meaning into new institutions. Article III's insulation of the judiciary from electoral politics, paired with the electoral accountability of the Congress and the presidency, spurred a vigorous struggle between judicial legalism and a rising democracy as contenders to shape republican governance. The democratic movement made itself felt in the elected branches, in political parties outside the government, and sometimes in the taverns, in the streets, and in the fields. Whatever the Framers and the ratifiers might have imagined, history demonstrated that the development of the Constitution would never belong wholly to the judiciary nor wholly to "the people." Rather, it would evolve, settle, lurch, and evolve again according to the twists of politics and the skills of those in the courts, in Congress, in the executive, in political parties and social movements.

Finally, whether this or that constitutional actor preferred the language of law or that of democracy, nearly everyone in public life – virtually all of them white and male – agreed that republican principles demanded the stark exclusion of most of the population from participation in republican governance. Although there was much talk in the Founding period to suggest some rethinking of the old exclusions and subordination of women, black Americans, and the indigenous peoples, developments of the next fifty years gave the lie to all that. The white men in power sometimes were open to this or that reform – an experiment with female suffrage in New Jersey, a fledgling movement to abolish slavery, an effort to protect the shrunken territorial rights of some few Indian tribes – but exclusion remained a dominant constitutional principle throughout the period of this book. Law and the judiciary did little for any of the excluded, and the rise of democracy rested openly on the declaration that America belonged to the white, male democracy and no one else.

## THE ASCENDANCY OF THE DEMOCRATIC PARTY

The conclusion of our story lies in the Democratic Party's triumphant claim to constitutional supremacy in the 1830s, substantially displacing the Supreme Court as preeminent interpreter of the Constitution and, indeed, displacing the original principles of the Constitution itself. The story of the struggles over the Indians' constitutional status revealed again the white basis of American democracy and the democracy's readiness to retake the Constitution from the Court. The white democracy's victory over the Court on the Indian question joined with other developments, summarized later, to galvanize white democrats north and south in the cause of states' rights and democratic control. But the ultimate triumph of the democratic, states'-rights Constitution depended on the novel construction of a mass political party devoted to those principles. This construction project was carried on for more than a decade before climaxing in the election of Martin Van Buren to the presidency in 1836.

Thomas Jefferson has often been thought the Founding Father of American democracy, largely because the founders of the Jacksonian Democratic Party advertised their creation as a mere restoration of the Jeffersonian Republican Party of 1800. The Democrats and their new Whig opponents were soon fighting over who more truly manifested Jeffersonian democratic principles, resistance to democracy now being self-defeating in American politics. But, in fact, the new constitutional orthodoxy deviated dramatically from the Jeffersonian Constitution.

Contrary to Jacksonian notions of rotation in office and binding popular instructions, Jefferson never suggested that the people themselves should rule via political parties or issue-driven popular campaigns. Never did he argue that positions of power should be accessible to all equally, nor that the holders of those positions should be mere conduits for the will of the untutored masses or the political parties that they might generate. Instead, he shared with Madison the belief that republican government required a constitutional structure that would deliver the best men into office and restrain them from factious legislating while there. Perhaps some insight into Jefferson's attitude is provided by the fact that, notwithstanding his deep-dyed racism, he was willing, apparently, to contemplate the "enfranchisement" of former slaves (at least as of 1774),[1] but never contemplated blacks actually holding positions of power. Rather, he viewed those of African descent as irrevocably inferior, lacking in the intelligence and character necessary to ascend to the role of a natural aristocrat, even if entitled as human beings to liberty and basic civil rights. He thought them, as a class, like many whites of little ability, entitled to their natural rights, responsible to spy and fend off would-be tyrants, but not fit to participate in actual governance.

The Convention of 1787 comprised delegates who mostly carried attitudes about race and government akin to Jefferson's. That is, for all their disagreements, they generally agreed that popular sovereignty should not imply democracy but rule by an elected elite. And they widely agreed that, although slavery was a regrettable institution, it must be accommodated for the foreseeable future. For most of the Framers, social class and race drew fundamental dividing lines that separated the civically responsible from the irresponsible. Few among the Framers or other supporters of ratification advocated democracy in any form, least of all a party-driven democracy in which the people's representatives would merely obey the will of the people as dictated to them through party structures.

Rather, as described in Chapter 1, the Framers designed the federal Constitution specifically to prevent the creation of durable factions or parties and to insulate the government from the influence of special interests. The new federal government was to be sufficiently distant from the people, sufficiently reserved for elite governance, and sufficiently controlled by checks and balances to prevent any self-interested coalition from diverting the government from justice and the public good. The framers further intended a substantial transfer of power from the states to the center. The federal government was to be, if possible, a white gentleman's government of far-seeing statesmen, kept on the straight and narrow by checks that pitted ambition against ambition and private interest against private interest.

---

[1] Jefferson, *A Summary View of the Rights of British America* 17 (Williamsburg, VA: Clementina Rind, 1774).

As the body of this book suggests, however, the realities of American politics never lived up to that model of partyless, elite governance. Rather, the durable conflicts that began in the 1790s yielded the gradual triumph of a kind of democracy. The localist and democratic traditions within the Anti-Federalists of 1788 survived to inform the subsequent opposition to Federalist rule. The plebeian rebellions and protests of the 1790s fed into the Jeffersonian movement of 1800. And the Revolution of 1800 seemed to Martin Van Buren and other Jeffersonians to vindicate the Constitution as a charter of democracy and states' rights – not elite governance and centralized power. The Jefferson and Madison administrations, for all their imperfections, kept the Federalist "aristocrats" on the margins. And waves of suffrage reform in the states, including the New York Constitutional Convention of 1821, built the framework for white democracy.

By the early 1820s, however, the ascendancy of states' rights and democracy seemed very much in danger of being rolled back. Danger lay especially in the *McCulloch* decision and other Marshall Court announcements of broad federal power and the supremacy of the common law over the people's and the states' own notions of justice and policy. If the Court was a major obstacle to popular sovereignty, so was the postwar, nationalist drift of President Madison (who signed the Second Bank of the United States into existence) and President Monroe (who compromised his former resistance to national funding of internal improvements). Both men had been old-school Republican leaders before the war but now pursued an antiparty politics of constitutional compromise rather than redoubling their support for the party of the democracy. With the Court doing all that it could to promote consolidation, the election of the National Republican John Quincy Adams in 1824 confirmed for Van Buren that consolidationism would return triumphant whenever the democracy failed to maintain party organization.

On the surface, the 1824 election was a model of the Framers' intended mode of electing a president. Multiple statesmen were in the field. Although an increasingly large segment of the white male population voted, their votes were safely divided and filtered through an electoral college that prevented an unmediated choice by the people. When the Electoral College yielded no majority choice for the office, the election went into the House of Representatives. The House would choose among the three highest vote-getters, who were, in order, the military hero Andrew Jackson, the New England ex-Federalist John Quincy Adams, and the party-nominated Republican William Crawford of Georgia.

When the erstwhile Federalist somehow beat both the popular Jackson and the certified Republican Crawford, Van Buren and democratic activists everywhere spied an "aristocratic" deal, allegedly arranged by the nationalist Henry Clay, that delivered the executive branch into consolidationist hands. The democratic Constitution's defective mode of presidential election had returned the government to a consolidationist "aristocracy" just a generation after the Revolution of 1800.

For Van Buren, only a reinvigoration of the Republican Party organization could restore the Constitution and its intertwined principles of states' rights and white democracy. Only through party organization could a scattered people ensure the implementation of majority will and the diffusion of power. But such a party was not to be just one of two parties in roughly equal competition under the Constitution. Rather, it would be the party of the entire democracy in defense of majoritarianism itself. And its destiny, according to Van Buren, was to recreate the "exclusive and towering supremacy"[2] that had supposedly belonged to the Republican Party in the wake of the Revolution of 1800. This single, dominant party was to defend the Constitution as a democratic, states'-rights document, as against aristocratic efforts to return the United States to British-style hierarchy and centralization. If the Constitution itself created a framework for democracy in its separation of powers and in its federal structure, experience had shown that even that was not enough. A democratic Constitution equally required the institution of the political party, by which the democracy could defend the Constitution against aristocratic sapping and mining.

Van Buren thus set out to secure the election of Andrew Jackson in 1828 but also "what is of still greater importance, the *substantial reorganization of the old Republican Party*,"[3] as he insisted in a letter to a leading Virginia Republican. By combining Jackson's personal popularity with the organizational prowess of Van Buren and his network, the democrats reclaimed the White House in 1828. And these democrats were, in significant part, radicals, the heirs of those who had resisted ratification in 1788, those who had resisted the Federalists in the Democratic–Republican Societies and even in the Whiskey Rebellion, those who had insisted on Georgia's right to declare the Yazoo land grant unconstitutional without the help of a court, and those who had

---

[2] Martin Van Buren, *The Autobiography of Martin Van Buren* (Washington, DC: U.S. Government Printing Office, 1920), 303.

[3] Van Buren to Thomas A. Ritchie, January 13, 1827.

impeached judges and resisted judicial review. Now, these democrats operated with a new theory of party organization and the new organizing tools that ensured Jackson's election.

It was no coincidence, then, that these years brought Georgia's insistence on the white democracy's control over the Indians, defying both federal law and ultimately a holding of the U.S. Supreme Court. With Jackson in office, they knew they had the sympathies of the federal government in defying the Court. Jackson similarly made his constitutional convictions clear on the question of internal improvements. In 1830, he vetoed a bill to fund the Maysville Road in Kentucky, signaling the return of Republican, strict-constructionist orthodoxy as against the loose-constructionist drift of Presidents Madison, Monroe, and Adams.

On the question of the constitutionality of the Bank of the United States, moreover, Jackson faced down the Court itself. The government's claimed power to charter a national bank had been hotly contested ever since Hamilton's original proposal in 1790. While Jefferson and Madison had futilely insisted on the unconstitutionality of the Bank from the beginning, both men as presidents allowed the Bank to operate through the end of its charter in 1811 rather than attempting to destroy it. And President Madison affirmatively supported the chartering of a second Bank after the War of 1812, accepting that its constitutionality had been affirmed by practice. When the Court's *McCulloch* decision resoundingly affirmed the government's power to charter banks, it explicitly declared that the Court held the final word on the meaning of the Constitution. It claimed superiority to the other branches of the government in its institutional aptitude for answering legal questions and superiority even to the people themselves until the latter should exercise their Article V power of amendment.

But the radical democrats had never accepted the Court's supremacy over the people, and Jackson affirmed that position as president. When presented in 1832 with a bill to renew the charter of the Bank, Jackson did not just veto the bill on policy grounds. Rather, he announced his obligation to declare it unconstitutional, notwithstanding the Supreme Court's holding to the contrary. In the face of that Marshall opinion, Jackson both defended a Constitution of limited powers and states' rights and embraced the departmentalist theory of constitutional interpretation, by which each branch of government exercised equal authority to interpret the Constitution within that branch's own sphere of action: "It is as much the duty of the House of Representatives, of the Senate, and of the President to decide upon the constitutionality of any bill or resolution which may be presented to them for passage or approval as it is of the supreme judges when it may be brought before them for judicial decision. The opinion of the judges has no more authority over Congress than the opinion of Congress has over the judges, and on that point the President is independent of both."[4] And, on the merits of the question, Jackson insisted on his own states'-rights version of the Constitution, which would invalidate any bank that carried the immunity from state taxation that Marshall had so firmly defended in *McCulloch*: "Nothing comes more fully within [the taxing powers of the states] than banks and the business of banking, by whomsoever instituted and carried on. Over this whole subject-matter it is just as absolute, unlimited, and uncontrollable as if the Constitution had never been adopted, because in the formation of that instrument it was reserved without qualification."

In this veto message, Jackson took his case to the people and found vindication in a resounding reelection. For constitutional democrats like Jackson and his new vice president, Van Buren, the democracy carried the ultimate authority to interpret the Constitution. It was superior to each of the coordinate branches because those branches only exercised their authority on behalf of the sovereign people. According to Van Buren,

'Each of the [federal branches] is the agent of the people, doing their business according to the powers conferred; and where there is a disagreement as to the extent of these powers, the people themselves, through the ballot-boxes, must settle it.'
This is the true view of the Constitution. It is that which was taken by those who framed and adopted it, and by the founders of the Democratic party.[5]

Indeed, Van Buren characterized most presidential elections as instances of this popular power of constitutional review, exercised through the mechanism of the Democratic Party. And the large Jacksonian majority of 1832 represented a vindication of the states'-rights, democratic version of the Constitution and a rejection of the judicial supremacy and centralizing constitutionalism of the Marshall Court.

The Jacksonian vindication of the white, states'-rights democracy on the questions of the Cherokees and the Bank expressed a rising identification of the Constitution with democracy, but not necessarily with party organization. Ultimately, though, the Jacksonian construction of a

---

[4] James D. Richardson, ed., *A Compilation of the Messages and Papers of the Presidents, 1789–1897* (Washington, DC: U.S. Government Printing Office, 1896), 2: 582.
[5] Martin Van Buren, *Inquiry into the Origin and Course of Political Parties in the United States* (New York: Hurd and Houghton, 1867), 330 (quoting Hugh Lawson White).

radically democratic Constitution triumphed only because Martin Van Buren and his allies tied it to a political party. Van Buren's Democratic Party (gradually leaving the "Republican" label behind) became the indispensable institution for securing a "democratic" Constitution. The necessity of a new institution defined by its commitment to states' rights and majoritarian democracy became that much clearer amid the Nullification Crisis. As explained in Chapter 6, the South Carolinian theory of nullification claimed the mantle of Jeffersonian states' rights but generated a constitutional crisis, defending even secession as the right of each sovereign state. Here, Jackson drew the line, publicly announcing the federal government's determination to enforce federal law within South Carolina. The particulars of Jackson's statement, however, seemed to swing back to consolidationism, portraying the Founding as the act of one consolidated people rather than a compact among the peoples of the several states. On the substance of the tariff question, a congressional compromise soon settled matters, but the episode demonstrated Van Buren's point about party organization and discipline. Even Andrew Jackson could not be relied on to get constitutional principles right on his own. Rather, Van Buren himself wrote the response of the New York Legislature, which forcefully reaffirmed a doctrine of states' rights that could unite the northern and southern democracies, condemned the nullifiers' secessionist distortions of that doctrine, and gently rebuked Jackson while reaffirming the democracy's faith in his leadership.

Most important, Van Buren renewed his determination to tie the democratic, states-rights Constitution to a permanent political party of the whole democracy, rather than to a single man or to the spontaneous action of the disorganized people. As Jackson's vice president and closest advisor, Van Buren was also the heir apparent to the presidency or at least to the Democratic nomination. But the very idea of a regular party nomination for the presidency remained controversial in the early 1830s. Van Buren could not ride into office on a wave of Jackson-like charisma and war heroism that he did not have, and the democratic Constitution could not depend on a lucky succession of charismatic tribunes for its preservation. Van Buren's job was to convince the nation that only the permanent entrenchment of a party of the democracy would preserve the Constitution against an ever-ready aristocracy.

The chief support for Van Buren's argument lay in the rise of the National Republicans and the partyless, "bargained" election of Adams in 1824. Aristocratic plans for internal improvements and protective tariffs under Adams, followed by a plan for an early rechartering of the

Bank under neo-Federalist leadership in Congress, accompanied further by the campaign to bring the federal government to support the colonization of free blacks – all of this resurgent aristocracy came from the slackening of party discipline. Although Jackson had ridden to the rescue in 1828 and 1832, the democratic Constitution would not be safe as long as an atrophied party organization allowed multiple, ostensibly democratic candidates in the field and thus the possible recurrence of a bargained House election.

When the Democratic convention nominated Van Buren in 1835, its first challenge was to justify the very practice of party nomination. And it did so entirely in terms of preserving a democratic Constitution. The Democratic address thus began with the startling premise that a fundamental obstacle to "public liberty and our happy system, next to revolution and disunion, *is an election of President by the House of Representatives*." Of course, election in the House was the very mechanism that the antidemocratic Framers had expected to complete most presidential elections. Yet the Democrats of 1835 deemed it "the Pandora Box of" a now-democratic Constitution. It was incompatible with popular sovereignty because it removed the choice of the president from the people. In fact, it allowed the distant, cloistered House to choose a president even in direct contradiction to the known preferences of the people, as in 1824.

The Democratic address allowed that one solution would be an "amendment of the Constitution ... to cut off the possibility of an election by the House of Representatives, and cause the will of the People to be respected in the choice of their Chief Magistrate." But, having failed to make headway via Article V, the more practical and comprehensive solution was rigorous organization of the entire American democracy into a political party: "[I]t should be the duty of the Republican party, either through National Conventions, or some other efficient mode, to concentrate their power, and produce harmony and union among their friends." Firm organization of the party would isolate all those who refused to adhere to the democracy's nomination. The result would be political competition only between, on the one hand, those *in* the party who would "secure the Constitution on a firm basis" and, on the other hand, those *outside* the party who would "overturn the Constitution."

When Van Buren won a clear majority in 1836 over a collection of antiparty candidates, he believed he had restored the Constitution to what it was before 1824. He had won the election of 1836 in the name only of party, democracy, and states' rights. The Democratic Party had thus accomplished a major amendment of the Constitution in all but name. Since then, no presidential election has been decided in the House, and the American Constitution has become a charter of "democracy." The anti-party, antidemocratic Constitution of the Founders was all but gone in its fundamentals, even as its particular provisions mostly survived. The new constitutional system would never play out exactly as Van Buren had theorized and hoped (more on that in a moment). But it would also never again be the Constitution of the Framers and Founders of 1787.

On taking the presidency in 1837, Van Buren believed that he and his party had effected not just the permanent organization of the democracy but also its corollary: the permanent elevation of states' rights and strict construction as core principles of the democratic Constitution. Looking back to the Founding in his inaugural address, he insisted that the party was only implementing the Founders' own "limits strictly drawn around the action of the Federal authority" and the states' "sovereign power over the innumerable subjects embraced in the internal government of a just republic."

Van Buren and the Democratic Party also understood the Founders to have founded a specifically white, male democracy, and in power the party never hesitated to act on that principle. Thus the Van Buren administration saw to the final removal of the Cherokees west of the Mississippi; the Democratic House extended its prohibition on even considering anti-slavery petitions; and Democrats as a whole resisted the sorts of public roles for women – especially petitioning on behalf of Indians and the enslaved – that the emerging Whig opposition often embraced.

Already by 1838, the disjointed opposition of 1836 had, out of necessity, coalesced into an organized opposition under the Whig party label. Rapidly now, two-sided party contests between Democrats and Whigs became a fixture of American elections. Indeed, by 1840, with the help of a severe depression on Van Buren's watch, the Whig party triumphed in the presidential election by organizing as thoroughly as the Democrats and beating them at their own game.

A stunned Van Buren firmly believed the election to be an aberration, with the democracy bound to return to itself on its "sober second thought." In the meantime, however, Van Buren warned the Whigs in his final annual message in 1841 that their electoral luck did not signify any change in the democracy's constitutional principles. States' rights and strict construction of federal power remained at the core of the people's constitutionalism, and the sovereign people remained the final word on the meaning of the Constitution. Indeed, Van Buren anticipated, as most did, that the Whigs' first order of business would be to restore the national bank that Jackson had vetoed in 1832. But Van Buren did not warn the Whigs that the now-Jacksonian Supreme Court would invalidate such an extension of federal power. He reminded them only of the sovereign people's commitment to strict construction. And through the 1850s, the Democrats in fact remained the dominant party and states' rights the dominant constitutional philosophy. For all those years, the party largely prevented the loose construction of the Constitution that would have produced a national bank, a national program of internal improvements, and federal intervention in the slavery question, among other policies. *McCulloch v. Maryland* was all but a dead letter for two generations, while the white democracy of states' rights, strict construction, and popular will marginalized the advocates of national economic ambition and common law constitutionalism.

As noted, however, the new system in which party was to be the primary safeguard and explicator of the Constitution never worked as Van Buren had hoped. There never was a party that achieved towering supremacy by organizing the entire democracy – allegedly nineteen-twentieths of the people – to isolate the few crypto-aristocrats. Rather, while the Democratic Party did become the most important institution in public life after 1836, it always struggled to keep its various divisions – especially that between the northern and southern states – from splitting the party into factions. And the Whig opposition, along with various third parties, always drew away far more than the aristocratic 5 percent that Van Buren imagined to be their proper constituency. While Van Buren succeeded in giving the nation a party-based "democracy" to replace the original aspiration to elite partyless rule, the party system turned out to be much more about alliances among factions than about a single constitutional party reliably isolating aristocrats and counterrevolutionaries.

### CODA

The death knell of Van Buren's vision and perhaps the birth announcement of a recognizably modern constitutional system came in the *Dred Scott* case of 1857. Begun as a freedom suit in Missouri by the enslaved Scott, it slowly found its way to the Supreme Court. There, it might have been decided on narrow, largely uncontroversial grounds. But it also bore the potential to address the most explosive political question of the era: whether the federal government could exclude slavery from the western territories. By Van Buren's lights, no court had any business answering such a constitutional question if it could avoid doing so because the people themselves, acting through the Democratic Party, were the ultimate authority on such matters. But by 1857, the party of the democracy had repeatedly failed to settle the issue. Worse, stymied Democratic politicians had resorted to the Federalist judicial heresy, that great constitutional questions belonged in the Supreme Court, not in politics, not in the hands of the people. The predominantly Democratic Court eventually agreed, turning the potentially trivial *Dred Scott* case into a judicial assertion of neo-Marshallian authority.

The Court delivered two major rulings as alternative ways of resolving the case. In the first, the majority held that it lacked jurisdiction because persons of African descent, like Scott, could not count as "citizens" within the meaning of Article III of the Constitution. It is not always recognized that this holding was actually endorsed by many northern whites, including Van Buren, a position that should not be surprising in a founder of the white democracy. In 1857, American constitutionalism, both north and south, remained predominantly racist, reserving full constitutional status and rights for white males only.

The second holding of the *Dred Scott* case split the sections more starkly and demonstrated the failure of Van Buren's hopes for a dominant democratic party in control of the Constitution. The Court accepted the invitation of the frustrated politicians and held that the Missouri Compromise was unconstitutional; the Due Process clause of the Constitution barred the federal government from excluding the slave property of American citizens from the territories. The Democratic Party had persistently failed to carry out the function Van Buren had assigned it, providing the final resolution to this constitutional question by majority rule. And the Democratic President James Buchanan – a Federalist in his youth! – could be heard calling on the nation to defer to the Court on the greatest question of the day, a heresy that Van Buren lamented at length in his memoir.

The result was exactly the emboldening of the Supreme Court that the founders of the Democratic Party had feared and famously overcome. Like Marshall in *Marbury, McCulloch,* and *Worcester,* the *Scott* Court again presumed to resolve a question that lay at the heart of the dominant political controversy of the day, rather than deferring to the democratic will and process. Van Buren roundly rejected the Court's grasping control of a constitutional question that belonged in the hands of the white democracy. He rejected the *McCulloch* notion, soon to become conventional wisdom, that "it belonged to the judicial power to decide upon [the] constitutionality" of laws while only "their expediency" lay with Congress.[6]

Van Buren had supplied the nation with party organization and white democracy to supplant the fundamentals of the original Constitution. In only a single generation, however, he had seen persistently factional and sectional competition supplant his model of a single, supreme party of the states'-rights democracy. The failure of the fractured party to express a clear majority will left the nation without its proper explicator of the Constitution. Into the void returned the Supreme Court. Equipped with the doctrine of substantive due process, the resurgent Court would supervise the legislation of the nation, much as the Marshall Court had done for a time through the Contracts Clause.

No case brings more immediate and, one may say, bipartisan condemnation today than does *Dred Scott*. Yet *Scott* was arguably the founding act of the modern Supreme Court, articulating its essential doctrine of substantive due process and playing its now familiar role of settling constitutional questions whenever the politicians have left the Court the space to do so. Modern Americans are obliged to reject *Scott* out of hand because it was an open expression of judicial racism. But that racism was an honest reflection of the constitutional order that the white democracy had created. In important ways, then, *Dred Scott* survives today in the Court's continuing, constitutional supervision of major political controversies, and even our escape from its racist premises remains a work in progress.

---

[6] Van Buren, *Inquiry*, 374.

# Bibliographical Essay

This book covers a pivotal period in American constitutional history and development: the time between the American Revolution and the rise of Jacksonian Democracy. Including the period often known as the "Founding Era," a term that itself is freighted with ideological significance, this period indisputably encompassed an extended period of constitution making and an almost incessant struggle to define the meaning of American constitutionalism. Understanding this history requires an immersion in a voluminous literature, that includes myriad primary sources and an ever expanding and rich scholarly literature scattered across the fields of history, political science, law, and a host of other disciplines in the humanities and social sciences from philosophy to anthropology. The purpose of this series is to both synthesize this vast body of scholarship and where appropriate integrate new research and insights. This book is also aimed at multiple audiences, from lay readers and undergraduates to law students and serious scholars. It would be impossible to do justice to all of the fine scholarship that has informed this project. Citations in the body of the text have been kept to a minimum, and historiographical asides have been purged from the final manuscript so that the narrative can read as crisply as possible. The bibliographical essay that follows is far from exhaustive and can only partially repay the enormous debt that this book owes to countless scholars.

Traditional constitutional history has often been court-centered and focused primarily on legal doctrine. The approach taken in this volume unites aspects of the traditional internalist, top-down approach of constitutional history, with a more wide-ranging externalist, bottom-up approach. Writing this history and understanding the historical dynamics of constitutional government, consequently, requires moving beyond courts and legal decisions to analyze the way a broad range of actors were shaped by and transformed American constitutionalism.

Although the Supreme Court was the not the sole actor and in many instances not even a significant player in constitutional development on a wide range of questions, its importance is difficult to dispute. General histories of the Supreme

Court worth consulting include: Robert G. McCloskey, *The American Supreme Court* (Chicago: University of Chicago Press, 1960; 4th ed. 2005); and David P. Currie, *The Constitution in the Supreme Court: The First Hundred Years, 1789–1888* (Chicago: University of Chicago Press, 1985). Several volumes of the *Oliver Wendell Holmes Devise History of the United States Supreme Court* cover the time span analyzed in this volume, including George Lee Haskins and Herbert Alan Johnson, *Foundations of Power: John Marshall, 1801–15* (New York: Macmillan, 1981); and George Edward White, *The Marshall Court and Cultural Change, 1815–35* (New York: Macmillan, 1988). John Marshall and his tenure on the court has generated a large literature. Two excellent studies include R. Kent Newmyer, *John Marshall and the Heroic Age of the Supreme Court* (Baton Rouge: Louisiana State University Press, 2007); and Charles F. Hobson, *The Great Chief Justice: John Marshall and the Rule of Law* (Lawrence, KS: University Press of Kansas, 1996). A superb biography of Marshall's great ally on the Court is R. Kent Newmyer, *Supreme Court Justice Joseph Story: Statesman of the Old Republic* (Chapel Hill: University of North Carolina Press, 1985).

Although the Marshall Court has drawn the most interest of scholars, other periods in the court's early history have also prompted important work, including William R. Casto, *The Supreme Court in the Early Republic: The Chief Justiceships of John Jay and Oliver Ellsworth* (Columbia: University of South Carolina Press, 1995); Scott Douglas Gerber, ed., *Seriatim: The Supreme Court before John Marshall* (New York: NYU Press, 1998); and Stewart Jay, *Most Humble Servants: The Advisory Role of Early Judges* (New Haven, CT: Yale University Press, 1997).

It is impossible to understand early American law without addressing English legal and constitutional thought. The influence of English law and political theory on early American constitutional culture was enormous. On the common law legacy, see David Lieberman, "The Mixed Constitution and the Common Law," in *The Cambridge History of Eighteenth Century Political Thought*, eds. Mark Goldie and Robert Wokler, 317–346 (Cambridge: Cambridge University Press, 2006); and H. T. Dickinson, "The British Constitution," in *A Companion to Eighteenth-Century Britain*, ed. H. T. Dickinson, 3–18 (Oxford: Wiley, 2002). On the common law in America, see Kunal Madhukar Parker, *Common Law, History, and Democracy in America, 1790–1900: Legal Thought before Modernism* (Cambridge: Cambridge University Press, 2013); William E. Nelson, *The Common Law in Colonial America* (New York: Oxford University Press, 2008); Peter Charles Hoffer, *Law and People in Colonial America*, Rev. ed. (Baltimore: Johns Hopkins University Press, 1998); and Sally E. Hadden, "Magna Carta for the Masses: An Analysis of Eighteenth-Century Americans' Growing Familiarity with the Great Charter in Newspapers," *North Carolina Law Review* 9 (2016): 1681–1724. These developments are placed in their trans-Atlantic context by Mary Sarah Bilder, *The Transatlantic Constitution: Colonial Legal Culture and the Empire* (Cambridge, MA: Harvard University Press, 2008) and Daniel J. Hulsebosch, *Constituting Empire: New York and the Transformation of Constitutionalism in the Atlantic World, 1664–1830* (Chapel Hill, NC: University of North Carolina Press, 2005). A good survey of the eclectic range of influences shaping American constitutional thought may be found in Forrest McDonald,

*Novus Ordo Seclorum: The Intellectual Origins of the Constitution* (Lawrence, KS: University Press of Kansas, 1987). The democratization of American constitutionalism in this period is central to the story of this volume. Understanding the changing meanings of democracy in Anglo-American history prior to the American Revolution is key, and the best place to deal with this is James T. Kloppenberg, *Toward Democracy: The Struggle for Self-Rule in European and American Thought* (New York: Oxford University Press, 2016), and Jack P. Greene, *The Constitutional Origins of the American Revolution* (Cambridge: Cambridge University Press, 2011). John Phillip Reid's four-volume *Constitutional History of the American Revolution* (Madison: University of Wisconsin Press, 2003) is also indispensable, and the main contours of his argument are readily available in his one-volume, abridged edition, *Constitutional History of the American Revolution* (Madison: University of Wisconsin Press, 1995).

The colonial influences on early American political and constitutional culture are examined in Gordon S. Wood, *The Radicalism of the American Revolution* (New York: Alfred A. Knopf, 1992), which provides a sweeping story of social, political, and constitutional change from prerevolutionary America into the early decades of the nineteenth century. Virtually every major political question in this period implicated some aspect of the Constitution, so the rich literature on early American political history has much to teach constitutional scholars. Two important surveys of this period are Gordon S. Wood, *Empire of Liberty: A History of the Early Republic, 1789–1815* (New York: Oxford University Press, 2011) and Sean Wilentz, *The Rise of American Democracy: Jefferson to Lincoln* (New York: W. W. Norton, 2005). Each provides comprehensive narratives of this period, highlighting different ideological strains in American political and constitutional development.

The problems posed by America's first constitution, the Articles of Confederation, are analyzed in George William Van Cleve, *We Have Not a Government: The Articles of Confederation and the Road to the Constitution* (Chicago: University of Chicago Press, 2017), and Peter S. Onuf, *The Origins of the Federal Republic: Jurisdictional Controversies in the United States, 1775–1787* (Philadelphia: University of Pennsylvania Press, 1983). On the efforts of the Continental Congress to grapple with governing the new nation, see Jack N. Rakove, *The Beginnings of National Politics: An Interpretive History of the Continental Congress* (New York: Alfred A. Knopf, 1979).

The transformation in constitutional thought in the period between the American Revolution and adoption of the Constitution has also spawned a large and rich literature. The essential starting point remains Gordon S. Wood, *The Creation of the American Republic 1776–1787* (Chapel Hill: University of North Carolina Press, 1969), which casts this evolution in ideological terms. Jack N. Rakove, *Original Meanings: Politics and Ideas in the Making of the Constitution* (New York: Alfred A. Knopf, 1996) views the transformation of constitutional ideas less in ideological terms and more in pragmatic terms. Max M. Edling. *A Revolution in Favor of Government: Origins of the U.S. Constitution and the Making of the American State* (New York: Oxford University Press, 2003) offers yet another perspective, focusing on the task of state building. It has been over a century since Charles Beard, *An Economic Interpretation of the Constitution of the United States* (New York: MacMillan, 1913) framed the origins of the Constitution in socioeconomic terms. The most recent and elegant study to stress the elitist nature of the Constitution and the economic motivations of the Framers is Michael Klarman, *The Framers' Coup: The Making of the United States Constitution* (New York: Oxford University Press, 2016), which demonstrates that Beard's insights continue to inspire important work in this area. The best account of the Philadelphia Convention is Richard R. Beeman, *Plain, Honest Men: The Making of the American Constitution* (New York: Random House, 2010).

There has been a considerable amount of work on the role of property and rights of contract in Founding-era constitutional thought. See Steven R. Boyd, "The Contract Clause and the Evolution of American Federalism, 1789–1815," *William and Mary Quarterly* 44 (July 1987): 529–548; Jennifer Nedelsky, *Private Property and the Limits of American Constitutionalism: The Madisonian Framework and Its Legacy* (Chicago: University of Chicago Press, 1990); James W. Ely, Jr., *The Guardian of Every Other Right: A Constitutional History of Property Rights* (New York: Oxford University Press, 1992); and James W. Ely, Jr., *The Contract Clause: A Constitutional History* (Lawrence, KS: University Press of Kansas, 2016). Veneration for property rights existed alongside a robust conception of the early American state's police powers. The extensive tradition of regulation in early America is explored by William J. Novak, *The People's Welfare: Law and Regulation in Nineteenth-Century America* (Chapel Hill: University of North Carolina Press, 1996). There has been a renewal of interest in the early American state, which played a more active role in using the law to advance the agendas of different political factions in this period. See William J. Novak, "The Myth of the 'Weak' American State," *American Historical Review* 113 (June 2008): 752–772; Brian Balogh, *A Government out of Sight: The Mystery of National Authority in Nineteenth-Century America* (New York: Cambridge University Press, 2009); and Jerry L. Mashaw, *Creating the Administrative Constitution: The Lost One Hundred Years of American Administrative Law* (New Haven, CT: Yale University Press, 2012).

There is a vast literature on the "Founders," but the notion that there was a single monolithic group of individuals that might be described as Founders is itself a modern invention and somewhat anachronistic. On this point see Richard B. Bernstein, *The Founding Fathers Reconsidered* (New York: Oxford University Press, 2009). Neither Jefferson nor Adams were participants in the Constitutional convention and hence were not "Framers of the Constitution," but both were major figures in shaping early American constitutionalism more broadly. There is a voluminous literature on Thomas Jefferson. Of particular importance is Peter S. Onuf, *Jefferson's Empire: The Language of American Nationhood* (Charlottesville: University of Virginia Press, 2000) and Annette Gordon Reed and Peter Onuf, *Most Blessed of the Patriarchs: Thomas Jefferson and the Empire of the Imagination* (New York: W. W. Norton, 2017). Other useful interpretations of Jefferson include Richard K. Matthews, *The Radical Politics of Thomas Jefferson* (Lawrence, KS: University Press of Kansas, 1984); Garrett Ward Sheldon, *The Political Philosophy of Thomas Jefferson* (Baltimore, MD: Johns Hopkins University Press, 1991); Gordon S. Wood, *Revolutionary Characters: What Made the Founders Different* (New York: Penguin Press, 2006); and Peter S. Onuf, *The Mind of Thomas Jefferson* (Charlottesville: University of Virginia Press, 2007).

On the important friendship of Thomas Jefferson and James Madison, see Andrew Burstein and Nancy Isenberg, *Jefferson and Madison* (New York: Random House, 2010). James Madison's central role in shaping the contours of early American constitutional history is evidenced in the vast literature that has emerged on his thought. One of the organizing issues in this literature deals with the issue of how much Madison's views shifted over the course of his career. A good starting point to understand this critical issue is Alan Gibson, "The Madisonian Madison and the Question of Consistency: The Significance and Challenge of Recent Research," *Review of Politics* 64 (Spring 2002): 311–338. For a view of Madison as a pragmatist, see Jack N. Rakove, "The Madisonian Moment," *University of Chicago Law Review* 55 (1988): 473–505. The strongest argument in favor of continuity in Madison's thought is Lance Banning, *The Sacred Fire of Liberty: James Madison and the Founding of the Federal Republic* (Ithaca, NY: Cornell University Press, 1996) and Drew R. McCoy, *The Last of the Fathers: James Madison and the Republican Legacy* (Cambridge: Cambridge University Press, 1989). On the composition of his *Notes of Debates in the Federal Convention of 1787* and what they reveal about Madison's evolving constitutional thought, see Mary Sarah Bilder, *Madison's Hand: Revising the Constitutional Convention* (Cambridge, MA: Harvard University Press, 2015).

One important nexus of scholarly interest is *The Federalist*, the collection of pro-Constitution essays authored by James Madison, Alexander Hamilton, and John Jay. A good starting place is Todd Estes, "The Voice of Publius and the Strategies of Persuasion in The Federalist," *Journal of the Early Republic* 28 (2008): 523–558. Hamilton's constitutional thought has generally not garnered enough attention, outside of the context of his contribution to *The Federalist*. An exception to this general neglect is Kate Elizabeth Brown, *Alexander Hamilton and the Development of American Law* (Lawrence, KS: University Press of Kansas, 2017). Alexander Hamilton's reinvention as a multicultural hero in Lin Manuel Miranda's award winning musical has spawned its own interesting literature. The Hamilton phenomenon has been dissected by a number of scholars in a forum on *"Hamilton, An American Musical" Journal of the Early Republic* 37 (Summer 2017). Although one of the most important legal thinkers in post-revolutionary America, James Wilson has not spurred nearly as much interest. A good starting place is Aaron T. Knapp, "Law's Revolutionary: James Wilson and the Birth of American Jurisprudence," *Journal of Law & Politics* 29 (2013): 189–307. Although not a framer of the US Constitution, John Adams was among the most creative constitutional thinkers and influential actors in this era. Two essential guides to his thought are Richard Alan Ryerson, *John Adams's The One, The Few, and the Many* (Baltimore: Johns Hopkins University Press, 2016) and C. Bradley Thompson, *John Adams and the Spirit of Liberty* (Lawrence, KS: Univ. Press of Kansas, 1998).

A panoramic and wide ranging analysis of the dynamics of ratification is Pauline Maier, *Ratification: The People Debate the Constitution, 1787–1788* (New York: Simon and Schuster, 2010). The diversity of Anti-Federalists, the "Other Founders," and original opponents of the Constitution is surveyed in Saul Cornell, *The Other Founders: Anti-Federalism and the Dissenting Tradition in America, 1788–1828* (Chapel Hill, NC: University of North Carolina Press, 1999). The transformation of Anti-Federalism into a loyal opposition is charted in David J. Siemers, *Ratifying the Republic: Antifederalists and Federalists in Constitutional Time* (Stanford, CA: Stanford University Press, 2002). The origins of the Bill of Rights are analyzed in Richard Labunski, *James Madison and the Struggle for the Bill of Rights* (New York: Oxford University Press, 2006) and Paul Finkelman, "James Madison and the Bill of Rights: A Reluctant Paternity," *Supreme Court Review* 9 (1990): 301–350. The first ten amendments were not known as the Bill of Rights until long after the Founding era. On this point see Gerard Magliocca, *The Heart of the Constitution: How the Bill of Rights Became the Bill of Rights* (New York: Oxford University Press, 2018). Legal scholars, particularly those of an originalist bent, have explored most of the provisions of the Bill of Rights in some detail, but most of this scholarship is marred by anachronism and presentism. Examples of genuinely historical discussions of various amendments include: Jud Campbell, "Natural Rights and the First Amendment," *Yale Law Journal* 127 (November 2017): 246–289; Saul Cornell, *A Well-Regulated Militia: The Founding Fathers and the Origins of Gun Control in America* (New York: Oxford University Press, 2006); James W. Ely, Jr., "The Oxymoron Reconsidered: Myth and Reality in the Origins of Substantive Due Process," *Constitutional Commentary* 16 (Summer 1999): 315–345; and F. Thornton Miller, *Juries and Judges versus the Law: Virginia's Provincial Legal Perspective, 1783–1828* (Charlottesville, VA: University of Virginia Press, 1994).

Although modern Americans are most focused on the provisions of the first eight amendments, it was the Tenth Amendment's federalism-enforcing provisions that drew the most interest in this period. Among the most important works on federalism, are Forrest McDonald, *States' Rights and the Union: Imperium in Imperio, 1776–1876* (Lawrence, KS: University Press of Kansas, 2000); Richard E. Ellis, *The Union at Risk: Jacksonian Democracy, States' Rights and the Nullification Crisis* (New York: Oxford University Press, 1987); Andrew C. Lenner, *The Federal Principle in American Politics, 1790–1833* (Lanham, MD: Madison House, 2001); Mark R. Killenbeck, "Pursuing the Great Experiment: Reserved Powers in a Post-Ratification, Compound Republic," *Supreme Court Review* 1999 (1999): 81–140; Alison L. LaCroix, *The Ideological Origins of American Federalism* (Cambridge, MA: Harvard University Press, 2010); and Edward A. Purcell, Jr., *Originalism, Federalism, and the American Constitutional Enterprise* (New Haven, CT: Yale University Press, 2007).

The two best surveys of the contentious decade of Federalist rule are Stanley Elkins and Eric McKitrick, *The Age of Federalism* (New York: Oxford University Press, 1993); James Roger Sharp, *American Politics in the Early Republic: The New Nation in Crisis* (New Haven, CT: Yale University Press, 1993). The political culture of this era was deeply informed by constitutional discourse. For pioneering studies of popular political culture, see David Waldstreicher, *In the Midst of Perpetual Fetes: The Making of American Nationalism, 1776–1820* (Chapel Hill, NC: University of North Carolina Press, 1997); and Simon P. Newman, *Parades and the Politics of the Street: Festive Culture in the Early American Republic* (Philadelphia: University of Pennsylvania Press, 1997).

There is a significant literature on various aspects of the constitutional ferment of this pivotal decade, including Jonathan Gienapp, "Making Constitutional Meaning," *Journal of the Early Republic* 35 (2015): 375–418; Todd Estes,

*The Jay Treaty Debate, Public Opinion, and the Evolution of Early American Political Culture* (Amherst, MA: University of Massachusetts Press, 2006); Albrecht Koschnik, "The Democratic Societies of Philadelphia and the Limits of the American Public Sphere, Circa 1793–1795," *William and Mary Quarterly* 58 (July 2001): 615–636; K.R. Constantine Gutzman, "The Virginia and Kentucky Resolutions Reconsidered: An Appeal to the 'Real Laws' of Our Country," *Journal of Southern History* 66 (August 2000): 473–496; Wendell Bird, "Reassessing Responses to the Virginia and Kentucky Resolutions," *Journal of the Early Republic* 35 (Winter 2015): 519–551; and Tadahisa Kuroda, *The Origins of the Twelfth Amendment: The Electoral College in the Early Republic, 1787–1804* (Westport, CT: Greenwood Publishing, 1994).

The Founding era's antipathy to party and the rise of partisanship was given elegant treatment in a classic text by Richard Hofstadter, *The Idea of a Party System: The Rise of Legitimate Opposition in the United States, 1780–1840* (Berkeley: University of California Press, 1969). Hofstadter's argument has been revised by Gerald Leonard, *The Invention of Party Politics* (Chapel Hill, NC: University of North Carolina Press, 2002) and Gerald Leonard, "Party as a 'Political Safeguard of Federalism': Martin Van Buren and the Constitutional Theory of Party Politics," *Rutgers Law Review* 54 (Fall 2001): 221–282. Also on this subject, see Ronald P. Formisano, "Deferential-Participant Politics: The Early Republic's Political Culture, 1789–1840," *American Political Science Review* 68 (June 1974): 473–487; Ronald P. Formisano, "Federalists and Republicans: Parties, Yes – System, No," in *Party Spirit in a Frontier Republic: Democratic Politics in Ohio, 1793–1821*, Donald J. Ratcliffe ed. (Columbus, OH: Ohio State University Press, 1998); and Ralph Ketcham, *Presidents Above Party: The First American Presidency, 1789–1829* (Chapel Hill, NC: University of North Carolina Press, 1984). Closely related to the rise of parties were the methods of electing presidential electors and the adoption of the Twelfth Amendment. Daniel Peart and Adam I. P. Smith, *Practicing Democracy: Popular Politics in the United States from the Constitution to the Civil War* (Charlottesville: University of Virginia Press, 2015); Brian Schoen, Peter S. Onuf, Robert G. Ingram, and Patrick Griffin, *Between Sovereignty and Anarchy: The Politics of Violence in the American Revolutionary Era* (Charlottesville: University of Virginia Press, 2015); Caroline F. Sloat, "A New Nation Votes and the Study of American Politics, 1789–1824," *Journal of the Early Republic* 33 (Summer 2013): 183–186; Lance Banning, *The Jeffersonian Persuasion: Evolution of a Party Ideology* (Ithaca, NY: Cornell University Press, 1978); Doron Ben-Atar and Barbara Oberg, eds., *Federalists Reconsidered* (Charlottesville: University of Virginia Press, 1998); Jeffrey L. Pasley, *"The Tyranny of Printers": Newspaper Politics in the Early American Republic* (Charlottesville: University of Virginia Press, 2001); Joanne Freeman, *Affairs of Honor: National Politics in the New Republic* (New Haven, CT: Yale University Press, 2001); Jeffrey Pasley, *The First Presidential Contest: 1796 and the Founding of American Democracy* ( Lawrence, KS: University Press of Kansas, 2013).

The meaning of Jefferson's election in 1800 is discussed in James Roger Sharp, *The Deadlocked Election of 1800: Jefferson, Burr, and the Union in the Balance* (Lawrence, KS: University Press of Kansas, 2010); Susan Dunn, *Jefferson's Second*

*Revolution: The Election Crisis of 1800 and the Triumph of Republicanism* (Boston: Houghton Mifflin, 2004); James Horn, Jan Ellen Lewis, and Peter S. Onuf, eds., *The Revolution of 1800: Democracy, Race, and the New Republic* (Charlottesville: University of Virginia Press, 2002). Making sense of Jefferson's presidency in constitutional and legal terms poses a number of interpretive puzzles arising from his unprecedented use of executive and federal power in a variety of contexts. See Jeremy D. Bailey, *Thomas Jefferson and Executive Power* (New York: Cambridge University Press, 2007). The constitutional implications of the Louisiana Purchase and the legal consequences of its incorporation into the United States raise a variety of questions about race, citizenship, and geopolitical concerns as well. See Peter J. Kastor, *The Nation's Crucible: The Louisiana Purchase and the Creation of America* (New Haven, CT: Yale University Press, 2004); Roger G. Kennedy, *Mr. Jefferson's Lost Cause: Land, Farmers, Slavery, and the Louisiana Purchase* (New York: Oxford University Press, 2003). On impeachment, see Peter Charles Hoffer and N.E.H. Hull, *Impeachment in America, 1635–1805* (New Haven, CT: Yale University Press, 1984). The legal issues emerging from the treason trial of Aaron Burr are charted in R. Kent Newmyer, *The Treason Trial of Aaron Burr: Law, Politics, and the Character Wars of the New Nation* (New York: Cambridge University Press, 2012).

The War of 1812 was a transformative moment in American constitutional development. See J. C. A. Stagg, *Mr. Madison's War: Politics, Diplomacy, and Warfare in the Early American Republic, 1783–1830* (Princeton: Princeton University Press, 1983); Alan Taylor, *The Civil War of 1812: American Citizens, British Subjects, Irish Rebels, & Indian Allies* (New York: Vintage, 2011). On James Monroe, see Noble E. Cunningham, *The Presidency of James Monroe* (Lawrence, KS: University Press of Kansas, 1995), and the essays in Stuart Leiberger, *A Companion to James Madison and James Monroe* (Malden, MA: Wiley-Blackwell, 2013). The relationship between Jacksonian politics and constitutionalism is explored in Gerald Leonard, *The Invention of Party Politics: Federalism, Popular Sovereignty, and Constitutional Development in Jacksonian Illinois* (Chapel Hill, NC: University of North Carolina Press, 2002). See also John L. Brooke, *Columbia Rising: Civil Life on the Upper Hudson from the Revolution to the Age of Jackson* (Chapel Hill, NC: University of North Carolina Press, 2010).

Until recently, a standard citation for the early history of judicial review was Sylvia Snowiss, *Judicial Review and the Law of the Constitution* (New Haven, CT: Yale University Press, 1990). But a raft of more sophisticated work has emerged in recent years, and Snowiss's work has been seriously undermined by Dean Alfange, Jr., "Marbury v. Madison and Original Understandings of Judicial Review: In Defense of Traditional Wisdom," *Supreme Court Law Review* (1993): 329–446, and Gerald Leonard, "Iredell Reclaimed: Farewell to Snowiss's History of Judicial Review," *Chicago-Kent Law Review* 81 (2006): 867–882. More importantly, new and better accounts of the origins of judicial review have appeared in Larry D. Kramer, *The People Themselves: Popular Constitutionalism and Judicial Review* (New York: Oxford University Press, 2004); Mary Sarah Bilder, "The Corporate Origins of Judicial Review," *Yale Law Journal* 116 (2006): 502–556; William Michael Treanor, "Judicial Review before Marbury,"

*Stanford Law Review* 58 (2005): 455–562; William Michael Treanor, "The Case of the Prisoners and the Origins of Judicial Review," *University of Pennsylvania Law Review* 143 (1994): 491–570; Donald F. Melhorn, "*Lest We Be Marshall'd*": *Judicial Powers and Politics in Ohio, 1806–1812* (Akron, OH: University of Akron Press, 2003); Keith E. Whittington, *Political Foundations of Judicial Supremacy: The Presidency, the Supreme Court, and Constitutional Leadership in United States History* (Princeton: Princeton University Press, 2007); Maeva Marcus, "Judicial Review in the Early Republic," in *Launching the "Extended Republic": The Federalist Era*, eds. Ronald Hoffman and Peter J. Albert (Charlottesville: University of Virginia Press, 1996); Gordon S. Wood, "The Origins of Judicial Review Revisited, or How the Marshall Court Made More Out of Less," *Washington and Lee Law Review* 56 (Summer 1999): 787–809; Gordon S. Wood, "The Origins of Vested Rights in the Early Republic," *Virginia Law Review* 85 (1999): 1421–1445; William E. Nelson, *Marbury v. Madison and the Origins and Legacy of Judicial Review* (Lawrence, KS: University Press of Kansas, 2000).

Treatment of the judiciary by the public political process is analyzed in Richard E. Ellis, *The Jeffersonian Crisis: Courts and Politics in the Young Republic* (New York: Oxford University Press, 1971); Wythe Holt and James R. Perry, "Writs and Rights, 'Clashing Animosities': The First Confrontation Between Federal and State Jurisdictions," *Law and History Review* 7 (1989): 89–120; Brian Carso, *Whom Can We Trust Now?: The Meaning of Treason in the United States, from the Revolution through the Civil War* (Boston: Lexington Books, 2006); Maeva Marcus, ed., *Origins of the Federal Judiciary: Essays on the Judiciary Act of 1789* (New York: Oxford University Press,1992); Kathryn Turner, "Federalist Policy and the Judiciary Act of 1801," *William and Mary Quarterly* 22 (January 1965): 3–32; Kathryn Turner, "The Appointment of Chief Justice Marshall," *William and Mary Quarterly* 17 (April 1960): 143–163; Kathryn Turner, "The Midnight Judges," *University of Pennsylvania Law Review* 109 (1961): 494–523; Charles Warren, "Legislative and Judicial Attacks on the Supreme Court of the United States – A History of the Twenty-Fifth Section of the Judiciary Act," *American Law Review* 47 (1913), 1–34, 161–189; and Jed Handelsman Shugerman, *The People's Courts: Pursuing Judicial Independence in America* (Cambridge, MA: Harvard University Press, 2012).

The constitutional meaning of citizenship is also central to the history of law in this period. The issue has been analyzed by Rogers M. Smith, *Civic Ideals: Conflicting Visions of Citizenship in U.S. History* (New Haven, CT: Yale University Press, 1997); and Kunal M. Parker, *Making Foreigners: Immigration and Citizenship Law in America 1600–2000* (Cambridge: Cambridge University Press, 2015). On suffrage, see Alexander Keyssar, *The Right to Vote: The Contested History of Democracy in the United States* (New York: Basic Books, 2000).

Several of the landmark early Supreme Court Cases have prompted book length treatments. *Chisholm v. Georgia* and the passage, in reaction, of the Eleventh Amendment are described in Clyde E. Jacobs, *The Eleventh Amendment and Sovereign Immunity* (Westport, CT: Greenwood Press, 1972); John V. Orth, *The Judicial Power of the United States: The Eleventh Amendment in American History* (New York; Oxford University Press, 1987); William Fletcher,

"A Historical Interpretation of the Eleventh Amendment: A Narrow Construction of an Affirmative Grant of Jurisdiction Rather than a Prohibition Against Jurisdiction," *Stanford Law Review* 35 (1983): 1033–1131; and John J. Gibbons, "The Eleventh Amendment and State Sovereign Immunity: A Reinterpretation," *Columbia Law Review* 83 (December 1983): 1889–2005. The crucial case of *Fletcher v. Peck* inspired a classic account by C. Peter Magrath, *Yazoo: Law and Politics in the New Republic: The Case of Fletcher v. Peck* (New York: W.W. Norton, 1967), which has now been joined by Charles F. Hobson, *The Great Yazoo Lands Sale: The Case of Fletcher v. Peck* (Lawrence, KS: University Press of Kansas, 2016). Other cases are treated in William R. Casto, "The Early Supreme Court Justices' Most Significant Opinion," *Ohio Northern University Law Review* 29 (2002): 173–207; Mark Robert Killenbeck, *McCulloch v. Maryland: Securing a Nation* (Lawrence, KS: University Press of Kansas, 2006); Richard E. Ellis, *Aggressive Nationalism: McCulloch v. Maryland and the Foundation of Federal Authority in the Young Republic* (New York: Oxford University Press, 2007).

The literature on "popular constitutionalism" seeks to broaden historical inquiry by including non-elite actors and understanding their contributions to American politics and law. The essays in Jeffrey Pasley, David Waldstreicher, and Andrew Robertson, eds., *Beyond the Founders* (Chapel Hill, NC: University of North Carolina Press, 2003) is an indispensable starting point for any inquiry into popular constitutional belief in this period. Alfred F. Young, Gary B. Nash, and Ray Raphael, *Revolutionary Founders: Rebels, Radicals, and Reformers in the Making of the Nation* (New York: Vintage, 2012), extends this project. Other important contributions to this burgeoning field of study include Christopher L. Tomlins, *Law, Labor, and Ideology in the Early American Republic* (Cambridge: Cambridge University Press, 1993); Seth, Cotlar, *Tom Paine's America: The Rise and Fall of Transatlantic Radicalism in the Early Republic* (Charlottesville: University of Virginia Press, 2011); Gary D. Rowe, "Constitutionalism in the Streets," *Southern California Law Review* 78 (2005): 401–454.

The impact of gender on constitutional and political thought in this period has received far more attention in the last generation. The starting point for engaging this literature is Linda Kerber, *No Constitutional Right to Be Ladies: Women and the Obligations of Citizenship* (New York: Hill and Wang, 1998). Other important contributions to this body of scholarship include Catherine Allgor, *Parlor Politics: In Which the Ladies of Washington Help Build a City and a Government* (Charlottesville: University of Virginia Press, 2000); Susan Branson, *These Fiery Frenchified Dames: Women and Political Culture in Early National Philadelphia* (Philadelphia: University of Pennsylvania Press, 2001); Sandra F. Van Burkleo, *"Belonging to the World": Women's Rights and American Constitutional Culture* (New York: Oxford University Press, 2001); Linda K. Kerber, *Women of the Republic: Intellect and Ideology in Revolutionary America* (Chapel Hill, NC: University of North Carolina Press, 1980); Woody Holton, *Abigail Adams: A Life* (New York: Simon and Schuster, 2010); Harriet B. Applewhite and Darline G. Levy, eds., *Women and Politics in the Age of the American Revolution* (Ann Arbor, MI: University of Michigan Press, 1990); Sheila L. Skemp, *First Lady of Letters: Judith Sargent Murray and the Struggle for Female Independence* (Philadelphia: University of Pennsylvania Press, 2009); Rosemarie Zagarri,

*Revolutionary Backlash: Women and Politics in the Early American Republic* (Philadelphia: University of Pennsylvania Press, 2007); Jeanne Boydston, "Making Gender in the Early Republic," in *The Revolution of 1800: Democracy, Race, and the New Republic*, ed. James J. Horn, et al. (Charlottesville: University of Virginia Press, 2002); and Carole Shammas, *A History of Household Government in America* (Charlottesville: University of Virginia Press, 2002).

The complex connections between the Constitution and race are explored in David Waldstreicher, *Slavery's Constitution: From Revolution to Ratification* (New York: Hill and Wang, 2009). On the pro-slavery character of early constitutionalism, see Paul Finkelman, *Slavery and the Founders: Race and Liberty in the Age of Jefferson*, Rev. ed. (New York: Routledge, 2001). On forms of African American resistance, see, e.g., Douglas R. Egerton, *Gabriel's Rebellion: The Virginia Slave Conspiracies of 1800 & 1802* (Chapel Hill, NC: University of North Carolina Press, 1993); Richard S. Newman, *The Transformation of American Abolitionism: Fighting Slavery in the Early Republic* (Chapel Hill, NC: University of North Carolina Press, 2002); Joanna Brooks, "The Early American Public Sphere and the Emergence of a Black Print Counterpublic," *William and Mary Quarterly* 62 (January 2005): 67–92; Richard S., Newman, and Roy E. Finkenbine "Black Founders in the New Republic: Introduction," *William and Mary Quarterly* 64 (January 2007): 83–94.

The many roles of race in the constitutional politics of the early nation and especially the constitutional issues posed by western expansion have been explored by a number of authors. John Craig Hammond, *Slavery, Freedom, and Expansion in the Early American West* (Charlottesville, VA: University of Virginia Press, 2007); Matthew Mason, *Slavery and Politics in the Early American Republic* (Chapel Hill, NC: University of North Carolina Press, 2008); John Craig Hammond, Matthew Mason, eds., *Contesting Slavery. The Politics of Bondage and Freedom in the New American Nation* (Charlottesville, VA: University of Virginia Press, 2011); Don Fehrenbacher, *The Dred Scott Case: Its Significance in American Law and Politics* (New York: Oxford University Press, 1978); Donald L. Robinson, *Slavery in the Structure of American Politics, 1765–1820* (New York: Harcourt Brace Jovanovich, 1971); Christopher L. Tomlins, *Freedom Bound: Law, Labor, and Civic Identity in Colonizing America, 1580–1865* (Cambridge: Cambridge University Press, 2010); John Wood Sweet, *Bodies Politic: Negotiating Race in the American North, 1730–1830* (Baltimore: Johns Hopkins University Press, 2003); Alexander Saxton, *The Rise and Fall of the White Republic: Class Politics and Mass Culture in Nineteenth-Century America* (New York: Verso, 1990); Don Fehrenbacher, *The Slaveholding Republic: An Account of the United States Government's Relations to Slavery* (completed and edited by Ward McAfee; New York: Oxford University Press, 2001); George William Van Cleve, *A Slaveholders' Union: Slavery, Politics, and the Constitution in the Early American Republic* (Chicago: University of Chicago Press, 2010); Padraig Riley, *Slavery and the Democratic Conscience: Political Life in Jeffersonian America* (Philadelphia: University of Pennsylvania Press, 2016); Adam Rothman, *Slave Country: American Expansion and the Origins of the Deep South* (Cambridge, MA: Harvard University Press, 2005); Gary J. Kornblith, *Slavery and Sectional Strife in the Early American Republic, 1776–1821* (Lanham,

MD: Rowman and Littlefield, 2010); Joshua Michael Zeitz, "The Missouri Compromise Reconsidered: Antislavery Rhetoric and the Emergence of the Free Labor Synthesis," *Journal of the Early Republic* 20 (Fall 2000): 447–485; Mark A. Graber, *Dred Scott and the Problem of Constitutional Evil* (New York: Cambridge University Press, 2006); Robert Pierce Forbes, *The Missouri Compromise and Its Aftermath: Slavery and the Meaning of America* (Chapel Hill: University of North Carolina Press, 2007); Sean Wilentz, "Jeffersonian Democracy and the Origins of Political Antislavery in the United States: The Missouri Crisis Revisited," *Journal of the Historical Society* 4 (2004): 375–401; Paul Finkelman, "Prelude to the Fourteenth Amendment: Black Legal Rights in the Antebellum North," *Rutgers Law Journal* 17 (1986): 415–482; David L. Lightner, *Slavery and the Commerce Power: How the Struggle against the Interstate Slave Trade Led to the Civil War* (New Haven, CT: Yale University Press, 2006); H. Robert Baker, "The Fugitive Slave Clause and the Antebellum Constitution," *Law and History Review* 30 (Nov. 2012): 1133–1174; Eva Shepard Wolf, *Race and Liberty in the New Nation: Emancipation in Virginia from the Revolution to Nat Turner's Rebellion* (Baton Rouge, LA: Louisiana State University Press, 2006); Lacy Ford, "Reconfiguring the Old South: 'Solving' the Problem of Slavery, 1787–1838" *Journal of American History* 95 (June 2008): 95–122; Jan Ellen Lewis, "What Happened to the Three-Fifths Clause: The Relationship between Women and Slaves in Constitutional Thought, 1787–1866," *Journal of the Early Republic* 37 (Spring 2017): 1–46; and William W. Freehling, *The Road to Disunion: Secessionists at Bay, 1776–1854* (New York: Oxford University Press, 1991).

The constitutional status of indigenous nations and their effect on early American constitutional development, has also generated an increasingly rich body of scholarship, including Reginald Horsman, *Expansion and American Indian Policy, 1783–1812* (East Lansing: Michigan State University Press, 1967); Anthony F. C. Wallace, *Jefferson and the Indians: The Tragic Fate of the First Americans* (Cambridge, MA: Harvard University Press, 1999); Stuart Banner, *How the Indians Lost Their Land: Law and Power on the Frontier* (Cambridge, MA: Harvard University Press, 2005); David Andrew Nichols, *Red Gentlemen and White Savages: Indians, Federalists, and the Search for Order on the American Frontier* (Charlottesville: University of Virginia Press, 2008); Frank Pommersheim, *Broken Landscape: Indians, Indian Tribes, and the Constitution* (New York: Oxford University Press, 2009); Lindsay G. Robertson, *Conquest by Law: How the Discovery of America Dispossessed Indigenous Peoples of Their Lands* (New York: Oxford University Press, 2005); Blake Watson, *Buying America from the Indians: Johnson v. M'Intosh and the History of Native Land Rights* (Norman, OK: University of Oklahoma Press, 2012); Eric Kades, "History and Interpretation of the Great Case of *Johnson v. M'Intosh*," *Law & History Review* 19 (Spring 2001): 67–116; Gregory Ablavsky, "The Savage Constitution," *Duke Law Journal* 63 (February 2014): 999–1089; Jill Norgren, *The Cherokee Cases: Two Landmark Federal Decisions in the Fight for Sovereignty* (Norman, OK: University of Oklahoma Press, 2004); Tim Alan Garrison, *The Legal Ideology of Removal: The Southern Judiciary and the Sovereignty of the Native American Nations* (Athens, GA: University of Georgia Press, 2002).

Efforts to understand the broad arc of American constitutional development include Bruce Ackerman, *The Failure of the Founding Fathers: Jefferson, Marshall, and the Rise of Presidential Democracy* (Cambridge, MA: Harvard University Press, 2005) and *We the People: Foundations* (Cambridge, MA: Harvard University Press, 1991); and Akhil Reed Amar, *The Bill of Rights: Creation and Reconstruction* (New Haven, CT: Yale University Press, 1998). On Jacksonian politics as a constitutional moment largely neglected by Ackerman and Amar, see Gerard N. Magliocca, *Andrew Jackson and the Constitution: The Rise and Fall of Generational Regimes* (Lawrence, KS: University Press of Kansas, 2007). More theoretical treatments of constitutionalism may be found in Keith E. Whittington, *Constitutional Construction: Divided Powers and Constitutional Meaning* (Cambridge, MA: Harvard University Press, 1999); Scott Gordon, *Controlling the State: Constitutionalism from Ancient Athens to Today* (Cambridge: Cambridge University Press, 1999); Sidney M. Milkis, *Political Parties and Constitutional Government: Remaking American Democracy* (Baltimore: Johns Hopkins University Press, 1999).

The emergence of externalist, context-focused histories has radically transformed the writing of legal and constitutional history over the past couple of generations. See Kermit L. Hall, "American Legal History as Science and Applied Politics," *Benchmark* 4 (1990): 229–242; Robert W. Gordon, "Critical Legal Histories," *Stanford Law Review* 36 (1984): 57–125; Hendrik Hartog, "Introduction to Symposium on 'Critical Legal Histories,'" *Law & Social Inquiry* 37 (2012): 147–154. On the interdisciplinary character of much recent externalist legal history, see Catherine Fisk and Robert W. Gordon, "Law As ... Theory and Method in Legal History" *UC Irvine Law Review* 1 (2011). Much of the legal scholarship on the Founding era has been dominated by forms of originalist analysis. For a range of historical critiques of originalism, see "Forum: Historians and the New Originalism," *Fordham Law Review* 84 (2015). The best introduction to contemporary writing about American constitutional history, including this period, is Michael Grossberg and Christopher L. Tomlins, *The Cambridge History of Law in America*, 3 vols. (Cambridge: Cambridge University Press, 2008). Another important survey of the developments in this field worth consulting is Alfred L. Brophy and Sally Hadden, *A Companion to American Legal History* (Wiley-Blackwell, 2013).

# Index

Adams, Abigail, 66
Adams, Henry, 134
Adams, John, 8–9, 67, 73, 78–79, 84, 86,
    89, 91, 115, 139
Adams, John Quincy, 163, 179, 214, 218
Alabama, 106, 113, 157, 195
Alien and Sedition Acts, 44, 53, 74, 76–77,
    86, 99, 106
American Colonization Society, 151,
    155–157, 164
American Revolution, 4, 10, 13, 21, 30, 32,
    55, 59–60, 63, 71, 139
Ames, Fisher, 55
Anti-Federalists, 5, 29, 31–32, 34, 46, 130
    and Bill of Rights, 39
    and constitutional review, 94
    and criminal law, 36
    elite, 34
    and militia, 37
    moderate, 35
    opposition to Constitution, 31
    and Tenth Amendment, 38
    weaknesses of, 33
    wealthy planters, 31
antislavery societies, 62, 155, 158
aristocracy, 4, 167, 169
    artificial, 82
    and Constitution, 85, 215, 218
    defense of liberty, 49
    and Federalists, 109, 111
    natural, 18, 31, 50–51, 56, 213
    and parties, 219
    populist opposition to, 3

republican alternative to, 8
special interests, 176
and Van Buren, 178, 215
aristocrats
    and Federalists, 214
    planters, 31
Articles of Confederation, 4, 10, 27, 40, 103
    attempt to revise, 9, 17, 33
    creation of, 10
    and Indians, 191
    lack of judiciary, 25
    and state sovereignty, 30, 38, 44, 195
    weakness of, 8, 10–16, 39

Bacon, Ezekiel, 173, 175
*Bayard v. Singleton* (1787), 94
Bill of Rights, 35–36, 38, 40, 102
Bishop, Abraham, 108–109
Black Americans, 2, 10
    Black Laws, 122
    black women, 64
    and Constitution, 5
    and Democratic Party, 6, 146
    elites, 121
    exclusion, 2, 82, 123, 147, 212
    free blacks, 43, 62–63, 69, 120, 122, 148,
        150, 155, 162–163, 166, 169, 219
    migration, 122
    voting rights, 43, 68, 82, 168, 170, 172
    and white democracy, 116, 165, 175
Bonaparte, Napoleon, 118
Bonus Bill, 138–139, 141
    Madison's veto, 138

Briggs, Olney, 173
Bucktails, 167
Burr, Aaron, 80–81, 128–129

Calhoun, John C., 130, 138
Canada, 128, 130
  border with, 124, 128
checks and balances, 10, 22, 139, 210, 213
*Cherokee Nation v. Georgia* (1831), 179, 202
Cherokees, 6, 179, 201–203, 207–208
*Chisholm v. Georgia* (1793), 104, 109
Claiborne, William, 121
Clay, Henry, 130, 138, 156, 160, 165, 179,
  215
Clinton, George, 31, 137
*Cohens v. Virginia* (1821), 178, 182
common law, 59, 129, 181, 214, 221
  and Constitution, 5, 40, 102–103, 105,
    136
  and contracts, 178, 188–189, 197
  definition of, 13
  and democracy, 25, 207
  and Eleventh Amendment, 105
  and federalism, 101
  and Federalists, 107
  and free speech, 36, 74
  and Indians, 190
  and legalism, 85, 108
  opposition to, 13, 91, 98, 106, 109, 113
  and Supreme Court, 23
  and women, 69
Congress
  House of Representatives, 27, 40, 72, 81,
    98, 110, 130, 141, 148, 160, 165, 214,
    216, 219–220
  Senate, 18, 27, 35, 40, 72, 90, 93,
    98–100, 119, 130, 148, 160, 169, 208,
    216
congressional veto, 24
Connecticut, 18, 20–21, 33, 69, 79, 100,
  108, 130, 132, 166
Connecticut Compromise. *See* Great
  Compromise
consolidation, 9, 34, 46, 53, 102, 105,
  138–139, 218
  and the Constitution, 103
  and courts, 103, 179, 214
  and Hamilton, 53
  opposition to, 29, 75
Constitution, United States
  Constitutional Convention, 9
  Eleventh Amendment, 104–105, 109
  First Amendment, 35, 74

Framers of, 1–2, 9–10, 19, 21, 23, 27, 32,
  40, 43, 50, 66, 81, 97, 145, 184, 194,
  196, 211, 213–214, 219–220
ratification of, 1–3, 10, 28, 30, 32–37,
  39–40, 43–44, 47, 75, 82, 84, 94, 103,
  113, 116, 130, 135, 147, 193, 211,
  213, 215
Second Amendment, 36–37
Tenth Amendment, 36, 38, 58, 103, 185
Continental Congress, 10
Contracts Clause, 23, 25, 27, 95, 102, 112,
  188–189, 198, 223
courts, 3, 78, 93, 211
  adjudication, 107, 131
  and Anti-Federalists, 94
  Articles of Confederation, 11
  check on democracy, 1
  checks and balances, 93
  circuit, 25, 87, 95
  closing of, 14
  and common law, 101
  in the Constitution, 23
  and Democratic Party, 2
  district, 25
  federal, 5, 25–27, 39–40, 76, 85, 88, 104,
    124–125, 178, 180–181, 187
  and federalism, 101, 103
  and Indians, 191
  judicial interpretation, 96
  local, 14
  and national bank, 136, 183
  opposition to, 3, 75, 97–98, 113
  and Republicans, 84, 86
  and sovereignty, 108
  state, 24, 26, 103, 180–182
  and state sovereignty, 34
  state sovereignty, 182
  and women, 69
Cumberland Road, 141–142
  Cumberland Road bill, 142

*Dartmouth College v. Woodward* (1819),
  179, 188
Davis, John, 147
Dearborn, Henry, 130
Delaware, 21, 33, 62, 100
democracy, 1, 168–169, 172, 214, 217, 220
  balance of, 8, 39
  and common law, 25
  and Constitution, 1, 3, 24, 220
  control of, 84, 101
  and courts, 23
  and Democratic Party, 3, 146, 219

excess of, 4, 16, 32, 40, 51, 181
Founders' view, 1–2, 18, 23, 27, 56
and irresponsible voters, 171
populism, 82
populist, 57
proponents of, 2, 17, 58
and race, 43, 64, 82, 116, 147, 166, 178
rise of, 167, 169, 178, 211
and slavery, 222
and states, 9
white democracy, 146, 163, 165, 168,
    172, 174–176, 179, 190, 207–209,
    212, 214–215, 221, 223
and women, 71
Democratic Party, 2, 4, 6, 70, 166, 176,
    207, 212, 222
Jacksonian, 200, 210
racism, 171, 177
slavery, 177
Democratic-Republican Societies, 43, 57,
    78, 82, 84, 87, 215

economy, 11–12, 31, 45, 48, 88, 116, 125,
    129, 133, 135, 137, 152, 159
Hamilton's plan, 45
policy, 13, 40
problems, 8–9, 12, 14
elections
Congressional, 98
local, 79–80
of 1796, 72
of 1800, 44, 68, 78, 80–81, 87, 89, 143,
    146, 214–215
of 1804, 100
of 1824, 214
of 1836, 219
electoral college, 22, 27, 81, 214
elitism, 2, 10, 40, 43, 57
and Constitution, 166
and democracy, 56
and republicanism, 10, 39
embargo, 117, 133
Essex Junto, 119
*Ex-Parte Gilchrist* (1808), 126

factions, 2, 9, 16, 33, 40, 47–48, 75, 139, 167
farmers, 12–13, 31, 39, 167, 199, 205
federal government, 1, 9, 16, 18, 34–35, 40,
    45, 51, 102–103, 117, 125, 129, 132
federalism, 2, 41, 49
and Anti-Federalists, 29, 31, 39
and Britain, 30
and democracy, 40

and the Constitution, 4, 185
and the courts, 101
debate over, 101, 134, 136
and Democratic Party, 7
and Embargo Act, 125
and First Amendment, 35
and Indians, 205
and localism, 58
and the militia, 130
praise for, 29
and the press, 73
and Second Amendment, 36–37
and Sedition Act, 74
and separation of powers, 101, 127
and states' rights, 32, 77, 102
and Supreme Court, 105
and taxation, 186
and Thomas Jefferson, 34
Federalists, 34, 39, 52, 140, 210
and Alien and Sedition Acts, 74
attacks on Jefferson, 79, 81
and central government, 32
and criminal law, 36
decline of, 99, 133
and democracy, 79, 101, 111, 170–171
and Democratic–Republican societies,
    55–56, 60
divisions between, 44, 80
and French Revolution, 71
and Haitian Revolution, 62
and Hartford Convention, 132
and impeachment of judges, 100
and Jay Treaty, 72
and Judiciary Act of 1801, 90
and judicial review, 94
and judicial supremacy, 95
and judiciary, 85, 126
and Judiciary Act of 1801, 89, 114
and legalism, 113
and Lousiana Purchase, 118
and militia, 130
and moderate Republicans, 6
and national bank, 48
and New Orleans, 118
and party organization, 56
and poor whites, 171
and popular sovereignty, 107
and slavery, 151–152
and states' rights, 124–125, 132
and War of 1812, 130
and Whiskey Rebellion, 57–58
and women's rights, 64, 68
and Yazoo scandal, 107

Federalists (cont.)
economic plan, 45
judiciary, 129
Madison's split with, 47, 52
moderate, 46
opposition to, 5, 32, 72
revival of, 117, 125
strengths of, 33
support of Constitution, 29
support of Jefferson, 81
First Bank of the United States, 48, 144
*Fletcher v. Peck* (1810), 25, 101, 105, 111,
179, 197, 201
foreign affairs, 9, 40, 72–73, 125, 132, 206,
210
Articles of Confederation, 9, 39
Barbary States, 11
Constitution, 28, 39
and democracy, 4
France, 44, 71
Indians, 192
Forten, James, 4, 123
France, 93, 118, 121, 124, 129
American relations with, 73, 124
French Revolution, 44, 63, 71, 79
Quasi-War, 74
Franklin, Benjamin, 15, 27, 72
Fuller, Timothy, 159

Gallatin, Albert, 63, 74, 110, 119, 133, 135,
138
General Survey Act of 1824, 143
Georgia, 88, 104, 110, 112, 188
border disputes, 195
and Cherokees, 6, 201–203, 207
Constitution of 1798, 111
defiance of Supreme Court, 203, 208
and Indians, 192–193, 197–198, 200, 206
and ratification, 33
and slavery, 19–21, 149, 153
states' rights, 106, 197, 206
and white democracy, 216
Yazoo scandal, 87, 97, 101, 105–113, 188
Gerry, Elbridge, 24, 27, 32
*Gibbons v. Ogden* (1824), 187
Great Britain, 9, 11–13, 46, 71, 124, 204
American colonies, 30
impressment, 124
Jay Treaty, 72
system of government, 8, 16, 39, 45
trade, 12
War of 1812, 129–130, 132, 140
Great Compromise, 18–19, 40

Hamilton, Alexander, 4, 107, 116
and Aaron Burr, 81
on Articles of Confederation, 16
and central government, 5, 16, 82
and Constitutional Convention,
9, 15
economic plan, 45–46, 49
and faction, 47, 72
federalism, 134, 186
*The Federalist*, 29, 47, 105
and French Revolution, 71
and judicial review, 94
national bank, 48
national debt, 46
opposition to, 46, 49–51, 53–54, 135,
140, 144
political views, 45
split with Madison, 53
and state building, 43
state building, 45
supporters of, 79
vision for presidency, 22
Whiskey Rebellion, 57–58
Harper, Robert Goodloe, 107
Hartford Convention, 132–133
*Hylton v. U.S.* (1796), 95

impeachment
of judges, 91–92, 98, 114, 216
Ohio policy, 98
political use, 99–100
Indians, 3, 67, 196, 198, 204, 206
Articles of Confederation, 191
assimilation, 121, 196
conflicts, 208
Constitution, 5, 193, 203, 212
and Democratic Party, 7, 220
dispossession, 194, 197, 199–200,
205–206
diversity among, 192
land sales, 191
property rights, 190
support for, 70
trade, 11
treaties, 192, 195
and white democracy, 166, 168
white democracy, 216
internal improvements, 133

Jay Treaty, 44, 72, 195
Jay, John, 72
*The Federalist*, 29, 47
Jay, Peter, 170, 173

Jefferson, Thomas, 9, 33, 53, 72–74, 78, 91, 96, 114–116, 130, 144, 146, 196, 211–212
  and courts, 84, 90, 97, 100
  and democracy, 56
  and expansion, 116–117, 196
  and nullification, 207
  and race, 62, 120–121, 124
  and slavery, 120, 151, 153
  and states' rights, 102, 106, 143
  election of, 5–6, 44, 78, 81
  Louisiana Purchase, 118
  national bank, 48
  opposition leader, 5, 47, 75, 77
  peaceable coercion, 124, 129
  presidency, 6, 115
  Shays' Rebellion, 14
  trade embargo, 124
  view of parties, 34, 57, 212
*Johnson v. M'Intosh* (1823), 179, 191, 196, 198, 204
Johnson, William, 126, 180
judicial review, 3, 99, 113, 127, 210, 216
  and Constitution, 24–25, 27
  and democracy, 95, 106
  and Federalists, 94
  and judicial supremacy, 96
  and states, 94
  debate over, 24
  opposition to, 97
Judiciary Act, 105, 180
  1801, 97
  of 1789, 25, 87–88, 103
  of 1801, 87–88, 90, 92, 104, 114
juries, 56, 61, 63, 65, 95, 124, 129
  and black communities, 166
  as a check on government, 60, 86, 125
  and democracy, 13, 89, 125
  and judicial review, 94

Kentucky, 88, 130, 216
  Resolution of 1799, 77, 84, 87
  states' rights, 75–76, 102, 106, 207
  tax protests, 57

land sales, 106
legalism, 85, 89, 106, 112–113, 178, 185, 187, 211
  definition of, 85
  opposition to, 50
liberty, 2, 4, 15, 19, 42, 53–54, 58–61, 63, 75, 81, 100, 144
  and aristocracy, 49

  and Bill of Rights, 38–39
  and confederation of states, 4
  and Constitution, 1
  and courts, 94, 104
  and Embargo Act, 144
  empire for, 116, 118–119, 123
  and federalism, 75, 103, 132
  Founders' view of, 1–2
  and militia, 37
  and popular unrest, 14
  and racism, 213
  and slavery, 19, 21, 40, 60, 62, 152–153, 160
  and states, 51, 82
  and the Constitution, 181
  and the press, 54
  and white democracy, 165
  and women, 64
liberty pole, 59
Lincoln, Levi, 110
Livermore, Arthur, 158
Livingston, Brockholst, 129
localism, 4, 16, 31, 34, 40–41, 43, 58, 105, 139, 214
Louisiana Purchase, 116–118, 123, 132, 144, 146, 150
Louisiana Territory, 116, 118
loyal opposition, 34

Macon, Nathaniel, 156
Madison, Dolley, 133
Madison, James, 4, 15, 31, 91, 96, 146, 161, 210, 216
  Bonus Bill, 138
  in Congress, 35
  constitutional amendments, 34–35, 38
  and Constitutional Convention, 9
  Constitutional Convention, 15, 17, 28
  congressional veto, 24
  and democracy, 1, 16, 24
  and factions, 16, 51, 56
  federalism, 77, 134
  French Revolution, 71
  and Indians, 192
  internal improvements, 137
  and judicial review, 210
  Kentucky and Virginia Resolutions, 75, 77
  and militia, 131
  and the press, 53
  and slavery, 19, 154, 161
  Lousiana Purchase, 120
  national bank, 48, 134–137, 184, 216

Madison, James (cont.)
  national debt, 46
  National Republicans, 140
  opposition to Hamilton, 43, 46–47
  state governments, 53
  states' rights, 53, 77
  *The Federalist*, 29, 33, 47
  view of parties, 34, 52, 57
  Virginia Plan, 17
  War of 1812, 117, 129–130
  Yazoo scandal, 107, 110
Manning, William, 50–51, 53–54, 57
*Marbury v. Madison* (1803), 89–91, 95,
  101, 113, 127, 222
Marshall, John, 4, 6, 89, 91, 112, 126, 178,
  197, 206–207, 216–217, 223
  appointment of, 90
  as Chief Justice, 5, 92, 114
  and Indian policy, 198–201, 203–204
  and judicial supremacy, 95–97
  and legalism, 102
  Marshall Court, 179–190, 210
  as Secretary of State, 90
  and state governments, 102, 105, 109
  and Yazoo, 112
*Martin v. Commonwealth* (1805), 69
*Martin v. Hunter's Lessee* (1816),
  178, 180
Maryland, 15, 21, 62, 152, 185
Mason, George, 15, 19, 22, 27, 149
Massachusetts, 32, 50, 69, 111, 130, 151
  Alien and Sedition Acts, 76
  Embargo Act, 125
  Hartford Convention, 132
  militia, 130
  Shays' Rebellion, 14
  and slavery, 21, 61, 159
*McCulloch v. Maryland* (1819), 179, 183,
  221
middling politicians, 5, 12–13, 31, 78, 82
Mifflin, Thomas, 147
militia, 13–14, 32, 36–37, 56, 58, 63, 95,
  122, 125, 129–131, 167, 169, 172,
  174
  and black communities, 121, 166
  and popular protest, 56, 58, 81, 125
  and Second Amendment, 37
  Second Amendment, 36
  and slave rebellions, 37
  and states' rights, 124, 131
  and voting rights, 172
  and the War of 1812, 130

Mississippi, 193, 195, 220
  and Indians, 201
  and slavery, 150, 157
Mississippi River, 118, 149, 192
  Yazoo scandal, 106, 113
Missouri Crisis, 147, 150, 157, 159,
  162–163, 165, 176, 182
monarchy, 4, 8, 22, 52, 71, 169
Monroe, James, 139, 142–144, 146, 163,
  176, 216
  and free blacks, 120
  as president, 140
  Cumberland Road veto, 142
  election of, 117
  internal imrpovements, 214
  political views, 140
  states' rights, 131
Murray, Judith Sargent, 4, 65

Natchez, 149
national bank, 45, 48, 134, 137, 216, 221
National Republicans, 117, 133, 139,
  143–144, 146, 163, 165, 176, 179,
  207, 210, 214, 218
New Hampshire, 33
New Jersey, 18, 33, 43, 67–68, 82, 159, 212
  and slavery, 21
New Orleans, 118, 121, 123, 133–134,
  149
New York, 78, 81, 143
  Anti-Federalists, 31
  Constitutional Convention, 15, 26
  Constitutional Convention of 1821, 166,
  214
  Embargo Act, 124, 128
  national bank, 134
  political parties, 80, 84, 207
  ratification debate, 29, 33
  rise of democracy, 167
  and slavery, 21, 62, 151
  states' rights, 218
  voting requirements, 167
  white democracy, 169, 173, 175
  and women's rights, 70
newspapers, 3, 29, 42–43, 50, 59, 69, 73,
  86, 94, 124, 136
  Alien and Sedition Acts, 74
  Federalists, 33
  judicial review, 25
  on the Constitution, 16, 28
  partisan, 52, 79
  political organization, 78

rise of, 52, 54
states' rights, 34
*The Federalist*, 29
Non-Importation Act (1806), 124
North Carolina, 24, 33, 94, 156, 193, 195
Northwest Ordinance, 149–150, 193
Northwest Territory, 119, 122
nullification, 76–77, 207, 218

*Ogden v. Saunders* (1827), 179, 189
Ohio, 98–99, 122, 149–150, 187, 192, 195–196
*Osborn v. Bank of the United States* (1824), 179, 187

parties, 77, 99, 211–213
    Anti-Federalists, 31
    Black Laws, 123
    Constitutional Convention, 15
    formation of, 1, 34, 73
    founders' view of, 52, 73
    free blacks, 61, 166
    fugitive slaves, 147
    militia, 81
    Pennsylvania, 13, 37, 58, 80, 88, 95
    and political parties, 78, 80
    populism, 58
    protests, 59
    and ratification, 33
    ratification debate, 28, 42
    and slavery, 21, 61–62
    tax protests, 57, 64
    third parties, 221
    Whiskey Rebellion, 57
    and women, 65
Pickering, Timothy, 119
Pinckney Treaty, 195
Pinckney, Charles, 19
Pinckney, Charles Cotesworth, 19, 90
Pinckney's Treaty, 118
popular sovereignty, 4–5, 17, 25, 51, 56, 60, 92, 94–95, 97, 102, 106–107, 109, 113, 135, 213–214, 219
populism, 3, 14, 23, 32, 34, 50–51, 54, 57–58, 84, 87, 97, 110, 113
property rights, 10, 13, 20–21, 23–24, 27, 40, 85, 95, 112, 148, 153, 188, 190, 197
Publius, 29, 42, 47, 131

Randolph, Edmund, 27, 58
Randolph, John, 110, 143

Republican Party, 52, 80, 97, 106–107, 110, 143, 215
    and Jacksonians, 212
    and slavery, 151–152
republicanism, 15, 47, 50, 74, 82, 102, 111, 115, 145, 176
    and central government, 32, 210
    and courts, 181
    democracy, 13, 39, 174
    elitism, 10, 39
    *Federalist 10*, 33
    Hamiltonian view, 45, 49
    Jeffersonian view, 102, 124
    and political parties, 80, 143
    and the press, 52
    public virtue, 8, 34
    and race, 121, 123
    Republican view, 51–52
    and slavery, 160
    and violence, 59
    and women, 64, 68
Rhode Island, 21, 33, 62, 76, 95, 130
Roane, Spencer, 136
Rodney, Caesar, 127
Ross, John, 169, 208

Saint-Domingue, 62
Sanford, Nathan, 168–169
Second Bank of the United States, 134, 137, 163–164, 179, 183, 214, 216
Shays' Rebellion, 23, 50
    Daniel Shays, 14
    elite reactions to, 15
    Shaysites, 14
Singletary, Amos, 32
slavery, 11, 40, 120
    "diffusion," 156
    abolition, 20–21, 61–62, 155–156, 158, 160
    and expansion, 121
    colonization, 154–156, 158, 219
    contradictions of, 64
    Denmark Vesey conspiracy, 163
    emancipation, 20–21, 61–62, 149, 151–156, 158–159, 163–164, 166
    Fugitive Slave Act of 1793, 148
    Fugitive Slave Clause, 20
    Gabriel's Rebellion, 63
    Gag Rule of 1836, 165
    international slave trade, 19–21, 40, 149, 151, 153–155
    interstate slave trade, 20, 154
    Three-Fifths Compromise, 19

smuggling, 124, 128
South Carolina, 19–21, 42, 77, 104, 107,
    149, 153, 158, 206–207, 218
Spencer, Ambrose, 169, 172
state governments, 1, 74, 129, 193, 206
    criminal law, 36
    election of Senators, 18, 27
    electoral college, 22
    factions, 16, 73
    federal courts, 124
    and Indians, 193
    and public opinion, 53
    and Republicans, 75, 89
    and slavery, 155–156
    states' rights, 77–78
    and Supreme Court, 102, 179
    in Virginia Plan, 17
states' rights, 2, 34, 44, 82, 104, 129, 141,
    146, 178, 189, 211
    Democratic Party, 3, 144, 165, 176, 179,
        216, 218–221
    Federalists, 124–125, 134
    Hartford Convention, 132
    and Indians, 200, 206, 208, 212
    party organization, 78, 80, 215
    Republican Party, 5, 106, 116, 132, 143
    Supreme Court, 5, 101–102, 187–188,
        207, 214
    Tenth Amendment, 103
    Yazoo scandal, 108
*Stuart v. Laird* (1803), 92, 95
*Sturges v. Crowninshield* (1819), 179, 189
suffrage, 100, 115
    and Andrew Jackson, 6, 208, 216, 221
    and circuit courts, 87
    constitutional interpretation, 1, 102
    creation of, 23, 25
    and Democratic Party, 178, 212, 222
    and Embargo Act, 125
    expansion, 167, 169, 173, 175, 214
    and Federalists, 5, 113
    and George Washington, 85
    impeachment of judges, 98
    and Indians, 190–191, 197, 201, 203, 208
    poor whites, 172
    property requirements, 167–168
    and race, 169–170, 173, 175
    and slavery, 221
    and state courts, 26, 103, 180
    state laws, 18
    and states, 101, 182

Supremacy Clause, 24, 95, 181
Supreme Court, 3
    tax requirement, 172
    women, 64, 66–68, 212

Tallmadge, James, 158–159
taxation, 4, 12, 14, 17, 19, 27, 46, 51, 80,
    117, 172, 174, 183, 185–186, 217
    and voting rights, 68, 167, 169, 172
    protests, 57, 82
Tennessee, 130, 195
Treason Clause, 128
Treaty of Paris (1783), 11, 95, 192
Turnbull, Robert, 164

*United States v. Hoxie*, 128

Van Buren, Martin, 172, 214
    and Aaron Burr, 81
    and aristocracy, 178
    and Bucktails, 167
    and courts, 181
    and Democratic Party, 4, 179, 218, 222
    and denial of suffrage, 172–174
    Election of 1824, 215
    Election of 1828, 215
    Election of 1836, 219
    Election of 1840, 220
    and party organization, 6, 143–144, 167,
        214–215, 218
    and slavery, 175
    as vice president, 217–218
    and white democracy, 165, 178, 207
*VanHorne's Lessee v. Dorrance* (1795), 95
Vermont, 124, 128
Virginia, 34, 51, 84, 87–88, 130, 141, 162
    Constitutional Convention, 15, 17
    free blacks, 120, 122
    Gabriel's Rebellion, 63
    and Indians, 191
    militia, 81
    ratification debate, 33
    and slavery, 19, 21, 62, 147, 152
    state court, 180
    states' rights, 53, 75, 77
    Supreme Court, 95, 105
Virginia Plan, 18

War Hawks, 130
*Ware v. Hylton* (1796), 95
Washington, George, 5, 15, 29, 57, 211

and Constitutional Convention, 9
Constitutional Convention, 15
and democracy, 84
Farwell Address, 72
Haitian Revolution, 62
Jay Treaty, 72
and political parties, 55
as president, 43
Supreme Court, 86, 93
Whiskey Rebellion, 58–59
Webster, Daniel, 140, 156
Webster, Noah, 151
Whig (English), 49–50, 89
Whig Party (American), 70, 165, 212, 220–221
Whiskey Rebellion, 57–60
Wollstonecraft, Mary, 65–66
women, 2, 10, 64, 69
    and Constitution, 5, 64–71
    and Democratic Party, 6, 220
    division of labor, 66
    and education, 65
    exclusion, 2–3, 67, 70, 166, 212
    and French Revolution, 71
    moral role, 65
    New Jersey Constitution, 67
    property rights, 70
    protests, 125
    voting rights, 43, 64, 66–68, 82, 168, 170
*Worcester v. Georgia* (1832), 179, 203

Yazoo land scandal, 87, 97, 101, 105–111, 113, 188, 197, 200, 215
yeomanry, 118, 196
    Jefferson's vision, 44, 116
    white, 116–117, 144
    yeoman empire, 118
Young, Samuel, 171